JAPANESE PAPERMAKING

JAPANESE PAPERMAKING

TRADITIONS, TOOLS, AND TECHNIQUES

by TIMOTHY BARRETT

with an appendix on alternative fibers
by Winifred Lutz

New York · WEATHERHILL · *Tokyo*

Publication of this book was assisted by a grant from the Japan Foundation.

Drawings on pp. 91–110 by Howard Clark; all other drawings by Richard J. Flavin. Photographs by Timothy Barrett (Figs. 75, 83, 92, 94, 97–101, 104, 105, 107, 112, 115, 118–21, 123), Richard J. Flavin (Figs. 91, 106, 111), and Nicholas Graetz (remaining photographs). Originals of 37 of the Flavin drawings are in the collection of the University of Delaware Library.

A NOTE ON THE DECORATIONS. The frontispiece shows a nineteenth-century Japanese papermaking village with workers soaking bark in a river, brushing paper on boards and placing them in the sun to dry, forming sheets at the vat, and transporting bundles of finished paper.

NOTE: With the exception of references in the notes and bibliography, all Japanese names in this text appear in the Japanese order, surname first.

WARNING: Some of the chemicals and equipment described in this book can be dangerous and should be used with due care.

First edition, 1983
First paperback edition, 1992

Published by Weatherhill, Inc., 420 Madison Avenue, 15th Floor, New York 10017

Printed in Mexico.
Library of Congress Cataloging in Publication Data: Barrett, Timothy. / Japanese papermaking. / Bibliography: p. / Includes index. / 1. Japanese paper. I. Lutz, Winifred. II. Title / TS1130.B37 1983 676′.2′0952 83-5790 / ISBN 0-8348-0255-4

To early unknown craftspeople,
Eastern and Western,
who left behind paper that speaks for itself,
and to those today
who emulate their work.

Contents

Preface

DURING TWO YEARS of research in Japan between 1975 and 1977, I believe I acquired a new, deeper understanding of the Japanese craft of making paper by hand. To learn, on occasions I had to inquire, at other times I was shown without asking, and at still other moments I learned by osmosis, by watching and listening alone. Whatever the means, I am convinced that little by little I was permitted a special intimacy with the craft. If only a small part of that privileged view of Japanese papermaking comes across in this book I will consider it a success. There is great joy in learning things for the first time, but even more reward if one is able to share those discoveries with others who care. This book has been written with exactly that goal in mind.

In order to successfully communicate the intricate workings of Japanese papermaking, presented in these pages is a detailed but composite view of what are actually slightly different crafts used to make a tremendous range of papers.

Much of this book is the result of the steady goodwill and encouragement of Henry Morris of the Bird and Bull Press. Mr. Morris urged me to write my first book about Japanese papermaking and then published it in a handsome and very successful limited edition. The majority of the text and drawings from that book appears as Part I in the present volume. Part II, the more instructional portion of the text, was made possible by a grant from the National Endowment for the Arts that funded a large part of the research on tools and techniques and allowed me time to write. A Fulbright Fellowship and its renewal provided for all of my initial study and travel in Japan between 1975 and 1977. I am also grateful to the Japan Foundation for their grant supporting publication of this book.

While I was in Japan no teacher inspired me more than Katsu Tadahiko, apprentice of National Living Treasure Abe Eishiro. Katsu gradually helped me see that young papermakers today must consider seriously the importance of past traditions. "We," he said, "are the last link with the best of the old craft. The quality of our work today will determine the spirit of the craft in the future. It is up to us. If we let the traditional attitudes and techniques pass unnoticed, they may be gone forever. And we will be to blame." Katsu's spirit runs throughout this text and underlies my present interest in early Western papermaking techniques as well.

Winifred Lutz has contributed a great deal to this book, beyond her highly informative appendix, by generously sharing her own thorough understanding of the Japanese papermaking process during preparation of the manuscript. For the drawings I could not have wished for more talented artists than Howard Clark and Richard Flavin. Each artist's own strong feelings for the craft show clearly in his work. Richard Flavin has also helped immeasurably with final manuscript and drawing preparation. Dr. Raymond L. Janes, Barbara Meijer-James, and Jesse Munn have all given generously of their time during editing of technical passages in the text. Any inaccuracies that remain are entirely my own.

I will never forget the many Japanese artisans who offered me their hospitality and a chance to learn their craft as well. I cannot begin to thank them all for what they gave me, but many of their names appear below, along with those of other individuals or organizations who, by their action or encouragement, have helped make this book a reality.

Abe Eishiro, Dr. and Mrs. Laurence Barrett, Kathryn Clark, The C. H. Dexter Division of the Dexter Corporation, Betty Fiske, Vera Freeman, Fukuiishi Masao, Nicholas Graetz, Simon and Remy Green, Dr. Gail Griffin, Dr. Raymond L. Janes, Kume Yasuo, Dr. Machida Seishi, Moriki Yasumi, Morita Yasutaka, Nakane Aiko, Dr. Nichikori Sadanori, Pamela Pasti, the staff of the Saitama Prefectural Paper Experimental Station, Seki Yoshikuni, Shimura Asao, Rob Singer, Ruth Stevens, Yagihashi Shin, and Paul Wills.

Finally, I would like to thank three master papermakers—Kubota Yasuichi, Naito Tsuneo, and Naruko Tetsuo—for graciously providing samples of their paper for inclusion in this book.

PART ONE

The Craft in Japan

Paper Samples (*facing page*)

Note: In celebration of this first paperback edition of *Japanese Papermaking: Traditions, Tools, and Techniques*, all paper specimens were made at the University of Iowa Center for the Book research and production papermaking facility. All sheets were made by the author and apprentice Bridget O'Malley, with the assistance of co-workers Jason Brickey, Jeff Fullam, Arla Mattock, and Peter Pascale.

Common technical details include cool or cold winter working conditions, cooking in soda ash (20% of dry fiber weight), the use of *tororo-aoi* formation aid grown in Iowa from Japanese seed, and drying on a steam-heated indoor stainless steel surface. Individual details are as follows:

1. KOZO, made from Japanese *Nasu kozo* white bark imported from Ibaragi Prefecture. Cooked 2½ hours, beaten by hand for 2½ hours, and finished with 15 minutes of treatment in the *naginata* beater. Finished sheet size: 60 by 90 centimeters (23½ by 35½ inches).

2. MITSUMATA, made from imported Japanese fiber. Cooked 2 hours, beaten by hand for 1½ hours followed by 5 minutes of treatment in the *naginata* beater. Finished sheet size: 31 by 42 centimeters (12¼ by 16½ inches).

3. GAMPI, made from imported Japanese fiber. Cooked 5 hours, beaten by hand for 2 hours followed by 3 minutes of *naginata* treatment. Finished sheet size: 31 by 42 centimeters (12¼ by 16½ inches).

1

2

3

INTRODUCTION

It is not an easy task for an outsider with only beginning language skills to acquire a knowledgeable view of Japanese papermaking in a brief two years in that country. That, however, was the nature of my research in Japan between 1975 and 1977. Part 1 of this book presents detailed observations made during those years with as much accuracy as possible.

All discussion of making Japanese paper in the West is reserved for Part 2 in order that the reader first obtain a prerequisite, clear understanding of the craft as it is practiced by professionals in Japan.

CHAPTER ONE

Japanese Paper: Past and Present

Past Uses

CENTURIES BEFORE the average European had even heard of paper, the Japanese were surrounded by it. At the time that Gutenberg was printing the Bible on some of the first Western handmade paper, the Japanese had long since been using paper for every imaginable purpose. Japanese papers were employed not only for books, calligraphy papers, letters and envelopes, bags, umbrellas, lanterns, and sliding screens but also for clothing. Raincoats of oil-impregnated paper were in use throughout the country as were kimonos, called *kamiko,* fashioned from sheets of paper and even special kimonos of fabric, called *shifu,* woven from threads of twisted paper.[1] For generations, *washi* (Japanese handmade paper) was used in making fireworks, since in addition to being strong and able to contain the rapid burning of explosive powder, it is also thin and light, an important consideration in the manufacture of large aerial bombs. Japanese paper was used in place of canvas for the waterproof side curtains of cabs, for string or light rope, and for medical plasters. Twisted into threads (called *koyori*), woven into intricate patterns on forms, and painted with lacquer, it was used to make protective cases for pipes, eyeglasses, and similar articles. *Washi* also made excellent toilet paper.

I learned of the latter use in the midst of an argument I once had with a famous but grumpy kimono maker about my samples of American handmade paper. They were, of course, made using the Western papermaking process and were considerably thicker than what he knew as handmade paper. He inspected them briefly and then barked, "Ha! Handmade paper?

This is cardboard! I'll show you what *real* handmade paper looks like." At which point he sent his elderly wife scuttling upstairs to bring down some of their old-fashioned, high-class toilet paper. "This!" he said, shaking the article in my face, "is real handmade paper!" And just so I knew what it was without having to strain my limited Japanese, he graphically motioned a wipe and a quick nose blow. I was duly impressed and humbly withdrew my paper samples. His paper was admittedly very fine.

Washi has also been used successfully for generations to suffocate those one wishes to be rid of but leave no marks upon. In this rather macabre use of Japanese paper, the killer first watches the intended victim in his sleep for a few moments. With carefully executed movements, he then lays a wet piece of *washi* over the victim's mouth and nose just after a breath is exhaled. Immediately the killer throws himself upon the victim and does whatever is necessary to keep the victim from removing the paper. This may require some exertion and forethought on the part of the killer but will probably be worth his trouble since in the end all he has to do is peel away the damp paper. The victim shows no signs of foul play, and, once dried, the highly durable *washi* proves perfectly serviceable for sending letters or writing poems.

In addition to the above, *washi* has contributed its share to death-dealing efforts throughout history. It was reportedly used to make a cannon that was actually fired once or twice. More incredibly, during World War II, papermakers all over Japan worked long hours making paper for balloons sent to North America bearing incendiary and antipersonnel bombs.

These balloons, with envelopes made entirely of Japanese handmade paper, were developed between 1942 and 1944 during research aimed at retaliation for Allied attacks on the Japanese mainland, notably the Doolittle raid on Tokyo in April 1942. Unbelievable as it seems, testing promised a transpacific travel time via high-altitude jet streams of only thirty to one hundred hours, or an average of sixty hours. Given 9900 total kilometers, computation shows a speed range of 100 to 320 kilometers per hour with an average air speed of 170 kilometers per hour.

One of the major design problems during development was to produce a balloon that would maintain a constant high altitude during the gradual escape of hydrogen gas and the drastic changes in temperature from day to night. The problem was solved by loading each balloon with thirty-two sand-filled ballast bags in addition to its bombs. The ballast bags were wired

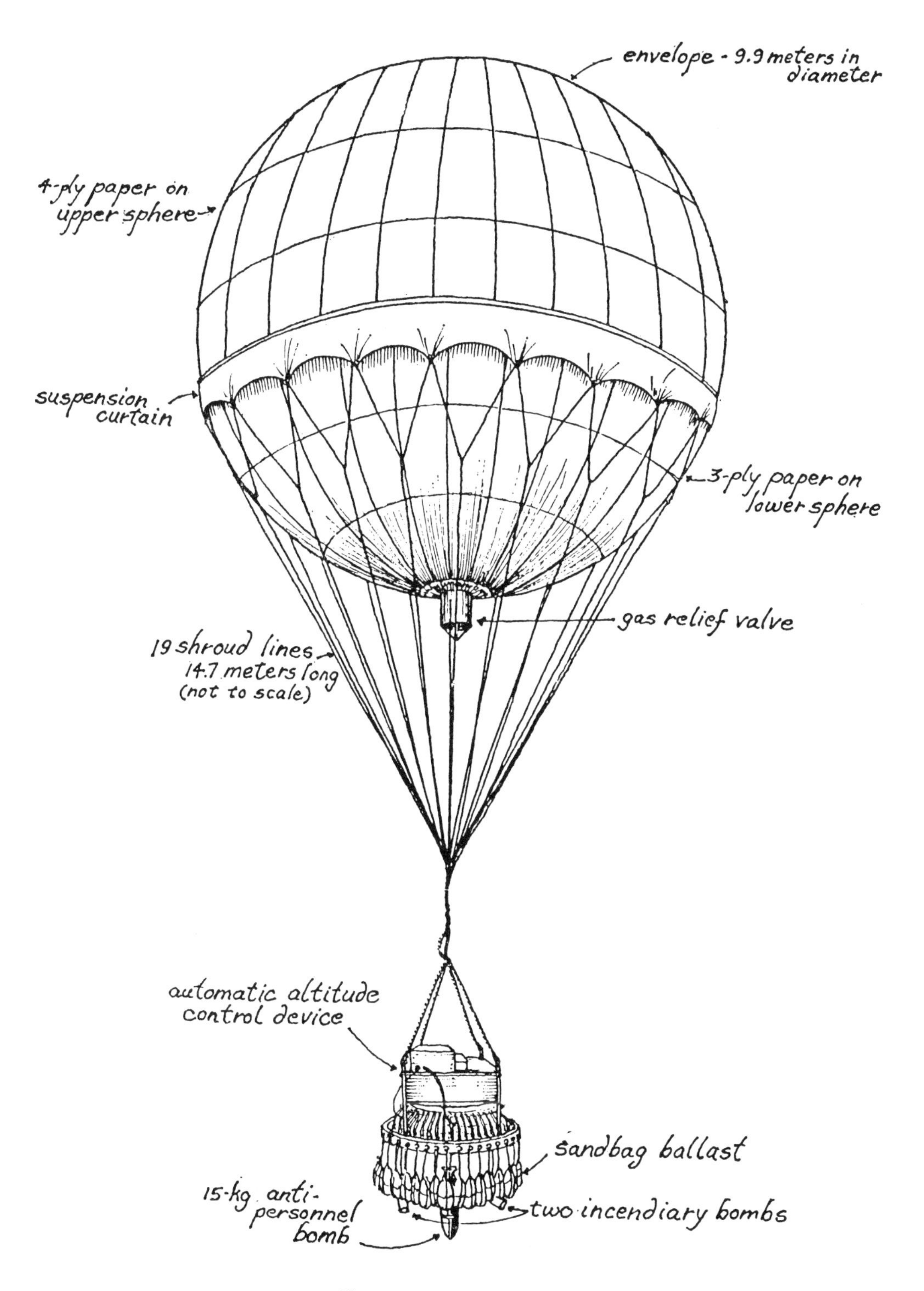

1. Japanese bombing balloon

to a device that not only automatically dropped two bags at a set minimum altitude to keep the balloon at the correct height as it drifted toward North America but also, upon arrival, released the bombs on anybody or anything below.

Paper for the 10,000 balloons in the 1944–45 project was made by hand by hundreds and hundreds of papermakers in famous *washi*-producing areas all over Japan. Many of the craftspeople I visited told stories of papermaking for the "balloon bombs," though few of them had known what they were contributing to at the time. Many laughed when I brought up the subject, but when pressed, they spoke seriously of the heavy production demanded by the military government at the time. "Oh yeah, I remember making that paper. I think I still have a few sheets of it tucked away somewhere. All we did for months and months, day in, day out, was make that paper. And all we had to eat was potatoes, because they sent all the rice to the soldiers. That paper was incredibly thin. I remember we used it to re-cover the shoji (sliding partitions), and it was so thin you could see the ridges of the distant hills right through it."

According to Robert C. Mikesh, the handmade sheets for balloon manufacture weighed about fifteen grams per square meter.[2] At various assembly locations the paper was laminated alternately with and against the grain, three or four layers thick, with an adhesive made from a type of Japanese potato called *konnyaku* (*Amorphophalus konjac* K. Koch). Once dried, the paper was softened by dipping it in a solution of soda ash, a water wash, and then a solution of glycerine. This treatment kept the paper from cracking and hardening in severe high-altitude temperatures. The paper was trimmed and pasted together; each balloon, measuring 9.9 meters in diameter, consisted of six hundred separate pieces. Much of the final assembly work was performed by high-school girls carefully trained to glue the seams. When completely assembled, the balloon was coated with a waterproof lacquer. The finished product was not only light in weight and strong but adequately airtight as well.

During the war, American security imposed a news blackout on any balloon-related stories, and in the spring of 1945, disruption of supplies in Japan and a lack of reports of successful crossings put a halt to the project. Only an estimated 1000 of a total 9000 balloons sent actually completed the crossing, but they traveled as far north as the Aleutian Islands, as far south as Mexico, and as far east as Michigan. They killed only six people and did very little material damage, but in larger numbers their potential for causing fear and confusion, forest fires, and death (especially if chemical or germ warfare bombs had been considered by the Japanese) was much greater than most Americans realized.

It seems likely that the Japanese bombing balloons were the last massive testimony to *washi's* incredible strength and versatility; it is doubtful that a handmade-paper project of this magnitude will ever be undertaken again. For this reason alone it is a fascinating story. The interested reader would do well to consult Mikesh's thorough report on the project and America's reaction to it.

The word *washi* conjures up a wide variety of images and feelings in older Japanese who grew up using handmade paper daily. For them, it has a meaning and nuance very different from what the word "paper" can have for us. In addition to its wide range of practical uses, *washi* can have religious significance as a Shinto purity symbol. On festival days, small strips of paper are often hung from rice-straw ropes as talismans, usually on shrine grounds. In fact, the Japanese papermaking craft itself has many more religious ties than does its Western counterpart.

During the New Year holiday I once saw small offerings of paper, rice, and tangerines placed on a papermaker's cooking cauldron and in his vat. Another papermaker had set the same objects on the electric pump at his well head. When I asked about the meaning of the offerings, there was some embarrassment, but eventually the papermakers agreed on the word *gokurosama,* a term spoken to one's inferiors meaning basically "thank you for what you did." In the case of the papermaking appliances at the New Year, the sentiment was more like "thank you for your previous year's service." The gesture was also somehow reminiscent of kiln gods in a Japanese pottery shop and Christmas wreaths in America. Some papermaking shops have a small Shinto shrine mounted on a wall to ensure the well-being of the shop and the people who work there.

Past Production

For most of *washi's* history, papermaking was primarily the off-season winter work of farmers. Coincidentally or not, at just about the time when rice harvesting and related field work was finished (November to Decem-

2. Cleaning kozo bark in winter

ber), the leaves would fall off the kozo (paper mulberry) trees, signifying the proper time for harvesting. Only enough kozo and formation aid plants were grown and harvested to last through the winter months. When spring came, papermaking tools were put away, and everyone returned to farming.

Many early Japanese papers were of exceptional quality because they were made during the cold winter months. Winter-made paper has a reputation for looking, feeling, and smelling a great deal better than paper made in the summer. Much of this is due to cold working conditions, which keep the inner bark fiber from spoiling even slightly after preparation. Also, vegetable matter collected for its formation aid secretions requires no chemical preservative in cold weather, and its viscosity lasts much longer and is more effective in cold water than in the lukewarm water of summer.

There are other reasons for the exceptional quality of papers made using the old routine and methods besides the cold seasonal working conditions. Papermaking used to be a life style requiring total commitment, with someone in the household rising at four or five in the morning to make paper and someone else working late at night hand-beating fiber for the next day's work. Households concentrated on and became very skilled at making one or at the most only a few types of paper, quickly developing very high quality control. In addition, in the days of the feudal system, all farmers had a lord and belonged, in a sense, to the lord's household. The quality of everything the farmers did affected the stature of the lord's house name. If poor-quality work was discovered, the responsible party might end up paying with the loss of one of his appendages or even his life. Therefore, everyone making paper went to a great deal of trouble to implement any specific requests from above. Those in power were in a position to initiate experimentation and gradually perfect the process. The top priority was to make good paper that the lord would appreciate; everything else came second. If he requested paper "free from a single speck," the object for those below was to get *all* the specks out, not to finish the job in a certain amount of time. There were no eight-hour days or paychecks—only house honor, pride, and proper implementation of the work at hand. At times, very high quality was the result. It is no wonder that contemporary papers rarely approach the quality of those made 150 or more years ago. The priorities then were entirely different.

Fiber was also prepared by each household, from beginning to end, and the resultant quality was usually far superior to that of currently available fiber. As a result of differences in species, habitat, farming, harvesting, and cleaning techniques, kozo, mitsumata, and gampi (the three main paper-making fibers) came in many different grades and qualities. The best fiber had been well tended during growing and meticulously cleaned after harvesting. People old enough to remember speak longingly and sadly of the superior-quality fiber available in days past. "You wouldn't believe how clean and white it was," one told me. "It was wonderful material, and I haven't seen anything like it since well before the war."

All the plants used in the process were planted and harvested according to set dates or standards tied to carefully observed phases of the moon. Drinking beer with a seacoast papermaker and a lumberman one afternoon, I was told, "Baretto-san,* you know all that old stuff about the moon and when to plant and when to harvest seems like bunk today, but you think about it a bit. You go out there and watch what happens to the level of the

* "Baretto-san" is roughly equivalent to "Mr. Barrett," Baretto being the closest approximation of Barrett possible in Japanese.—ED.

ocean because of the moon and then tell me the moon doesn't affect kozo and *tororo-aoi* (a plant raised for its formation aid secretions) as they grow, and everything else besides. There're lots of connections between the moon and our own bodies and minds. Crazy people go more nuts during a full moon, and that's a fact. Temples and shrines in Japan that are centuries old still stand because the wood used to build them was cut during a full moon and seasoned exactly two years before building. Certainly there was something right about the way they used to watch the moon and the dates in the old days, and today we're making a big mistake in letting it go by."

In the old days, fiber was treated gently during preparation. Past techniques never employed strong chemicals or bleaches because they were not available. Instead, since light-colored papers were desired, time-consuming stream or snow bleaching, thorough washing, and meticulous hand picking were relied on to render whiter papers. Cooking was always a long and gentle process in wood-ash lye over a wood fire. Employing a variety of tools and routines rarely used today, all cooked bark was beaten entirely by hand, preserving the natural character and length of the fiber in the finished sheet. The fiber, formation aid, and water were mixed by hand in the vat. The sheets were formed on small hand-held moulds that enabled a great deal of control and attention to the whole area of the sheet. Dyes used were natural vegetable dyes or pigments. After pressing, the parted paper was dried very gradually outdoors on boards in the sun. The whole process was carried out patiently, carefully, gently, and slowly. The quality of the paper, rather than time or profit, was the priority.

Contemporary Uses

Today the situation has changed drastically. Many traditional uses have been entirely replaced by the use of cheaper modern materials. The Japanese often prefer articles from Western culture over the traditionally made item—pop-up nylon umbrellas over oil-impregnated paper umbrellas, for example. Mass-production, machine-made paper products, modern packaging techniques, plastics, and Western culture in general have engulfed *washi* and its traditional place in Japanese life. In most homes it has already become history.

The various handmade papers still produced today are eventually sold as calligraphy papers, letter paper and envelopes, wallets, shoji papers, decorative papers, notebooks, business cards, postcards, and papers for artwork, to mention only a few uses. Demand for *washi* is still very much in evidence, and the contemporary market includes both domestic and export sales, but Japanese handmade paper is no longer the common, staple material it once was. It has become a specialty item, very much like handmade paper in the West, and its quality varies drastically.

Contemporary uses *do* include some traditional uses that demand durability and traditional high quality. Gold-leaf manufacture, scroll mounting and repairing, book and art conservation, important calligraphy and woodblock printing, and stencil making are all good examples. Today, however, the quality of even these papers may change unpredictably, and each new order is checked carefully by those who use the papers regularly.

The term *washi* still suggests "handmade paper" to many Japanese, but few realize how rare the traditionally made article is. Today anything, even machine-made paper, may be labeled and sold as *washi*. One traditionalist told me, "Baretto-san, a paper made with wood pulp in it, or made on a machine, even if it *is* all bast, is just rearranged fiber, and will never, never be *washi*. Don't ever forget it."

The majority of young people in Japan and many older people have no idea how *washi* is made nor do they come in contact with it in their daily lives. This is unfortunate, for if handmade paper is not used, felt, and seen in action, it will cease to exist. "Paper" in Japan is sadly but rapidly becoming the "paper" of the West.

Contemporary Production

Since 1868, when Western culture and techniques began to enter Japan, old papermaking methods have been in steady decline. There is little profit in the traditional techniques today. As one of the last farmer cum winter papermakers in the entire country put it, while we were cutting kozo, "I still do this because I enjoy it. I'd rather prepare kozo and make paper during the winter lull than carry a lunch box to a factory job, but I'd be a fool to think I could make any money at it."

Today, except in a few rare cases, *washi* production has changed to a year-round operation, including the hot summer months. Many households produce a wide variety of papers and are not especially skilled at making any one paper. *Tororo-aoi* is kept throughout the year in chemical preservatives that gradually lower its effectiveness.[3] Chemical substitutes for *tororo* have begun to appear, and although they seem benign, no extensive tests have been undertaken to assess their effects on the aging of paper. Fiber from all over the country is ordered through dealers, and the quality seems to fall yearly as the price rises. Land once used for fiber cultivation is more profitably used for other crops so fiber production as well is falling. Cooking with lime or soda ash is standard in the more traditional shops, but often poorer fiber is cooked in caustic soda and then chemically bleached. The cooked bast is beaten by machines and sometimes mixed and cleaned by machines. Foreign bast and wood pulp are commonly used to lower the proportion of expensive native bast. Chemical dyes are the predominant coloring agents; the result, although lightfast, lacks the subtlety of naturally dyed papers. Internally sized contemporary papers are treated with alum and rosin, contributing to a lack of permanence.[4] Finished sheets are often dried rapidly on hot sheet-metal dryers, and fresh sheets are sometimes even couched on a moving felt leading directly to a large heated drum dryer.

The dominant priority has changed from quality to profit. The larger the paper the better; hence the appearance of suspension systems and large moulds where there is less control and less uniformity. Many papermakers and distributors spend a great deal of time thinking about how to make paper faster and more cheaply. Only a few are concerned with rediscovering lost techniques or regaining the quality of the best papers of the past.

Machine-made papers have made considerable advances in simulating the most difficult handmade papers. With the use of *tororo* or other formation aids, sheets of very thin, long bast fiber can be successfully rendered as a continuous roll. Although the formation quality is not as good, the finished product is cheaper than the handmade item. A bar graph showing the decline of hand papermaking in a given locale corresponds in reverse, almost exactly, to a similar graph of the rise of machine papermaking in the same area. Most machine papermakers in *washi*-producing communities once made paper by hand.

The contemporary Japanese papermaking craft is characterized by a decline in the availability of quality fiber, tools, and water, and thus quality paper as well.

Future Prospects

In the heyday of *washi* production in the mid-1800s, before the introduction of Western culture and the paper machine, 100,000 households were making handmade paper.[5] By the early 1950s, the number had dropped to 9,000. In 1974, a survey by the Mainichi Daily News listed 756 households still working, and the number is now, in 1983, under 600.

The number of households in production just fifty or sixty years ago was considerable compared to today. On several occasions I visited Japanese villages where paper was still made, stopping to talk with the head of a household about the current state of affairs and then having a previously silent grandparent draw me aside. "There are only six houses in this village making *washi* now," he or she would say, "but let me tell you something. When I was young *everyone* around here made *washi*—sixty or seventy houses all told. I remember when, on a sunny day, there were drying boards all over the hillsides. My friends and I used to work helping clean kozo. All the children helped their parents. The whole village made paper then." The average age of fiber growers, toolmakers, and papermakers today is between fifty and fifty-five.

There *is* a group of young people aged twenty-five to forty, and numbering between fifty and one hundred, involved in the production of handmade paper on some level. They were very helpful and encouraging when I was in Japan. Although the older craftspeople were the teachers, the young folks and I shared a common concern for the future of the craft. But my contemporaries in Japan often have to fight a lack of peer-group and cultural support for their pursuits. The devoted student of the craft, unless working with a famous papermaker, is considered a bit of a fool, brave and diligent though he or she may be.

The hand-papermaking field is naturally associated with long hours and cold, boring work. In one area where papermaking had been prevalent before the war, there had been a saying among young women of a marriageable age that went something like "Sleeping on a bed of rose thorns is better than marrying a papermaker"—a quaint warning of the demanding work required of a papermaker's wife. Such negative peer-group pressure makes most young women, and young men as well, very reluctant to enter the field.

Many papermakers in Japan work long hours to get their children through the highly competitive educational system, into good schools, and *out* of the papermaking field. If all goes well the children will enter good universities and eventually find a comfortable spot in one of the major conglomerates, banks, or public-service organizations.

On many occasions, papermakers had a hard time understanding why I, a college graduate and an American, was studying their craft. After the initial introductions, as we sat around cups of tea, the head of the household would eventually say something like, "Now, excuse me, but I want to get this straight. You have a university degree, right? And you came all the way over here to learn this process? Why?" And I would respond by talking about the merits of well-made paper and the fact that the craft is declining and the knowledge of old techniques disappearing. This would all be met with affirmative nods and the conversation would gradually turn to detailed stories of how it was done in former times, and soon deep pride would begin to show on the papermaker's face. Still, they would often regard me with bewildered amazement.

The feeling that the craft is dying is pervasive. In fact, part of the reason my reception was so cordial may have been because of this sense and a resultant willingness on the part of the older artisans to share their knowledge and experiences with someone young and seriously interested.

Today in Japan there is a growing interest in *washi* and many other traditional crafts as well, but the demand for the traditionally made product and the willingness to pay the price are very rare.[6] The general public does not understand the difference between chemical cooking and bleaching techniques and the traditional process, nor the difference between wood pulp and the traditional fibers. If there were substantial renewed demand (either domestic or Western) for quality paper, people would come forward to fill the gaps being left by the dwindling population of fiber growers, toolmakers, and papermakers. But the consensus of authorities in the field is that the next fifteen to twenty years will see a drastic decline in the volume of *washi* produced in Japan.

There were times during my stay in Japan when I found myself thinking that I was too late, that real, traditionally made *washi* was already a part of the past. Paper produced only during the winter, of hand-beaten, lye-cooked fiber, and dried on boards was rarely if ever made anymore. If only I'd been here fifty years ago! I would lament. It seemed that the old techniques had been set aside and what I was seeing was just the shadow of a very honest and admirable craft. Yet in those moments, I also felt deeply honored to have been taught by several of the few remaining traditional craftspeople, to have heard their stories of the old methods, and to have seen and touched some of the fine early papers. Since then I have realized I was not too late. For together they taught me, and are teaching other young people, the spirit of the craft, and therein lies hope for its future.

CHAPTER TWO

Raw Fiber Production

THE MOST ELEGANT and unique fibers in the field of papermaking are, without doubt, those of young Japanese kozo, mitsumata, and gampi trees. Used from all three are the bast (inner white bark) fibers, and all are very expensive. Prepared for papermaking, one kilogram of any of the three is worth at least ten to twelve dollars (at two hundred yen to the dollar). In comparison, a fully prepared kilogram of bleached wood pulp costs around fifty cents, and new cotton rag, perhaps two dollars. The Japanese fiber may be well worth the price, however, for even after beating, the fiber retains a surprisingly long three-to-twelve-millimeter length. Beaten rag and wood pulps, on the other hand, are four millimeters or shorter in length. In addition to considerable length, the slender fiber shape, thin fiber walls, and large amounts of attached gluelike hemicelluloses make kozo, mitsumata, and gampi rare and unusual fibers. In an almost uncanny way, all three function superbly in the Japanese papermaking process and yield some of the thinnest, strongest, and most delightful handmade papers available anywhere in the world.

A look through a microscope at prepared slides gives some indication of the vast differences between bast fiber and rag or wood fiber. Through the eyepiece the long bast fibers look like buttered spaghetti, while cotton rag or wood fibers look more like a pile of twigs. These characteristics of the actual shape and surface of the Japanese fibers and their freedom from irregularity, though barely visible to the naked eye, are directly related to the special look and feel of the finished papers. Much of the warmth, suppleness, and luster of Japanese papers is a result of the nature of the fiber itself and nothing more. Just as a choice slab of walnut is naturally attractive and possessed of a singular beauty before the carpenter sets to work, so are the raw kozo, mitsumata, and gampi of Japanese papermaking intrinsically beautiful. The skilled craftsperson in both cases has learned not to interfere with that beauty but, instead, to work with it, preserving it in the finished product as much as possible.

Cultivation

The high price of Japanese fiber is mainly a result of the numerous time-consuming steps required to take it from nature and fully prepare it for papermaking. Depending on the locale, fiber-bearing trees are cultivated, or are found growing, on hillsides or on terrain unsuitable for crops. All papermakers once produced their own fiber, but today, with a few rare exceptions, non-papermaking farmers in different locations produce and process the trees as a supplement to their income from food crops.

Kozo trees are, in fact, one-year-old sprouts from old, gnarled, parent stumps. After a batch of trees is harvested in December, the stump continues living and gives forth new sprouts the following spring. If the stump is crowded with new trees, some of the sprouts may be thinned while young. The kozo parent stump is started initially from a root or plant cutting and bears usable trees after two years. Optimum harvests occur five to eight years after planting and decrease thereafter.

During the summer there is little maintenance of the trees save the occasional cutting of surrounding tall grasses or vines. In some parts of Japan, young lower branches are trimmed to make the plant grow straight, tall, and freer of forks. Kozo does not seem very particular about where it grows. A Japanese papermaker and I once cut kozo on the embankment below a two-lane highway, and we had to kick our way through tin cans and broken beer bottles to get to the trees.

Kozo grows fastest of the three trees, attaining in one year an average two-meter height and a two-centimeter diameter at the base. Its fiber is much longer than mitsumata (twelve millimeters versus three millimeters, on the average) and gampi (four millimeters average), and the finished paper is much stronger and tougher. Kozo accounts for ninety percent of the bast fiber produced in Japan for hand papermaking and is thus by far the most common fiber in Japanese papers.

3. Left to right: kozo, mitsumata, and gampi trees

Kozo is a mulberry of the family Moraceae and is closely related to the white and red mulberry trees common in areas of North America, and to *Morus alba* L., leaves of which are used in Japan for feeding silkworms. Although there are several varieties used for papermaking, *Broussonetia kazinoki* Sieb. is considered to yield the best fiber. Another variety, *Broussonetia papyrifera* Vent., commonly designated "paper mulberry," is occasionally found growing in Hawaii and in North America from New York to Missouri and south. *Broussonetia kaempferi* Sieb. is also cited as a variety of kozo.

While kozo is started from root cuttings, mitsumata is usually raised from seeds. As with kozo, however, the cut stump will yield new growth each successive spring. Mitsumata stumps bear usable sprouts for perhaps ten years, compared to twenty for kozo. Mitsumata takes three years to reach the proper 1.5-to-2-meter height and is usually 2.5 centimeters in diameter at the base. Although kozo and gampi were in use by the eighth century in Japan, mitsumata was not used for papermaking until the late sixteenth century. Its fiber is much shorter and weaker than kozo fiber, but it produces a shinier, slightly denser, crisper paper than kozo. In addition, mitsumata is resistant to harmful insect infestation.

4. Left to right: kozo, mitsumata, and gampi leaves

Mitsumata is usually cited as *Edgeworthia papyrifera* Sieb. et Zucc., or *Edgeworthia chrysantha* Lindley, but can be found listed as *Daphne papyrifera* Sieb. in some sources. Like gampi and bast fiber used for papermaking in Nepal, mitsumata is a member of the family Thymelaeaceae.

Gampi is normally considered impossible to domesticate, but with attention it *can* be cultivated. However, it takes five to seven years to reach the proper average height of two meters and is troublesome to produce profitably. As a result, gampi is invariably harvested where it grows wild—in deciduous forests on mountainous terrain. Gampi is usually cut from mid-March to late April, when fiber hardness and gloss are optimum and stripping is easiest. Gampi produces the finest, most dignified of the three papers. Sometimes called the king of all papers, it is unmatched in translucency, luster, and character. Humidity and harmful insects rarely damage paper made of gampi.

As with kozo, several varieties of gampi are used for papermaking, but *Diplomorpha sikokiana* Nakai is usually considered to yield the best fiber. Gampi is also cited as *Wikstroemia canescens* Meisn., *Wikstroemia trichotoma* Makino, *Diplomorpha gampi* Nakai, *Wikstroemia sikokiana* Franch. et Savat., and *Passerina gampi* Sieb. and Zucc.

For hundreds of years, rice straw and bamboo also held a traditional place in Japanese papermaking, but their use was limited in the past and is rare in Japan today. Both have much shorter fibers than bast and are occasionally used in making calligraphy papers. Their character and preparation are very different from that of the much more prevalent basts. Rice, except for the above-mentioned straw fiber (and very rare rice loading or sizing), has nothing to do with Japanese handmade paper. Thus the term "rice paper" is erroneous when applied to a typical Japanese paper made of bast fiber. Hemp, *Cannabis sativa* L., although commonly used at various points in the past, is rarely used today.

Bast-producing trees generally grow in the more temperate sections of Japan, although kozo does quite well in colder areas where prolonged freezes are not common. Kochi Prefecture, on the island of Shikoku, accounts for the majority of Japan's kozo fiber production, with Tochigi Prefecture a close second. Mitsumata is produced in Kochi, Ehime, and Okayama prefectures. Gampi, rarest of the three, comes largely from Yamaguchi, Shimane, Kochi, and Wakayama prefectures.

Harvesting and Stripping

While the wood core accounts for the bulk of all three trees, only the inner bark yields the fiber essential for papermaking. Every hundred kilograms of harvested trees produces only five kilograms of paper. Even a low-production shop must collect mounds of cut trees to extract one year's supply of fiber.

Although most contemporary papermakers buy their fiber from suppliers, some still harvest and strip bark in a small local group effort very similar to a corn shucking, barn raising, or quilting bee in America. I was allowed to participate in such a kozo harvest one year in the small papermaking community of Misumi in Shimane Prefecture, along the coast of the Japan Sea. What follows is a description of the process and equipment used in Shimane, but it is representative of similar methods used all over Japan.

From the start, hauling the cut trees down from the hillside, stripping off the bark, and then separating the unwanted black outer bark from the white inner bark (or bast fiber) was a laborious, sweaty job for most of the over-forty group I worked with; but all fifteen of them tore into it with a jovial, almost festive attitude. For all those participating, the two-week kozo harvest was an important annual social event, a time to gather with friends and relatives and catch up on events of the past year.

Harvesting began soon after the leaves fell from the kozo trees in November and December. At various plots where kozo was growing, they cut the trees near the ground with a hook-shaped knife and trimmed them to an even one-meter length with a device similar to a table-top paper cutter. They tied the trimmed lengths into bundles thirty or forty centimeters in girth,

5. Harvesting kozo

loaded them onto a cart or truck, and drove them to the central work site for steaming and stripping. Since large quantities of trees were required, within a week or so the work site was surrounded by a maze of walls and corridors of stacked kozo bundles.

To help ease the bark off the inner sticks, the bundles were bathed in steam in a confined space for two to three hours. In Misumi, they used a large cast-iron cauldron filled with water to generate steam. A rice-straw ring was placed around the top edge of the cauldron to act as packing, and on top of that a five-tiered wooden box was set. The middle three tiers consisted of only vertical walls. The bottom section had a thirty-centimeter-square hole in its floor, allowing steam to enter freely from the cauldron below. The top section was built with a solid cover to prevent the loss of steam.

To load for steaming, two people removed the tiers of the box to allow access to the bottom section. Then, with the assistance of others in the group, they loaded the bundles of cut trees, gradually restacking the box sections as they went. Once fifteen or twenty bundles were packed in, they lowered the top of the box and cinched all the sections together with rope to inhibit the escape of steam. The leader of the operation then fired up an oil burner under the cauldron, and within a short time steam filled the box inside and blew out any loosely sealed cracks. The pervading smell was of something green and nourishing cooking and bore a tinge of haylike sweetness. The steam, the roar of the burner, and the general hubbub of activity reminded me very much of maple sugaring in America.

The bark of properly steamed sticks shrinks back about a centimeter

6. Steaming box

from the end of the wood, but experience more than anything else told the steaming crew when a load was finished. After about two hours they unloaded the steamed bundles, and while they reloaded the box with fresh trees the rest of the group carried the steamed bundles into a large room where the hard work began. In the first step of the stripping process, they roughened the ends of the bundles with a mallet to loosen a starting end of bark. Steam filled the room, but through the haze I was amazed to see two wizened ninety-year-olds, normally prone to shuffling around the neighborhood, take up the large wooden hammers and start thumping the steaming bundles as if they were young men of thirty-five. Astonished, I started taking pictures to record the event, half expecting the two to expire on the spot, but they kept right at it. Much of their youthful energy and enthusiasm grew from the fact that they had helped strip kozo in that town, probably in the very same house, every year for the last eighty-five. It had become as important to them as the New Year's holiday—a mark of the season, a special gathering and sharing—and to let the event go by without participating to the fullest would be a sure indication of the end of their usefulness to

7. Stripping kozo

the group. Their pride in still working hard at ninety was evident, and I could tell that the younger workers were even prouder to have them along.

Once the bundles had been properly treated with the mallets, we all sat down on rice-straw mats on the floor and set to work stripping off the bark. Three or four sticks each of approximately 1.5 centimeters in diameter could be stripped at once. The woman across from me grasped the loosened bark of four sticks in her right hand, the bared wood at the same end of the four sticks in her left, and, in one opposing pull, peeled the bark off the inner wood somewhat like skin off a salami. Often she would use one outstretched foot as a wedge to separate the last length of bark from the wood. After stacking slick yellow sticks in one pile and the stripped, damp bark in another, she leaned forward to pick up another handful of warm sticks. Although individual styles differed slightly, we all sat and worked in essentially the same fashion.

Gradually our sitting positions and our stick and bark piles became established. Before long everyone fell into a relaxed routine and conversation began to lubricate the work. All of the people in the room with me were country folk who had never seen a real live American up close, let alone asked him questions in Japanese. The initial queries revolved around why I was sitting there on the floor stripping kozo with them when I had a college degree and why I was interested in handmade paper to begin with. But once we had covered the basics, curiosity got the better of them and they asked about anything and everything. We all laughed as I dealt with such series as:

"How old are you?"

"Are you married yet?"

"Don't you think it's getting a little late?"

"Are you going to marry an American woman or a Japanese woman?"

"Well, even if you're not sure, which do you prefer?"

"Let me see your watch there. Are the numbers the same as ours?"

"Do they tell time in America the same way we do here?"

"Why don't they eat raw squid and octopus in America?"

Not wanting to pry, they often changed the subject or paused in the conversation—or perhaps they tired of hearing me butcher their language when responding to their questions. All the while, though, we continued stripping. Children rode their mothers' backs papoose style if they were too young to foot it, and four- and five-year-olds ranged around the room looking for attention and tripping over the kozo sticks that covered the floor. The atmosphere throughout the day was warm, moist, and congenial, and the air was full of the slightly sweet smell of kozo.

When a full load from the steaming box was stripped, they gathered the fresh loose bark into handfuls and tied them together at one end with a strand of bark, leaving the opposite ends hanging loose and free. Then they loaded the bark onto open packframes, carried it a short distance outside, and hung each tied handful on bamboo drying racks. Everyone sat down for a brief break, but the next steamed load was ready shortly thereafter and we were soon back at work, pounding the steaming bundles with mallets. The stripping work continued from 7:30 in the morning until 5:30 in the evening.

For the leader of the operation, the hours were often longer. At dinner following a long harvest day, one papermaker told me, "I usually get up at six, but for two weeks a year during kozo steaming I get up at four to fire the cauldron and have the first load ready when the help comes. I go to bed at nine or ten at night. It's not bad, but let me tell you something: you have to drink lots of sakè to keep your stamina up. I have some at lunch and quite a bit at dinner every day. It's very important. You can't last without it."

In Shimane they cut and steamed mitsumata each year in much the same fashion as they did kozo. Stripping mitsumata, however, required a slightly different technique. Since the small mitsumata trunk branches repeatedly into threes, it is impossible for one person to draw the bark off in one hefty pull. Two people usually performed the task. One person would take a firm hold on the loosened end of the bark, the other, on the white tree trunk, and then they would pull, tug-of-war style, until one held a bare tree and the other held the limp bark. In response to the different stripping procedure, one old woman, after stripping several bundles of mitsumata, groaned and said, "Phew, I don't know what's worse—going home at the end of a day of mitsumata and having your back ache, or sitting down all day stripping kozo and going home with a sore rear end." Everyone in the room boisterously approved her observation.

As work continued past the first week, piles and piles of slick yellow kozo sticks and bone-white mitsumata trees were bundled and stacked outside for firewood much the way the brown trees had been piled before stripping began. In a day or two of exposure to sun and breeze the heavy bunches of leathery stripped bark were transformed into light, dried shells of the former trees. It was at that point that I first began to understand how much loss is incurred in gathering bast fiber for papermaking. After manhandling hundreds and hundreds of kilograms of kozo trees and moving load after load of damp bark strands, all that was left in the end was a small pile of shriveled bark that looked and felt more like a bundle of trimmed twigs for kindling than next year's papermaking fiber. I began to feel a little attached to the bark, to regard it with a certain amount of respect, having seen the time and effort invested in its harvesting.

Black, Green, and White Bark

At this stage, the crisp dried bark was called "black bark" because it still carried a thin, dark, outer layer. Black bark was often stored for later use. However, prior to making clean traditional papers, the outer black layer had to be removed. Two alternative approaches were used. In the first, a worker soaked the black bark in a nearby river for several hours to soften it. After repeatedly treading on the bark in the water to loosen the black outer layer, he carried the damp strands to a dry work area. Working against a small raised block, he then shaved off the remaining black outer bark by drawing the whole flat strand under a knife. Starting at the trunk

8. Scraping kozo bark

end, he worked carefully but quickly, holding the knife at just the right angle so that it scraped rather than cut as he pulled the strand. He also removed any tough areas or wounds in the bark by stopping to cut them out with the knife. By working in this fashion and removing only the black outer layer, he produced what I term "green bark" since a thin, green, middle layer still adheres to the inner white bark.[1]

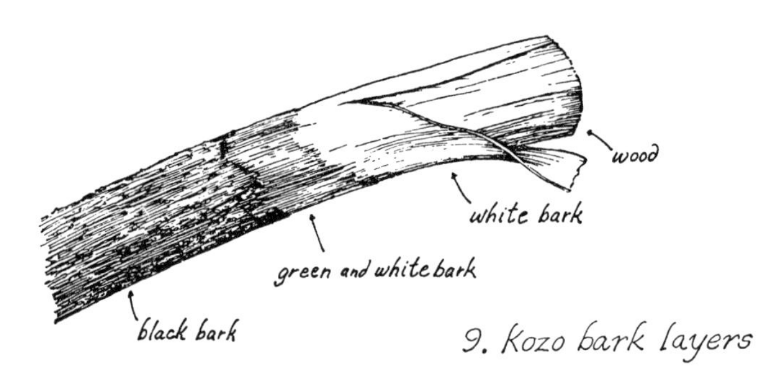

9. Kozo bark layers

In the second approach, since a white, fine paper was to be the finished product, the worker removed the black *and* green layer from each strand, leaving only the white inner bark. To do so, he used the knife to start a delamination between the white layer and the green and black layers. Then he grasped the two strands in opposite hands, white in one, green and black in the other, and peeled them apart as if he were peeling the backing off a long stick-on label. Invariably, bits of clinging bark had to be scraped away with the knife, but the technique allowed removal of most of the unwanted two outer layers in one pass.

In either approach, the next step was to wash the cleaned bark in clear water to free any remaining loose specks of black bark and then hang the strands to dry. Later, other workers baled and stored the fully cleaned bark for future use as required or for shipment to other papermaking areas.[2]

Final Thoughts on Raw Fiber

I remember walking alone into storerooms full of well-cleaned white bark, smelling the haylike aroma and feeling a certain presence. It was somehow very moving to stand next to the piled bales, each the precious end product of many hours of human labor and hundreds of kilograms of trees. In a well-stocked storeroom, I sensed bundles of invested time and dormant potential for the craftsperson. Realizing the fiber in its raw state was already worth four or five dollars a kilogram only increased my respect for it. The papermaker's storeroom reminded me very much of a woodworker's private stock of choice handpicked lumber, or a weaver's studio filled with boxes of carefully spun wool and raw flax. The smells and the crafts were different, but the admiration for the materials was the same.

Accurately judging the quality of raw fiber before it is prepared is a crucial step in hand papermaking. The artisan must have a sensitivity to raw fiber and know from experience the grade of paper it will yield. Before investing in fiber, he carefully balances the quality and price of the fiber, the intended use and quality of the paper to be produced, and the price the finished product will bring.

A number of factors may lower the quality of a bale of bast. When wounds and discolored areas in the bark are prevalent or have not been properly removed, the overall fiber grade declines. Such defects are often the result of abrasion between trees, climbing vines, diseases, insect infestation, or total neglect by the cultivator as the trees grow during the summer. Two- or three-year-old kozo fiber is larger and has thicker cell walls than the finer, one-year-old fiber and is coarse and tough in comparison. Thus, old fiber should not be found in a bale mixed with young fiber. The narrow upper branches of kozo trees yield bark that is harder to clean than the lower, thick bark so, when processed, it usually contains bits of black bark. An excess of bast from small upper branches, then, should not be found intermixed with quality fiber. All of these defects do not respond well to the cooking prior to beating and eventually yield flaws in the finished paper if not removed during processing. Very high quality fiber contains few, if any, of these defects.

Growing, harvesting, processing, and selecting a good bast fiber require time, experience, and pride. If the papermaker does not directly oversee fiber production himself, he must deal with a trusted intermediary. Even then, there is no way to avoid the fact that the quality and availability of raw fiber are declining, while the price is steadily rising.

CHAPTER THREE
Fiber Preparation

Cooking and Washing

ONCE HE HAS SELECTED a fiber type, the Western papermaker determines much of the character of the finished sheets during the beating process. The Japanese papermaker, on the other hand, controls the character of the finished paper primarily in the cooking and washing steps. If he cooks the bast too long or in too strong a chemical mixture, he will reduce the yield and produce a soft, weaker paper. If he cooks the fiber in too weak a chemical mixture or for an insufficient time period, he will end up with fiber that does not separate easily at beating and leaves tough strands and small clumps in the finished paper. Extended washing after cooking results in a lighter, softer paper, while slight washing produces a darker, crisper paper. Minor variations in cooking and washing can produce very different papers from the same fiber.

After actual fiber selection, cooking and washing are the most crucial preparatory steps in Japanese papermaking. All three steps, in fact, do much more than sheet forming to shape the paper's final identity. I was talking with a papermaker one day, lamenting and feeling a bit ashamed about my lack of hours at the vat versus time committed to fiber preparation study.

"Listen," he said, "I'll tell you something. Anyone can form decent sheets at a vat with a little advice and practice, but picking the fiber and cooking and washing it—getting the fiber just right—that's where the technique is. That makes the paper. Not many people are really good at it. Don't worry about the vat; you'll master that eventually. You understand me? You stay with fiber preparation—it's the secret to the finished paper."

The cooking process consists of boiling the fiber in a strong alkali solution to dissolve most of the lignin, pectin, waxes, and gums, leaving primarily the cellulose fiber and hemicelluloses required for papermaking. The largely unwanted nonfibrous constituents removed at cooking represent half the weight of the dry bark. If they were not removed, the fiber would not separate freely at beating, and an evenly formed finished sheet would not be possible.

The Japanese use several chemicals for cooking today, but the traditional alkali was potash made by leaching water through ashes. Hardwoods, reeds, rice straw, and buckwheat husks all yielded appropriate ash, although some papermaking areas preferred a single type. In very early times, ashes were mixed directly with the cooking water. According to B. Hickman, in premodern times in one locale, the ash produced by burning forty-five kilograms of straw or twenty-eight kilograms of reed was dissolved in about 180 liters of water. The resultant solution was suitable for cooking approximately forty kilograms of fiber.[1] Although it was hard to keep the strength of the alkali standard, many papermakers concede that the old wood-ash cooks were less likely to harm the fiber and produced better paper than the chemicals in common use today.

Old papers made of fiber cooked in wood ash seem to have a gentle crispness and life lacking in contemporary papers. This may be due to aging, a factor which, in its early stages, favorably affects most handmade papers just as time enriches the color and texture of a well-made wooden desk. However, it is more likely that the various metal salts present in potash, its relatively mild alkalinity, and the long cooking time required combined to give a superior character to the final papers. Whatever the technical factors, the wood-ash cook is to be highly commended for yielding papers of time-proven beauty and permanence.

Today, unfortunately, wood-ash cooks are rarely practiced in Japan. Aside from the time required to process the potash, large amounts of ash must be collected to keep one shop in operation. In the old days, cooking stoves and bathing cauldrons were always fired with wood, so ash was plentiful. But today, wood is seldom used for fuel. And perhaps more significantly, the available chemicals are quicker and much more convenient than potash. One expert at a testing institute told me, "I know you want to try a wood-ash cook, but there's no sense in your doing it. It's not worth your time. The only reason they used ashes in the old days was because they

10. Cooking fiber

didn't have the splendid chemicals we have today." Even the hard-core traditionalists, who maintain old standards at every other step of the process, cook with a chemical unless wood ash is specially ordered by the customer. Wood ash fell out of common use in most shops during the 1920s.

The contemporary Japanese papermaker usually cooks fiber in caustic soda (sodium hydroxide, $NaOH$) or soda ash (sodium carbonate, Na_2CO_3) using an average of fifteen percent of the weight of the dry fiber. (Water volume approximates fifteen liters for each kilogram of dry fiber.) Of the two, soda ash is preferred by traditionalists because it is gentler with the fiber and yields papers of a more natural tone. Very white papers are difficult to produce from fiber cooked in soda ash. Caustic soda, on the other hand, is a very strong chemical that will produce cleaner and whiter papers from lower quality bast. A caustic-soda cook is always the first step in making bleached white papers. In fact, a strong caustic cook in combination with chemical bleaching will produce bright white paper straight from black bark without the time-consuming hand removal of the black and green outer layers. Considerable money can be saved with this approach, but the finished product lacks the more natural warmth and integrity of papers made from white or green bark cooked in soda ash.

Some craftspeople consider slaked lime, $Ca(OH)_2$, to be a better substitute than soda ash for the old wood-ash cook. Lime tends to produce a sometimes preferred, softer, less glossy, lighter-colored paper than soda ash, but it is more unpredictable in daily usage and requires a longer cooking time. The chemical concentration is usually twenty-five to thirty-five percent lime vis-à-vis the dry fiber weight. Once the norm in some areas, lime is used only rarely today. Soda ash and caustic soda have gained a definite edge over other alternatives because of their speed, low cost, and reliability.

In a standard papermaking shop, the dried white or green bark is soaked in clear water from two hours to several days before cooking. The importance of high-quality water in this and all steps of the process has been impressed upon me more than once. Everyone claims his area has superior water and thus, of course, better paper than that of competing areas. I had an enlightening discussion one day with a famous maker of *hosho* (paper for woodblock printing). He was forming sheets, and I was standing next to the vat, watching.

"Everyone keeps telling me about water," I said. "I understand that good water is really important in making good paper, but how do you tell good water from bad water?"

"Come over here a minute," he said, as he moved away from the vat to a cement cistern in the back of the shop. "You see this?" He was pointing into the cistern at a layer of green on the wet inner wall. "See this green?"

"Ah. . . yes," I said.

"This shows you it's good water."

"Hmmm. . . ."

"You remember the creek down the hill that you crossed on the way up?" he asked. "You put those rubber boots on and go down and walk around in the water. You'll see the rocks are all slippery, and underneath the rocks there are crayfish and waterbugs and other living things crawling all over the place."

"Yes, but. . ."

"That means it's good water."

"But minerals and. . ."

"Do they have *hotaru* in America?" he asked.

"*Hotaru*?" I said, checking my dictionary.

"Yeah, you know, in the summertime after it gets dark. They blink yellow lights in the night. Especially on quiet evenings when it's warm and humid and the air is still. Do they have them in America?"

"Well yes, sure, in some places. Once in Indiana I saw so many of them I..."

"If you've got *hotaru* then somewhere nearby you'll find perfect water. You understand what I'm saying?"

"Ah, yes... that's amazing... yes, I understand."

"Iron and that sort of thing," he added, "are no good for paper. I'll tell you something, Baretto-san. When you get back to America and look for a spot to work, don't settle someplace just to be near your friends and family. You pick a good spot by the water. That should be your first concern. Excellent paper is impossible without excellent water. Do you understand me?"

"Yes... thank you...," I said, and found myself gazing quietly into the cistern at the green.

Depending on the area, there may be other steps taken to lighten or improve the bark prior to cooking. The bark may be whitened considerably in the presoaking process if it is river bleached—submerged in cold moving water in a sunny spot for a day or two. Snow bleaching is used in some regions and consists of spreading the bark in thin layers on the snow, covering it with snow, and turning it occasionally during the course of several days. Often, soaking white bark is given a second and final scraping with a knife to remove any remaining wounds or specks of black bark before cooking. All fiber is at least washed briskly in clear water after soaking to remove any loose black bark, since after cooking the bark becomes much harder to pick out.

In one house I visited, the papermaker began a typical cook by filling his large cast-iron cauldron with water at a ratio of roughly fifteen liters of water to each kilogram of dry bark. Since he had been soaking the bark, he shifted the ratio to about thirteen to one.[2] The craftsman fired the cauldron, and when the water approached the boiling point he added a measured amount of cooking chemical and stirred it in. Then he carefully added the wet bark to the cauldron so the strands were evenly distributed and the cooking liquid covered all of the fiber equally. Every thirty minutes or so he turned the bark in the cauldron with a stick to assure an even cook. As the boiling continued and steam rolled out from under the wooden lid, a wholesome, vegetable-like aroma filled the air. He continued cooking until a small strand of the bark separated easily when tugged lightly against the grain; his skill was in knowing just when to stop. (On the average, cooking takes about two hours but varies considerably depending on the fiber species, age, and quality; the alkali used; and the intended paper character and quality.)

After the cook, the liquid in the cauldron was brown and murky from the released soluble constituents in the original raw bark. Two hours after ending the cook, the papermaker removed the long but now soft and fragile strands and dispersed them in a low cement tank of clear water to wash out vestiges of the cooking solution. Then, since he desired a soft, white paper, he used gently flowing water to wash more remaining soluble hemicelluloses and impurities from the cooked strands. Had he washed the strands only slightly, a darker, crisper paper would have resulted.

Various types of fuel can be used for the fire in cooking. The oldest is, of course, wood. A few papermakers still use wood, claiming that the now-prevalent oil burners do not produce the same cook. Traditional though it is, this view did not seem reasonable to me. I was convinced that water at one hundred degrees centigrade would be one hundred degrees no matter how it was heated. I remember asking a famous and well-established paper dealer for clarification. His response came quickly and naturally. "Well," he said, "you'd think hot water was hot water, but I'll tell you something very interesting. I've got a bath at home that you can fire with wood or gas because I just had a new unit put on it last year. Now it seems crazy, but I swear the feeling of the gas-heated water just doesn't compare to wood-heated water. I can't tell you why, but it's true. You stay warmer longer after taking a wood-fired bath."

One possible advantage of wood occurs at the end of the cooking when remaining coals produce gradually diminishing heat. The result is a very slow decrease in the water temperature and additional gentle cooking well after the last stoking. The standard oil fire, on the other hand, is extinguished suddenly.

Rather than formulas, successful and consistent cooks require a sensitivity to equipment, raw fiber, chemicals, and the strength of the fire. The proper feel for the elements involved comes from experience as well as from what the Japanese call *kan,* or "sixth sense," a word that came up many times during my stay in Japan. In response to a question like, "When do you know it's time to stop cooking?" I would often get an answer like, "Oh, say . . . two or three hours . . . *kan* . . . you know, when it's time to stop." Most papermakers have general figures and patterns for most of their processes, but the fine tuning is ultimately done by feel. Strict formulas do not work in Japanese papermaking, particularly during cooking and washing.

Removing Foreign Particles

The next step, following cooking and washing, is certainly the most time-consuming. Working with their hands in water to enable easier inspection, a team of workers has to pick out any remaining specks of black bark, hard areas, and wounds, one strand of bark at a time, until the fiber is completely clean. (This cleaning is always conducted in cold water to retard spoilage of the fiber.) Working the fiber absolutely clean takes a great deal more time than picking until only a few specks remain. I was told that some of Japan's unbleached but perfect, spotless paper is made from fiber that was picked over two or three times in succession—the only way to be sure of absolutely clean fiber.

11. Cleaning fiber

The actual hours involved vary greatly, of course, with the type and quality of the fiber and the quality of the paper to be made, but one person needs at least a full nine-hour day to clean two kilograms. With few exceptions, the work is done by older women who are paid little but, according to the bosses, have the splendid chance to talk for hours on end. That does not seem to be much consolation to the women doing the work, and most are willing to admit they do not particularly enjoy the task.[3] Once picked clean, the cooked bark strands are kept cool and damp until beating, which follows shortly thereafter.

Due to the much shorter fiber lengths of gampi and mitsumata (three to four millimeters on the average) both can be cleaned effectively by a device called a flat diaphragm screen. This machine works by drawing a mixture

12. Flat diaphragm screen

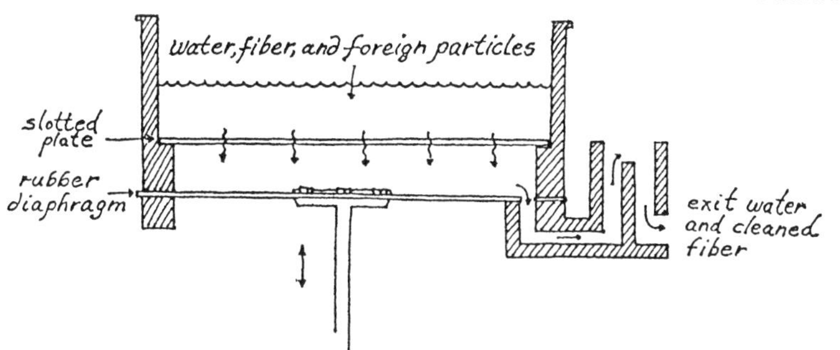

13. *Flat diaphragm screen (cross section)*

of beaten fiber and water through slotted brass plates. The width of the slots is small enough (.2 millimeter, or .008 inch) to strain out foreign particles while allowing the fiber and water to pass through. Similar to European jog knotters, flat screens can be purchased in Japan for around five thousand dollars. Such an investment will allow the mitsumata or gampi papermaker to skip the hand-picking process, and many manage to find the necessary funds. Although flat diaphragm screens require some nursing, lower the paper's gloss slightly, and usually do not produce perfectly clean fiber, they are unquestionably an advantage over hand picking.[4]

Kozo fibers are too long (twelve millimeters on the average) to be cleaned by any device developed thus far. Papermakers producing a 100-percent-kozo product by machine must employ hand pickers to go over the cooked bark. Even strongly bleached kozo fiber made from black bark contains some yellowed areas that must be removed by hand. The only cleaning devices kozo will cooperate with are human hands.

Beating

One of my more startling observations made during study in Japan concerned the drastic difference between Western and Japanese beating techniques. In the preparation of cotton rag, a common raw material in Western papermaking, beating is a loud and violent process. Small chunks of cloth must be torn and ripped apart into threads, and the threads must be pulled or torn apart until only single cotton fibers remain. It is really at this point that beating *begins;* the parted fibers are now hammered, sometimes lightly but nevertheless thoroughly, until they are softened and engorged with water molecules. This plasticization, or softening, of cellulose fiber is essential for strength in any finished paper. Rag fibers, especially those of cotton, have few if any hemicelluloses and a tight fibrillar structure. Both of these factors necessitate rather severe treatment during beating for proper plasticization. Rag beating creates a terrible din, takes time and energy, and most importantly, changes the length and surface of the fiber—greatly altering its original character.

Cooked bast for *washi* (Japanese handmade paper), on the other hand, is never beaten in this way. Instead of fiber twisted into thread and woven into tight patches of cloth, the Japanese papermaker begins with strands of cooked tree bark, each formed of millions of long straight fibers, all lying closely together along the same axis. Most of the lignin and natural gums holding the fibers together have been dissolved and washed away or at least softened by cooking. The fibers stand loose in the bark strand, more or less ready to come apart. As a result, Japanese beating is really only a sort of loosening process. The idea is to tease the fibers apart, but not to cut, macerate, or fibrillate them. Before my study of Japanese papermaking began, I was amazed by photographs of Japanese hand beating. I assumed that making paper as tough as *washi* would certainly require torturous and prolonged hand beating. Much to my surprise, I found that it actually goes rather quickly, generally not taking more than thirty minutes to fully beat a kilogram of fiber. "Beating" is actually a somewhat misleading term for what is done. The step might better be called "loosening" or "shaking down" the fiber. Treating bast severely like rag in a hollander beater would ruin it for *washi* by drastically lowering its freeness (drainage rate), shortening its length, and destroying its natural character.

This attitude toward beating was clarified for me in many discussions of the subject with Japanese papermakers. Referring to gampi preparation, a Japanese researcher once asked me, "What do you think is the best way to beat gampi in a regular roll beater?" "Lightly, right?" I said, thinking of the treatment rag receives in a hollander, a type of roll beater commonly used in the West. "Well, an old guy in Okayama told me one centimeter between the roll and bedplate for fifteen minutes." "But when do you lower the roll?" I said, assuming that at some point it had to happen. "You don't, except for maybe fifty or sixty seconds in the beginning." I found it hard to believe we were both talking about beating. Another papermaker secretly drew me aside one day and proudly told me his beater didn't have a bedplate. "What do you mean 'no bedplate'?" I asked him, convinced my Japanese was failing again. "I ordered it specially made," he said. "Produces superior stuff, no question. It's just smooth cement down there."

The strands of cooked bark are so soft and loose that his beater, like those with bedplates, is used as a kind of paddle-wheel thrasher. It really only looked like our typical rag beater. In fact, many of the Japanese beaters would probably not hold up or perform at all well with rag stuff in daily production.[5]

European-style hollander beaters *are* used for preparing mitsumata and gampi, but the roll is rarely, if ever, brought to bear on the fiber, and the

14. Stamper

beating time is usually kept below a thirty-minute maximum. If possible, when preparing kozo fiber, a Japanese papermaker avoids the hollander altogether because it tends to produce knots in the much longer kozo fiber.

In Japan, mechanical stampers were first built in the 1920s to substitute for hand beating. Their configuration, however, is very different from that of the traditional European trip-hammer, which was raised by hardwood pins set in a large, round, rotating shaft and allowed to fall. Japanese stampers usually consist of one vertical iron shaft approximately four centimeters in diameter and three meters long. The shaft is mounted onto a sturdy wood or iron framework at two points with bushings so that it will travel up and down freely. The bottom of the shaft is fitted with a hardwood striker approximately seven centimeters wide and sixty centimeters long. About two meters up the shaft from the striker, a large wooden weight is bolted solid to the shaft. A cam driven by an electric motor raises, rotates slightly, and lets fall the entire assembly of weight, shaft, and striker once every two seconds. Cooked bast is placed in a circular depression about twenty centimeters deep in the stamper's cement foundation. Stampers are often employed in working with kozo for a preliminary thumping that resembles hand beating. Stamping time averages thirty minutes, and stamped fiber is usually transferred to a regular hollander or a *naginata* beater for a final treatment.

The *naginata* is a specialized piece of beating equipment unique to Japanese hand papermaking. It was developed after the appearance of stampers for bast preparation, and it does a better job than a hollander of teasing the fiber apart, with minimal loss of freeness. *Naginata* is the Japanese term for a curved halberd used in former times to dispatch one's enemies. In the present-day beater, dull *naginata*-like blades are mounted on a shaft housed in a hollander-type tub that has a midfeather (middle partition) but no backfall (return ramp). Stamped bast is added to a load of clear water and dispersed by hand. The motor is switched on, and the blades begin hacking at the water and fiber. The mixture soon begins swimming around the oblong tub at a healthy clip, and treatment continues for one to twenty minutes, depending on the nature of the fiber. Kozo papers with very even fiber distribution are difficult to produce without a *naginata*.

Although hand beating was still practiced in many areas up until World War II, it is unfortunately rare in contemporary Japan. When employed,

15. Naginata beater

16. Naginata (halberd)

often it is followed by a very short one- or two-minute treatment in a *naginata* or hollander beater. Hand beating is believed to produce stronger papers by less shortening and washing of the fiber, but formation quality, particularly of contemporary hand beaten papers, may suffer somewhat.

Whatever the method, Japanese papermakers continue beating no longer than absolutely necessary for the paper type in production. One reason for this is a traditional inclination to be as gentle on the fiber as possible during preparation. Another is the more technical fact that very free (fast-draining), long-fibered stuff (prepared fiber) is essential to the Japanese process. The average papermaker in Japan may or may not consciously weigh both factors during preparation of the fiber. Usually, he evaluates the fiber's readiness by checking for finished length and dispersion in much the same way Western craftspeople inspect their beaten rag—in a clear glass or other small vessel of water. When the fiber is properly treated, he dumps it all into a box with a porous bottom, drains it, and then sets it aside, damp and concentrated, for papermaking in the next few days. (In the summertime, fiber cannot be left in this state for more than a few days or it will spoil. In the wintertime, however, it can be left a week or more in a cold room without any adverse effects.)

Finished Fiber

After many days of work, a batch of carefully prepared bast has been gently coaxed from its natural state into precious and fine material for papermaking. Many of its advantageous qualities are a result of the presence of large amounts of various hemicelluloses. Nonfibrous in nature, hemicelluloses have almost magical properties when they occur naturally with certain cellulose fibers. Water-loving and slightly mucilaginous, they greatly facilitate plasticization of the fiber during beating and improve deflocculation of the long fibers during mixing in the vat. Somewhat gluelike, they encourage bonding during drying. Hemicelluloses generally help to make much stronger, more transparent paper. Wood-pulp mills in the paper industry usually lose a good portion of various hemicelluloses when they put wood chips through the customary series of high-pressure cooking and bleaching processes. The Japanese papermaker, on the other hand, because of the low-lignin, high-hemicellulose content of the fiber, is able to cook in a relatively weak chemical and without pressure. This causes little damage to the fiber and leaves a large percent of the original hemicelluloses in the finished stuff.

Hemicelluloses produce a strong affinity for water molecules in bast fiber. As a result, in Japanese papermaking, a well-plasticized pulp is obtained with very little of the beating required of a rag fiber. The finished stuff is thus able to form strong bonds at drying, yet at papermaking it remains free, that is, willing to give up water at a rapid rate.

The gentleness of traditional bast preparation accounts for much of the strength and luster of *washi*. The tough, crisp quality of otherwise soft and flexible sheets is a result of the tight bonding of long, fine fiber made possible when thin bast cell walls, under the influence of plasticizing hemicelluloses, respond almost immediately to light beating by softening or collapsing. Fiber length is preserved, contributing to strength. Each fiber's smooth undamaged surface, combined with its uniformly long, thin shape, multiplied millions of times gives the finished sheet an enchanting surface sheen.

In addition to strength and beauty, it is apparent that some of the permanence of *washi* can also be attributed to the relatively mild treatment given the fiber during preparation.

Final Thoughts on Fiber Preparation

Finished bast ready for papermaking has a richness and sheen that makes it seem like fibrous gold. Knowing the time and energy invested in its production, Japanese craftspeople are very careful with their prepared stuff, and I was often reprimanded for not picking the last remaining lumps of fiber from the wall of a beater or bucket. ("Baretto-san, there's still lots of fiber in there. Make sure you get it all. You've got to have more respect for your stuff!") This attitude toward the fiber is born of the knowledge that seventy percent of the total working hours necessary to finish a batch of Japanese paper has gone into the preparation of the fiber. One person working all day and forming four hundred sheets at the vat will spend two more days pressing, drying, and inspecting those sheets. But, assuming the papermaker worked alone and started with harvesting the trees, the previous *seven* days would have been necessary for fiber preparation. In another light, 100 kilograms of harvested kozo trees yield 17 kilograms of black bark and 9 of white bark, but only 5 of finished paper. Likewise, the same quantity of harvested mitsumata or gampi yields 4.5 or 3.5 kilograms, respectively, of finished paper.

The processes of preparing the raw materials for a Japanese paper require considerable time and skill and are crucial to the quality and character of the finished product. These steps determine, in fact, the very essence of the paper, yet they take place long before anyone ever actually forms a sheet at the vat.

CHAPTER FOUR

Sheet Formation

HAND PAPERMAKING as it is known in the West is called *tame-zuki* by the Japanese. The term comes from the verb *tameru,* meaning "to retain or to fill and hold," plus *suku,* "to make paper." A rough translation would be "the fill and hold way to make paper." The phrase is, appropriately, descriptive of the sheet-forming action of *tame-zuki.* The Western papermaker dips his sievelike mould and deckle into the vat of stuff and scoops up a charge. Holding the mould parallel to the water's surface, he dexterously shakes the mould just enough to send waves running from side to side and then front to back across the mould. As he does this, all the drainable solution passes through the porous surface of the mould, leaving the fibers, including any knots or clumps, in an even layer. In this manner, a sheet of paper is formed in four to fifteen seconds with one charge from the vat.

On the other hand, the Japanese form sheets utilizing a unique method called *nagashi-zuki.* There is no appropriate term in English to differentiate it from the Western method except for "Japanese hand papermaking." The Japanese word comes from the verb *nagasu,* meaning "to flow or slosh," plus *suku,* "to make paper." A rough translation of *nagashi-zuki* might be "the flowing or sloshing way to make paper." Again, the phrase accurately describes the action involved at the vat, an awe-inspiring sloshing and splashing of water.

Grasping the two mould handles attached to the deckle, the papermaker uses the near edge of the mould to gently scoop up a charge from the vat. Then, tilting the mould, he sends the solution flowing rapidly across it, causing the excess to jump off the far side, and without pausing he scoops up another charge. This time, however, he keeps the liquid in the mould, amply contained by the deckle, which is three centimeters deep, and sloshes it repeatedly back and forth, and occasionally from side to side, across the surface of the mould. Gradually, water drains through and fiber builds up on the mould surface, but before the charge is exhausted the papermaker again tosses off much of the remaining solution and picks up a fresh charge. Without stopping, he continues sloshing the stock over the surface until a proper layer of fiber has accumulated. The final excess is then tossed back into the vat, and with it go large strands and knots of fiber, which are kept in suspension by the motion and do not form into the sheet. The charge–toss-off cycle may be repeated several times during the formation of one sheet of paper. Japanese sheets generally require between seven and ninety seconds at the vat, more time than needed for Western sheets.[1]

In addition to different action at the vat there are other important disparities in the two papermaking methods. In Western papermaking, paper is made from beaten linen or cotton rag. After formation of a sheet the deckle is removed, and the mould, with its fresh sheet adhering, is inverted and pressed against a felt with a slight rocking motion. The new sheet comes neatly off the mould and lies on the felt undamaged. A second felt is laid upon the new sheet of paper, and the papermaker returns to the vat with the mould to form another sheet. The second sheet of paper is also "couched" and covered with another felt. The process continues until a stack, or "post," of one hundred or more sheets interleaved with felts has been made. The post is then pressed for twenty minutes with a strong hydraulic press to remove most of the water. The paper is removed from the press, separated from the felts, restacked into a "pack," and pressed again lightly to remove more water and smooth the surfaces of the sheets. At this point, the sheets are usually set out to dry in a loft designed for the purpose. One papermaker working alone may make 250 sheets measuring fifty-five by seventy-five centimeters in a day.[2]

In Japanese papermaking, however, an entirely different process takes place. To begin with, the vat stock consists of water, a viscous formation aid, and very lightly beaten bast stuff.[3] After the papermaker forms a sheet, he unlatches and *opens* the deckle, since it is hinged to the mould at the far side. Then, carefully picking up the flexible *su,* or woven mould surface, with the new sheet adhering, he turns to a table behind him. Aligning one edge of the *su* with a post of previously couched sheets, the papermaker

17. Couching

carefully lowers the *su* with a rolling motion across the post until it lies flat and even on top. Then, picking up the near edge of the *su,* he carefully draws it away, leaving the new sheet of paper squarely on top of the post. He continues this form of couching, sans felts, accumulating between 200 and 500 sheets by the end of the day. He allows the post to stand and drain overnight. The following day he presses the post, gradually and very slowly increasing pressure. After pressing, the papermaker peels the fresh damp sheets off the pressed pack one at a time and brushes them onto a heated metal surface indoors or onto wooden boards outdoors for drying.

While modern *tame-zuki,* or Western hand papermaking, is a relatively familiar craft, *nagashi-zuki,* or Japanese hand papermaking, is, in essence, an entirely different process with unique dynamics at play. This chapter will explore *nagashi-zuki's* distinctive characteristics in detail.

Nagashi-zuki Action

When I went to Japan to study papermaking I had two years' experience in *tame-zuki.* While learning *nagashi-zuki* was always exciting, no aspect of the technique was quite as stunning as the sheet-forming action at the vat. It took me a long time to adjust from the stiff arms and shoulders and charge and shake of *tame-zuki* to the bent-kneed, curved-back posture and bouncing rhythmical action of *nagashi-zuki.* My initial critics kept pleading, "No, no, Baretto-san, you're trying to handle it like *tame-zuki.* You're just using your arms. This is completely different. You have to forget *tame-zuki.*" Even after months of practice, the advice was similar. "You're still too tight. Relax. You're working too hard. You work like that and you're going to be exhausted in seventy sheets. Get into a rhythm. Bend your knees and back. Only your knees should touch the vat. Use your whole body. You're too tight, Baretto-san."

Just getting the basic feel of *nagashi-zuki* action was a bit of a personal breakthrough, equivalent to successfully riding a bicycle for the first time. Part of the trick was learning to work with the system of overhead bamboo poles and lines that suspend the *nagashi-zuki* mould just clear of the stock in the vat. Without this spring-loaded support from above, working the charged mould would be quite difficult for anyone.[4] Trying to muscle the mould was, I quickly found, a sweaty and hopeless endeavor. One teacher made his point by working a large mould (sixty by ninety-five centimeters) with only his finger tips holding the handles. "See," he said, "you have to let the rigging above carry the weight; that's how it works. If you lift it and force it, you'll just kill yourself." His point was more easily understood than implemented. Simply scooping up some stock, allowing the rigging to bear the weight, and shaking or bouncing the mould was, to my dismay, not it. "No, no, no," my teachers patiently urged, "you're still moving *tame-zuki* fashion. Be loose. Be gentle. You have to roll and work with the bounce. Stop forcing it." I gritted my teeth and tried and tried and couldn't for the life of me generate the even waves and splashes, the rhythmical plops and swishes they all so gracefully produced. I watched and could see their movements were always the same, with never a mistake—dipping and sloshing, arms, legs, body, and back bent, all moving with the mould and splashing stock, bouncing and nodding together in the same movement, the same dance. I watched carefully and never was there a pause or a dead moment during the forming of a sheet. The mould and movement seemed like an extension of hands and body—as much a part of the papermaker as his fingers, and as easy as breathing. Each artisan had his own style, his own sounds at the vat, and each, the special grace and ease of action only time and practice can afford. By watching young, inexperienced workers next to those older and more skilled I saw how the dance grows on the clumsy student like running on a colt. Embarrassing, even comical at first, gradually the movement becomes steady and finally beautiful as all parts of the body move together in the same form, a joy to watch.

Several weeks after beginning, I had learned to use the spring from above and was forming sheets of fair quality. But forming sheets of identical thickness, for a full day and at a relaxed pace, is a skill born of long experience and one which I am just starting to acquire. Much of my time at the vat in Japan was spent practicing—making a post of fifty sheets, some of them perfectly good, and then throwing the whole lot back into the vat and starting over again.

It is difficult to fully describe the *nagashi-zuki* action with the written word alone. Because of this the reader should take advantage of any opportunity to see the actual process or a film or videotape of it. Styles may differ depending on the geographical area and the type of paper; for example, making thin tissue calls for a great deal of splashing action, while thicker papers require a more relaxed rolling of the stock back and forth across the *su*. But, while more will be said on *nagashi-zuki* action in a later chapter, for now suffice it to say that the basic idea during sheet forming is to keep the mould surface always awash with constantly moving stock.

Tororo-aoi: Key to Japanese Papermaking

The formation of very fine and delicate Japanese papers is made possible in the *nagashi-zuki* process largely by the admixture to the stock of a viscous agent called *neri*. (The term is related to the verb *nebaru,* meaning to be sticky or viscous.) Acting as a formation aid, *neri* serves to deflocculate the long bast fiber and to control drainage during sheet forming.

Neri is most commonly rendered from the roots of the Japanese *tororo-aoi* plant (*Abelmoschus manihot* Medikus or *Hibiscus manihot* L.) by pounding the roots with a mallet and soaking them in a tub of water. In a few hours the water in the tub takes on a curious thick and stringy texture. The first time I ran my hands through a tub of soaking *tororo-aoi* (also called *tororo*) it felt like a weird cross between honey and egg whites. But *tororo's* secretion is not sticky or gluelike; the terms "mucilage gum" and "size," used commonly to refer to this formation aid, are not appropriate. The secreted

18. Tororo-aoi

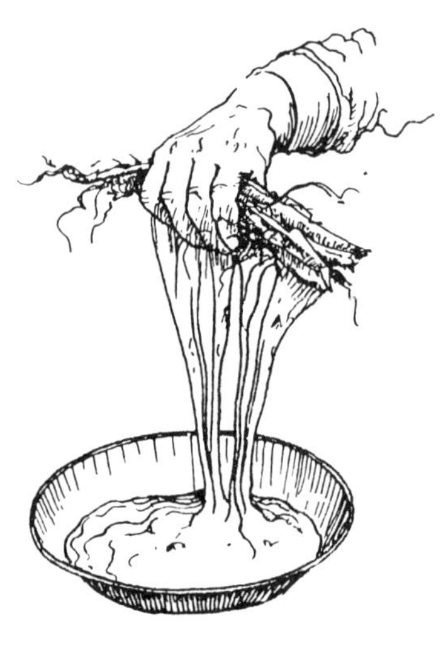

19. Tororo-aoi secretion after soaking in water

solution acts more like thick water, clear and viscous, free from an adhesive feeling. When rubbed between the fingers, although it feels slippery at first, it soon feels more like water.[5]

One of *tororo's* most obvious characteristics is its string-forming capability. If you pick up a bit of soaking root in one hand, raising it high, the water will fall away in one continuous hairlike strand, with no breaks and no sound of liquid falling into liquid. It is a surprising substance. Its ropiness will allow it to form its own siphon-like rope. I once scooped a bucketful of *tororo* from a larger tub without cutting the mass at the bucket's edge. Halfway across the room, I was dismayed to discover that the *tororo* was crawling out behind me and oozing across the floor entirely of its own accord. *Tororo neri* is a clear, slippery, viscous, stringy water—a kind of magic goo in the *nagashi-zuki* vat.[6] *Tororo's* various properties and effects during papermaking will be discussed below.

Tororo Cultivation

Tororo roots are raised annually from seeds, exclusively for papermaking. Seeds are usually planted in May. Later in the summer some leaves and the flowers are trimmed back to make the roots grow fatter. Only a few plants are left flowering for seed. As with fiber, few papermakers raise their own *tororo;* rather, it is done by full-time farmers who sell to dealers. During my stay in Japan, I met one exception, a sixty-five-year-old farmer and papermaker who gave me some enlightening advice on growing *tororo.* The conversation went somewhat as follows:

"Ah, Mr. Tanaka," I said, "about *tororo* and growing it.... I just want to ask a few things.... Is there anything difficult about planting?"

"Not especially," he said, "I usually plant in April or May, spacing the seeds about ten centimeters apart, and they come up fine. 'Course you have to thin them a bit later."

"I see," I replied. "What about rain?"

"Oh, you need rain all right. But *tororo* takes care of itself pretty well. You don't need to fool with it much. If you want you can put a little *jimpun* in the soil before planting."

"Uh...." (I was checking my dictionary. Finally, I found it: "human feces, human manure, night soil.") "Oh, really? That really helps, huh?"

"You bet it does," he said. "Makes an incredible difference in vegetables, too. New factory-made fertilizers never have matched it."

"I see," I said.

"Actually," he continued, "after you get it out of the pit it's best to mix it up really well and let it sit a while in a crock, maybe ten or fifteen days, till it gets soft and loosens up a bit."

"Hmm. . . ."

"Makes a surprising difference," he said. "People around here used to pay for it once a month at the grade school over the hill there. Strawberries turn out great . . . and watermelon! Watermelon gets very sweet and delicious."

I was checking my dictionary again. "Oh. . . ."

"Yes, indeed. You ask anybody around here. The taste of watermelon in the whole country has dropped a good bit since they came out with factory-made fertilizers. No sir, don't forget *jimpun* when you plant your *tororo*."[7]

Tororo roots are harvested, cleaned, and baled for shipment in fall. Papermakers then store a year's supply of the roots by submerging them in large cement tanks filled with a disinfectant diluted in water. If this is not done the roots will dry out or rot. There are several commercial agricultural disinfectants used in Japan, but cresol soap mixed with water in a one-percent solution is reportedly effective. The roots can be dried for later use, but the yield after resoaking and beating is poor. There is no concentrated powdered form of *tororo-aoi*.[8]

The Sheet-forming Process

Generally, a papermaker will add enough stuff to the vat of cold water to make fifteen or twenty sheets, taking into consideration the thickness of the intended paper and the need for an initial vat charging. The fiber is mixed first by hand with a bamboo stick and then with a rake or comblike mixer, usually referred to as a *mazè* in Japan. The *mazè* hangs from supports attached to the sides of the vat and is operated by pushing and pulling the device back and forth through the stock in the vat. When not in use, the *mazè* hangs above and in back of the vat. During preliminary mixing, which lasts about five minutes or for 125 strokes, the *mazè* is effective in breaking up clumps of beaten fiber and dispersing them evenly throughout the vat.

Tororo is then dipped from a barrel of mashed roots and poured through a cotton bag strainer into the vat. The strainer keeps any root chunks or specks from contaminating the vat. As with the fiber, the initial vat charge of *tororo* is greater than the amount required at subsequent rechargings as papermaking continues. Once added, the *tororo* is mixed evenly into the vat solution. This is done fairly quickly, first perhaps briefly with the *mazè,* then with the bamboo stick using wide circular but sudden strokes. Such action breaks up any large strands or concentrations of *tororo* remaining in the vat. Mixing is continued only as long as necessary, since prolonged agitation weakens *tororo's* effects. *Tororo's* concentration is often judged by observing its stringiness as a handful of the final vat stock falls from a raised hand.

In the mixed and ready vat the long fibers (three to twelve millimeters) stand still and evenly dispersed as if cast in jello. At the first charge, the papermaker works very quickly to dash the solution across the surface and off the far side of the mould. The charge immediately following is also handled quickly because the surface of the mould is quite porous and prone to rapid drainage. This means any large strands or clumps of fiber in the stock will be easily imbedded in the sheet if the mould is not operated quickly to keep them in motion. (If desired, the papermaker may stop and remove a clump or knot at the first charge.) At the second or third charge the papermaker shifts into a gentler motion. The mould surface by now has a slick base coating of fiber and *tororo* on which to work successive charges. Drainage decreases rapidly as a sheet accumulates thickness, so heavier and larger clumps may be more easily kept in motion and out of the sheet with less action.

Tororo's effect at this point is to control drainage enough to allow proper time for manipulation of the mould. If *tororo* were not present, the long fibers would sink and clump together in the vat, and drainage through the mould would be so fast that only a crude mat of fiber could be formed. The relatively unbeaten, free stuff of Japanese papermaking works with *tororo* and vice versa to produce a long-fibered, low-consistency stock of the proper freeness to be worked on a mould. If the stuff itself were not very free, its combination with the viscous *tororo* would yield a stock too slow to drain efficiently.

A sheet is slowly formed as charges are manipulated back and forth across the mould surface. (The deep deckle on the Japanese mould allows considerable action without loss of liquid over the edge.) Drainage through the mould surface and fiber mat pulls the fiber down and the long smooth bast fibers snag on those already intertwined on the mould surface.

The *nagashi-zuki* action and the string-forming nature of *tororo* serve to lay the fibers out evenly and along the same axis (parallel to the chain lines). This accounts for the very pronounced grain in many Japanese papers. Some well-made kozo papers cannot be torn against the grain without having the tear immediately switch to the direction of the chain lines.

In an effort to even out the grain difference, papermakers in some areas of Japan include a side-to-side motion in their sheet-forming technique. The predominant fiber orientation in all contemporary *nagashi-zuki* papers is, however, along the chain-line axis. Little or no grain in *tame-zuki* papers is considered to be one of their greatest advantages. The strong grain common to Japanese papers has been a fact of life for so long, however, that artisans using *nagashi-zuki* papers in other crafts have learned to work with the grain and often use it to special advantage.

Tororo in itself does not make *nagashi-zuki* happen. A sheet formed from the *nagashi-zuki* vat using the single-charge, gentle-shake action of *tame-zuki* will produce an uneven, thicker sheet. Only when *tororo* is used in combination with the distinctive sloshing action of Japanese papermaking does a thin and exceptionally uniform sheet result.

In *nagashi-zuki,* fibers are laid, pulled, and rubbed more snugly together than they would be in the simpler free-fall process of *tame-zuki. Nagashi-zuki* may be considered a controlled lamination process, while *tame-zuki* is a more random, "casting" form of papermaking. As a demonstration of the dif-

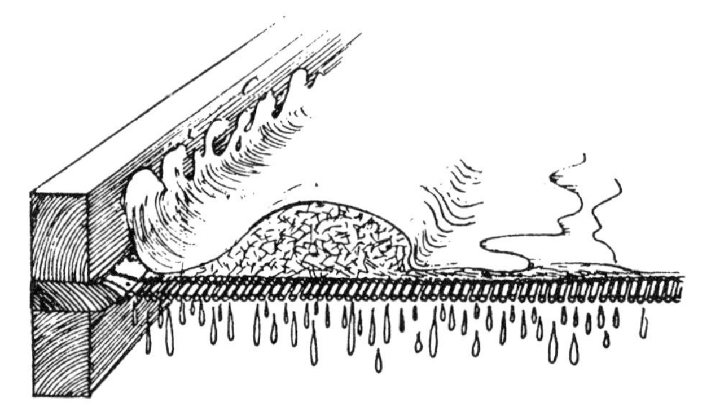

20. Cross section of mould during sheet forming (showing gradual lamination effect)

ference, a finished (dry) *nagashi-zuki* sheet can sometimes be peeled apart into several distinct layers.

A variety of considerations determine proper *tororo* concentration. However, since *tororo's* effects are never consistent, the main guide used by all papermakers is again *kan* and the knowledge born of experience. A feel for the air temperature, the condition of the *tororo,* the prepared fiber quality and type, the time on hand, and the desired quality and thickness of the finished sheets all bear on the final decision about quantity of *tororo* added to the vat. There is no standard formula. After making a few sheets the experienced papermaker knows if drainage and dispersion are correct.[9]

Control of paper thickness in *nagashi-zuki* is affected by fiber concentration in the vat as well as by *tororo* concentration and sheet-forming action and duration. When making thinner papers (tissues and some stationery), action must be lively. Although a high *tororo* concentration aids in making thinner sheets, too much *tororo* will cause problems later at parting. Accordingly, the stock is made with the minimal amount of *tororo* necessary, and more forceful action is used to help form clean and even sheets. In forming thicker papers, after the initial coating of the mould surface, action may become much more relaxed. Slower action permits better drainage, and drainage is a serious problem when making thicker papers. *Tororo* in combination with bast stuff, which bears large amounts of hemicelluloses, quickly builds up into a slick layer resistant to the passage of more stock. In making thick paper there may be pauses during the formation of a sheet when the handling of the mould is very much like that in *tame-zuki*—almost motionless, permitting maximum drainage.

Thickness is judged during papermaking by watching the slightly changing opacity of the sheet being formed. Thinner papers allow the mould surface to be easily seen through the sheet as formation proceeds. (Some of Japan's tissues, in fact, are so thin they seem absolutely nonexistent on the mould surface, requiring considerable experience for successful formation.) Thicker papers and all papers in general require a feel for how fast the fiber is accumulating. Consistency of style and routine is essential to forming several hundred sheets of the same thickness.

Each papermaker's sheet-finishing action is a bit different and varies with the paper being made. All, however, finish off smoothly, working the last charge to the far side of the mould and then tossing off the excess into the vat. Often a loud pop or crack accompanies the last wave of stock as it jumps off the mould and hits the thick stock below. It is a uniquely satisfying sound that those with long experience produce consistently at the close of each sheet's formation. A skilled papermaker is a pleasure to hear as well as to see.

Such noises in the vat help the craftsperson maintain rhythm and maintain consistency. I was told to "make it talk, make it speak—now! Right there!" when learning the proper sheet-forming action. Listening to one's own vat noises when practicing is as good a guide as watching the stock in the mould. Papermakers from the same shop can identify, with eyes closed, the person at the vat on the basis of the characteristic sounds alone.

A sheet completed, the papermaker rests the mould on two sliding mould supports in the vat and then unlatches and raises the hinged deckle, exposing the *su*. The *su* is really an oversized, refined version of a bamboo placemat, made of hundreds of rounded splints woven together with silk threads. In addition to the bamboo splints, a *su* has two outer edge sticks of Japanese cedar attached for strength and rigidity during use.

The papermaker removes the *su* from the mould by picking up the near edge stick with his left hand. He raises it in front of him until the far edge of the *su* is dangling free at about waist level. The new fresh sheet remains clinging to the opposite side of the *su*. The papermaker grasps the lower edge of the *su* with his free (right) hand and, as he rotates his body to the left 180 degrees, swings the *su* over his head so his left hand is now the lower and his right hand holds the *su* from above. The fresh sheet is still on the opposite side of the *su*. Carefully the papermaker lowers the *su*, easing the lower edge stick along upright guides on the couching table with his left hand. In the same motion, he continues lowering the *su* with his right hand, always maintaining a sharp curl where the new sheet meets the post of previously couched sheets, until it lies flat and even atop the post. Once the *su* is laid out flat, the papermaker carefully picks up the near edge stick resting against the couching guide and draws the *su* away, leaving the new sheet smooth and unwrinkled atop the post. The papermaker returns the *su* to the mould and, after closing the deckle and latching it, begins immediately to form another sheet. In one day of papermaking the craftsperson forms a pile perhaps twenty centimeters high, each sheet couched on top of the next.

A freshly finished stack in a damp and quiet shop after work has ended is a sight to see. It shines slick and wet, and *tororo* still shows its thick nature as the stack quietly releases strung-out drops around the edges. A fresh wet 400-sheet post is really a gentle laminate of laminates, like a fine pastry folded over so many times that you can barely see the individual layers, but you know they are there and that someone has worked long to produce them. The damp cool stack, though still far from finished paper, is a fragile, gentle creation that leaves its maker proud and protective.

This feeling struck home one day in Japan when I was practicing sheet forming while two older teachers dried paper at the other end of the room. They both were semiconscious of my work, watching me now and then out of the corners of their eyes. After two hours I had accumulated a solid five-centimeter post of sixty new, fragile sheets. I hung up my mould on the overhead rack and began running my hands through the post, tearing up the fragile sheets to return them to the vat. At that moment painful moans and cries ensued from the drying area. At first I assumed the teachers had uncovered a problem of their own, but I quickly realized they thought I had gone berserk and was ruining my fresh paper. As soon as I explained I was practicing, they were greatly relieved. Their initial spontaneous response, however, had revealed how second nature their protective feeling for new damp posts had become. The feeling one acquires is like that for a babe in a cradle—as if something very tender and precious is close at hand.

When first finished, the pile of sheets is quite fragile and should not be moved unless necessary. One Japanese papermaker I know learned this the hard way years ago. He had just finished work and, with several co-workers, was trying to move his pile into the press to sit until morning. Someone slipped, the board tipped, and the day's work slid off onto the dirty floor. Had the floor been clean, he could have put all of the fiber back in the beater and reworked it the next day. As it was, he lost most of the fiber in addition to his labor. Ever since that accident, he has kept the area in front of his couching table hosed clean. The same person also gets nervous with children in the shop. A quick grab by a two-year-old hand can destroy the corners of two hundred sheets in an instant. Once a child threw a stick across the shop and it landed in the middle of the unlucky fellow's post, puncturing most of the day's work.

Because there are no felts separating the sheets of paper and protecting them, pressing is a delicate process. Pressing too fast will slightly alter the stratification between the individual sheets, causing problems at parting, and may, in its extreme, turn the entire pile into a fluid mass, most of which will be pushed out from under the press boards for disastrous results. A general rule of thumb is: the slower, the better. The faster the post is pressed, the more trouble one is likely to encounter at subsequent steps in the process. Normally, after the paper drains naturally for the night, a press board, blocks, and a small hydraulic press are set atop the paper and left, with no other pressure exerted, for an hour or so. Then, during the course of the next five to seven hours, pressure is slowly applied, making the stack "weep" a bit each time until eighty percent of the water is removed. (As the hours pass, the viscosity of the formation aid breaks down, and the overall moisture distribution in the post equalizes.) At the end of the squeeze a twenty-centimeter post will be reduced to a thickness of five centimeters. Maximum pressure on a *nagashi-zuki* post is about 1.2 kilograms per square centimeter as opposed to 15 to 30 kilograms per square centimeter applied to a typical *tame-zuki* post. The pressure required in the Japanese process is so light that a simple lever device or stones piled on top of the upper press board will suffice. Such simple methods were, in fact, universal during the early days of the craft.

Most Japanese papermakers today use gaugeless screw or hydraulic presses to exert pressure and, once again, judge by feel, taking into consideration fiber type, paper thickness, and qualities desired in the finished paper. Thin papers, oddly enough, need to be pressed *harder* than other papers so that they are dry and strong enough at parting to withstand the handling. Kozo, because of its longer fibers, can stand higher pressure with less trouble at parting. Light pressure tends to produce a softer paper, while higher pressure yields a denser, crisper sheet.

21. Early pressing methods

22. Japanese screw press

After pressing, the compressed pack is moved only if necessary and then only with the care and attention worker bees show the queen of the hive. The human eye cannot detect individual sheets in the pack, but they are there and precious indeed. With a little picking, a corner of the first sheet can be raised, and incredible though it seems, a full sheet of damp paper can be peeled away from the pack in one smooth continuous movement.

The main factor permitting this surprising parting of paper pressed without felts, is the compact integral nature of each sheet produced in the *nagashi-zuki* process. During sheet forming, abnormally long, thin, well-plasticized fibers are laminated into a cohesive sheet with an internal strength that far surpasses the forced contact between sheet surfaces during pressing. Hemi-celluloses and *tororo* both greatly facilitate the mutual attraction of fibers within this compact sheet by associating well with cellulose, water, and each other.[10]

As one might suspect, parting is not always easy. In order to avoid problems, many professional, full-time papermakers lay a length of string or long grass along the inside edge of each new sheet after it is couched to indicate divisions between sheets. The step is bothersome during paper-making but saves time at parting. In making very thin papers, before couch-

23. *Parting sheets from the pressed pack*

ing, the near edge of the *su* is sometimes used to fold over five millimeters at the edge of the sheet. These double-thickness edges are staggered at the near edge during couching and, like the strings or grass lengths, serve to make parting easier.

Papermakers producing their standard paper in a customary thickness generally have few problems during parting. Students, however, and anyone dealing with an unfamiliar fiber or thickness may well have trouble. A common experience is to get a sheet well started only to have the last corner stick to the sheet below and finally tear, leaving the corner adhered to the lower sheet and spoiling one or sometimes both sheets. Pressing and final moisture content of the pack are critical to successful parting. A drier pack will yield strong paper that may part with difficulty if it is too dry. A wetter pack may separate more readily, but the sheets are likely to lack strength and be difficult to handle during the drying stage.

I once saw a papermaker throw a 250-sheet pack of 60-by-130-centimeter gampi paper back into the beater because he could not get the sheets apart after pressing. This person was highly experienced at making traditional kozo paper, but since he was unfamiliar with gampi and only worked with it occasionally, he had problems.

Mitsumata and gampi are known for being troublemakers at parting. Compared with kozo, the fibers of both are much finer and only a third as long. This means less wet-web strength, more free fiber ends, and a greater chance of picking between sheets at separation. The presence of more hemicelluloses in mitsumata and gampi (sixteen to twenty-three percent vs. nine percent in kozo) means better plasticization and more intimate fiber contact everywhere, including at the sheet interfaces. Thus, in most cases very large amounts of hemicelluloses, particularly in short fiber, contribute to problems at parting.

I myself have fussed and fumed over a troublesome pack of kozo sheets only to see another papermaker start four corners of her own paper and, staggering them a centimeter apart, draw all four off the pack in one effortless movement. Experience and the paper itself are great teachers.

Drying

After pressing and parting, each damp sheet is brushed onto a smooth surface for drying. Traditionally, wooden boards (usually ginkgo or pine) were used for this purpose, but since World War II, steam-heated metal dryers have

24. Drying boards

become widespread. Whatever the surface, learning to handle a thin, damp sheet and apply it flat and smooth to the drying surface without wrinkles or tears is not easy. Doing so quickly on a very warm or hot metal surface can be nerve-wracking. As a beginner I felt as if I were trying to brush a sheet of Saran Wrap onto plate glass with a whisk broom. Eventually, I was able to smooth out the paper before it started drying, but I am still working on doing it without leaving wrinkles behind. Papermakers in Japan brush sheets on a dryer or board so fast one would swear there are creases and folds, but close inspection reveals no such defects.

Steam-filled, metal-plate dryers dry paper in a minute or two. Boards placed outside dry paper in fifteen minutes if the paper is thin and the sun is strong. A dry sheet feels warm and smooth to the hand. A still-damp sheet feels cool and resists the hand's sliding across it. Dried sheets pulled from the drying surface often come away with an extremely satisfying crack. It is a high point in the process when the craftsperson gets to see, for the first time, the character of the paper that has been so long in the making.[11]

25. Steam-heated dryer

Although metal dryers are often praised for producing strong, crisp papers with smooth, uniform surfaces at mass-production rates, whether day or night and in any weather, there continues to be some argument about their possible harmful effects. Most are made from unpainted sheet steel, but if used often, they do not rust, and only in a few instances have I seen foxing or other possible evidence of iron entering the paper from the dryer. Technically, high-intensity drying is known to cause a loss of brightness. Traditionalists in Japan, however, disapprove of metal dryers because they seem to yield paper that is more prone to instability with future changes in humidity and that lacks the subtle gloss and wood-grain imprint of board-dried papers. Traditionalists also note that the indoor artificial dryers do not yield the slight bleaching effect of board drying in the sun and that while the heated dryers consume large quantities of increasingly expensive fuel oil, the boards require none.

One traditionalist summed it up with an example of squid drying in the sun: "You remember last night when we were drinking beer and eating that dried squid? You remember how flat the squid was? Well, that's because it was dried slowly and naturally in the sun. You put that same raw squid on a hot griddle and it'll shrink and twist like you wouldn't believe. Same thing happens to paper fiber when you use one of those metal dryers. It changes the paper inside. It isn't right, it isn't natural, and that's all there is to it."

The Finished Sheets

Finished *washi* is quickly appreciated for its light weight, softness, translucency, gloss, natural color, and amazing durability and strength. Traditionalists claim its gloss and crispness increase with age.

Often, dried *washi* is found stacked in piles with fuzzy deckle edges protruding, inviting a touch. Riffling through a pile of *washi,* face and nose close to catch the haylike smell, is a distinct pleasure. And sitting in a room full of piles of well-made paper is a warm and quiet honor. There is more here than "just paper." While the Westerner is conditioned to think of paper as something cheap, lifeless, and expendable, like air, in Japan traditionally made paper speaks to the beholder in an unforgettable way, stirring the spirit and infusing the word "paper" with a deeper meaning. It has presence and dignity, and commands respect.

Nagashi-zuki sheets are usually quite thin and lightweight—ten to eighty grams per square meter. Relatively thick sheets made using the *nagashi-zuki* technique are either rough and uneven or are made up of two or three distinct sheets laminated together (formed and couched as separate sheets but dried as one). Making thick sheets using the *nagashi-zuki* process is not very practical due to decreasing freeness during sheet forming. Because of *tororo's* presence, the rate of drainage through a sheet slows rapidly as fiber accumulates on the mould surface. Cutting back on *tororo* content increases drainage but detracts from good formation; hence, a rough or uneven final sheet results. Lamination of sheets by parting and drying them two or three at a time after pressing yields very even and beautiful thick sheets but requires two or three times the work at the vat. Because of these problems, when making thicker papers, the Japanese often find the Western (*tame-zuki*) method more economical.

Final Thoughts on *Nagashi-zuki*

It is my feeling that good *nagashi-zuki* paper is not made but rather becomes. The sensitive craftsperson only helps the process along—as if just another element, equal to the water or the fiber or the sun. To believe that one has a more significant role, or to assume that by trying one can "make" the paper more beautiful, is a mistake. The finished paper is too fine, too possessed of its own life and spirit to be a "man-made" product. If a papermaker watches the paper, and listens, and feels, the paper will train him to improve. There are no lessons, no easy answers—only repeated papermaking until a natural dialogue develops between craftsperson and fiber; only watching and working until the language is learned and the hands, eyes, and ears understand intuitively. In a sense, it is a magical process, and the craftsperson, only an honored participant.

The *nagashi-zuki* craft today is the result of dialogues that have taken place between generations of unknown artisans and the same fiber over the course of 1200 years. Those exchanges have improved the craft century after century, and now we are the privileged inheritors of the process.

Although there is evidence to support earlier Chinese or Korean invention of the craft, most experts believe that *nagashi-zuki* sheets were first made in Japan around the year 800. Whenever and wherever it occurred, the development of *nagashi-zuki* marked the beginning of a way of making paper completely different from all other methods. The basic process evolved into a craft adapted to forming a variety of highly specialized long-fibered thin papers that until recently no machine could simulate. *Nagashi-zuki* is a craft in itself and only a distant relative of the felting processes of *tame-zuki* and machine papermaking. Its place in the history of hand papermaking is second only to the invention of papermaking itself.

PART TWO

The Craft in the West

INTRODUCTION

By this point, the reader is doubtless fully aware of the challenges to be faced in any attempt at *nagashi-zuki* in the West. The varied materials and tools required are not available off-the-shelf, and more important, it is extremely difficult to communicate the actual hands-on working of the craft in a book.

I am reminded of an important visit with one of my teachers in Japan. Together we were looking at a book the Japanese government had recently published to help preserve the craft of making his traditional paper. The amount of detail in the government report was astounding. Data on water quality, weather, soil conditions, equipment, tools, and papermaking procedures were all carefully presented. Not a stone seemed left unturned. I asked the artisan, "Kubota-san, aren't you concerned about this book? With it in hand, now anyone will know the details of your craft and be able to make your paper." He was quiet for a moment, then he looked me in the eye and said firmly, "You have to realize this book is almost useless." I was a little surprised. "Why do you say that?" I said. "They've covered everything. . . ." "Baretto-san, you can show a photograph of a drying brush, and you can print a perfect drawing of it in a book like this, but you cannot describe the slightly changing position of a person's hand as he brushes a damp sheet on a board. That, and all the other unspoken things that are essential to making my paper, can only be passed directly from one person to another, as they work together. That is the only way the craft can be preserved. You cannot learn the essence of it from a book, and it is foolish to think you can."

Kubota-san's comments are equally relevant here. *Nagashi-zuki* can never be fully presented in a book, no matter how lengthy or how carefully written the text. It *is* possible, however, to give the reader enough information to perform the basic technique in the West, with relatively simple tools and available materials. It is to this end that Part 2 is presented—not to transmit mastery of the craft, but to share its basic workings to the extent possible in book form, to allow the reader to delve into and use the process, and thus by touch and by experience, to lead him or her to a more intimate sense of the real mastery evident in well-made Japanese paper.

For those who actually try *nagashi-zuki* and especially for those who persevere, quiet but deep rewards lie in wait. Carry on and good luck!

CHAPTER FIVE

Tools and Equipment

As THE CRAFT of Japanese papermaking has evolved over the past 1100 years, several tools have also been developed that are now integral to the papermaking process. While Western items may be easily substituted in some cases, a few of the required tools are highly specialized items normally made only by full-time Japanese professionals. Although it was common practice for papermakers to build their own tools during the history of the craft, today these skills have become completely separate fields. Ironically, with the passing of the few remaining professional toolmakers, in-house tool production may again become a necessity for contemporary Japanese papermakers, as it already is for Western practitioners of the Japanese craft.

This chapter describes all tools essential to the Japanese process, beginning with the professionally made Japanese tools and advice on importing them. Subsequently explained is the construction of alternative tools in the West, proceeding from the simplest to production-level substitutes. For ease of reference the tools and construction procedures are listed below in order of appearance. Proper use of each item is explained here and in Chapters 6 and 7. Suppliers for tools are listed in Appendix 2.

Moulds
- Japanese Moulds
- Simple Mould
- Advanced Mould

Vats and Attachments
- Japanese Vats
- Simple Vats
- Traditional Production-Level Vats
- Attachments and Related Tools

Cooking Equipment
- Japanese Cauldrons
- Simple Pots
- Production-Level Pots
- Drain Basket
- Wood-Ash Lye Maker
- Washing Equipment

Beating Equipment
- Japanese Tools
- Beating Sticks
- Beating Surfaces
- Stamper
- *Naginata* Beater
- Hollander Beater

Cleaning Equipment
- Speck Removal by Hand
- Flat Diaphragm Screen

Tororo-processing Tools
- Mallet
- Strainer

Presses
- Japanese Presses
- Simple Weight System
- Lever Press
- Screw and Hydraulic Presses
- Press Boards and Felts

Drying Equipment
- Japanese Dryers
- Boards
- Heat-Lamp Dryer
- Steam-Heated Dryer
- Drying Brushes

Other Tools
- Work Table
- Mould Suspension System

The *Su*

Japanese Su There is no other item so tied to successful implementation of the *nagashi-zuki* process as the *su,* the flexible mould surface. Once the sheet is formed, it must be very gently stacked atop the post. A finely crafted Japanese *su* lies smooth and rigid on the mould, yet is porous during papermaking and curls loosely in one direction during couching (see Fig. 75).

In addition, it is very light in weight, even when wet—an important consideration when making sheets of at least 60 by 180 centimeters (about 24 by 71 inches). A poorly made *su,* on the other hand, is likely to be too stiff at couching and may slightly distort the sheets or cause bubbles between successive sheets, making parting of the sheets after pressing more difficult.

The traditional Japanese *su* is made from bamboo splints woven together with silk and nylon threads. The surface of the *su* actually consists of three sections—the main mat woven together with silk, and two short outer sections woven together with nylon where wear is the greatest. Nylon thread is considered inappropriate by Japanese *su*-makers for weaving the main mat because it stretches more than the silk and may cause distortion of the fresh paper during couching.

Because the grain changes radically at the nodes of a bamboo stem, only bamboo taken from between the nodes is used in making the main mat of the *su.* Since these sections are only about 30 centimeters (12 inches) in length, a series of butt joints are required when weaving the normally much-longer *su.*

The bamboo splints used in a *su* are actually bamboo dowels made from splints that have been drawn through a die four to six times each until they are perfectly round. The raw material for the splints is taken from bamboo growing among cedar trees. In such an environment, the bamboo has a tendency to grow straighter and with greater length between nodes, in its effort to reach the light above the cedars. At the splintmaker's house, the bamboo is cut into sections and the nodes are cut away, leaving open-ended tubes. Only the outer layer of wood is cut into slabs for splitting because the outer grain of bamboo is much tighter than the inner and produces a stronger, longer-lasting splint with a smoother surface. Each slab from the original tube is split into ten square splints, and then each splint is drawn through a series of five or six consecutively smaller holes until the entire batch is consistent in diameter. The action of finishing bamboo splints looks something like drawing wire except that the tool for making *su* splints gradually cuts and shaves material away from the core while wire is stretched and compressed to the appropriate diameter. Splints of many different diameters are produced for the range of *su* required for the tremendous assortment of papers made in Japan. The average *su* has splints approximately .625 millimeter (.025 inch) in diameter with a spacing of roughly eleven

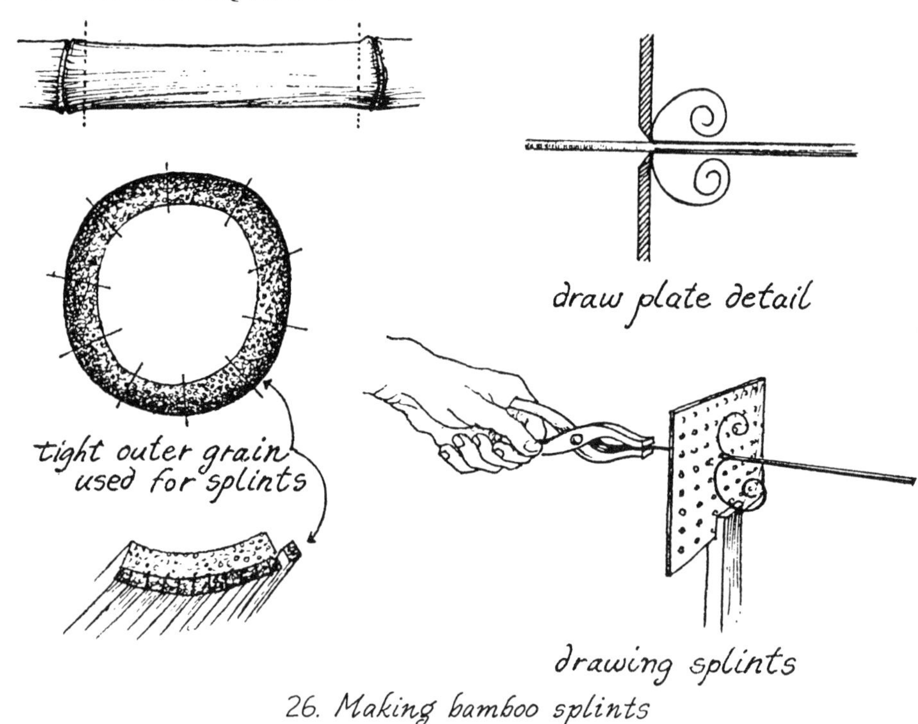

26. *Making bamboo splints*

laid lines to the centimeter (28 lines to the inch). Only one eighty-four-year-old woman in the entire country still makes bamboo splints, and presently no young people are learning her craft.

A finished *su* used daily will last between one and five years depending on how it has been cared for. During that period the threads may break and require mending in places. The bamboo splints will last many years. When a *su* begins to need frequent repairs, it is sent to the *su*-maker for reweaving. The old threads are cut completely away, the splints are cleaned and resorted, and the *su* is rewoven with new thread.

The silk threads used in making the *su* are also produced by only one forty-nine-year-old artisan. Just as the bamboo splints are finely crafted dowels, the silk threads are in fact three-ply threads made like rope. Spinning is done in a long narrow workshop by running lengths of silk fiber up and down the hall and attaching them to a series of bobbins on a spinning rig. Each of the small bobbins is driven by its own string belt that runs to a master drive-wheel manipulated by the craftsman. The drive wheel looks somewhat like a bicycle wheel with an attached hand crank. When spinning begins,

27. Spinning threads

the craftsman puts a set number of lefthand twists on each of the small bobbin threads by counting his turns on the drive wheel. He pushes the spinning rig down the hall as the threads shorten in length.

The proper number of turns completed, he stops, attaches three twisted strands to every third bobbin, and reverses the master wheel in a righthand direction, allowing the strands in each group of three to untwist a bit and intertwine. The whole operation is like making miniscule ropes. Like the bamboo splints, threads are made in an incredible variety of sizes depending on the nature of the finished *su* required by the papermaker.

Once the threads are finished they are strung out to air, requiring more trips up and down the long hallway. On a busy day the threadmaker, a human spider of sorts, walks or runs up and down the hallway the equivalent of forty kilometers. No young people are currently apprenticed to him.

While only one person still makes thread, and one makes splints, as many as ten people in Japan still weave the two components together into *su*. Weaving is performed on a long, low, upright stand set on small wheels so the whole assembly can roll back and forth across the floor. This saves the *su*-maker considerable leaning and stretching when working on a 180-centimeter (71-inch) *su*. For a detailed description of the weaving process, see Weaving the *Su* below.

Although nineteen people still weave *su* today, no more than two of them are below the age of fifty-five, and no one under thirty-five has shown a commitment to continuing in the field.

In addition to bamboo, *su* are occasionally made of lengths of pampas grass (*Miscanthus sinensis*). Stalks of the plant are cut from the wild and graded for size. Then, since the grass is hollow, rather than solid, and too short to run the full length of the *su*, sections are butt-spliced together with a short piece of bamboo. This bamboo splint must be just the right diameter so that when wet and swollen during papermaking it does not split the grass and weaken the joint.

Su made of pampas grass or other naturally occurring grasses were much more common in the early days of papermaking (prior to 1300), and horse-hair was used long before the highly refined silk threads of today. The coarse watermark produced by the pampas-grass *su* is still associated with earlier periods, hence its occasional use in producing paper having an "ancient" appearance. The longevity of pampas-grass *su* is less than that of regular bamboo *su*, since the hollow grass is not as resistant to water as the solid, tight-grained bamboo.

Very thin and delicate Japanese papers free of laid or chain lines are made on regular *su* faced with a specially made, very fine white silk mesh called a *sha*. No one continues to make the white fabric by hand today, and paper-makers have switched to more troublesome machine-made substitutes. Before the mesh can be attached to the *su*, it must be treated with fermented persimmon juice to toughen the silk fiber and keep it lying flat against the *su* during papermaking.[1] To apply the brown juice, the untreated fabric is laid on a smooth, tight-grained board and liberally wetted with water. The mesh is then brushed out flat against the board, with care being taken to smooth out any bubbles or folds. Without disturbing the mesh, thinned persimmon juice is then applied with a brush. The first application is allowed to dry, as are five or six successive applications. When finished, the fabric is stripped off the board, brown in color and having considerably more stiffness and body than the original white mesh.

Attaching the treated *sha* to the *su* also requires special skill. The two are sewn together along one outer support stick when both are wet so they

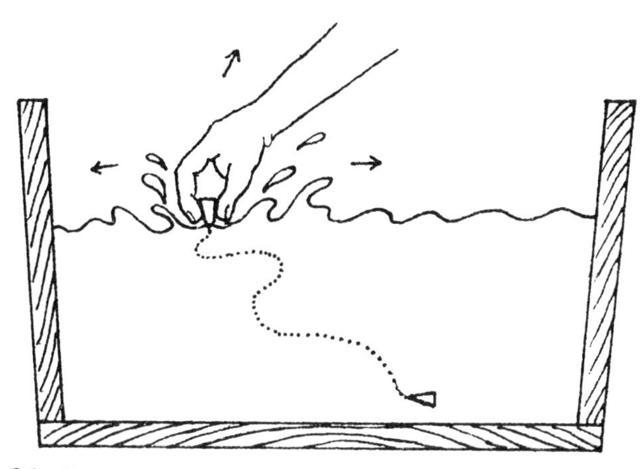

28. Rinsing su in rinse vat after papermaking

act as one uniform surface during papermaking. Unlike the regular *su,* the mesh-covered *su* is not flipped in the mould from one sheet to the next during papermaking.

At this writing, custom-made *su* (and occasionally attached *sha* as well) can still be ordered from Japan in any size and shape desired. A matching mould can either be ordered with the *su* from Japan or built in the West after the *su* arrives. Exact inner deckle dimensions and advance payment (foreign bank draft payable in Japanese yen) must accompany any order. Write Shimura Asao or Richard Flavin with your requirements and request a quote. Lee S. McDonald Fine Hand Papermaking Equipment, in America, sometimes has a stock of Korean *su* on hand. (See Appendix 2 for addresses.)

To care for your imported *su,* after papermaking each day rinse it *thoroughly* in clear water until few or no stray fibers remain adhered to the surface. (See Fig. 28.) Then roll up the *su* and shake it out thermometer-style, using your whole arm. Then switch ends, shake it again, and hang it up to dry in a place with good air circulation. Hanging the *su* on a clothes line (clip it with clothes pins at one of the edge sticks, or at the sewn edge, if covered) is recommended. The *su* should not be left to dry when rolled up or when hanging in a damp place. Doing either increases the chance of mold formation and thereby promotes deterioration of the silk threads.

Placemat Su (Refer to the vat and *su* terminology chart in Fig. 29 to clarify descriptions of tools described here and below.) The placemat *su* is a very crude substitute for the superbly made professional Japanese tool, but

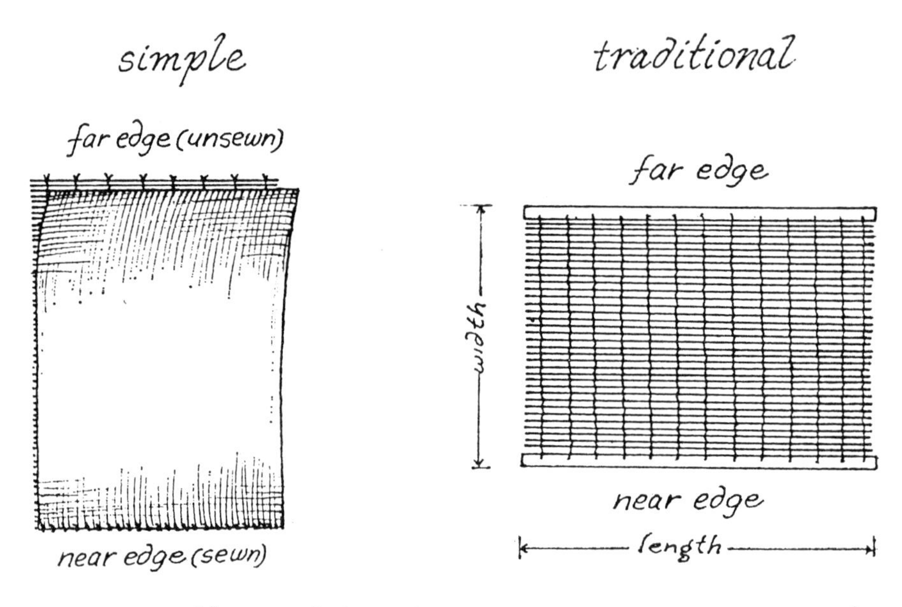

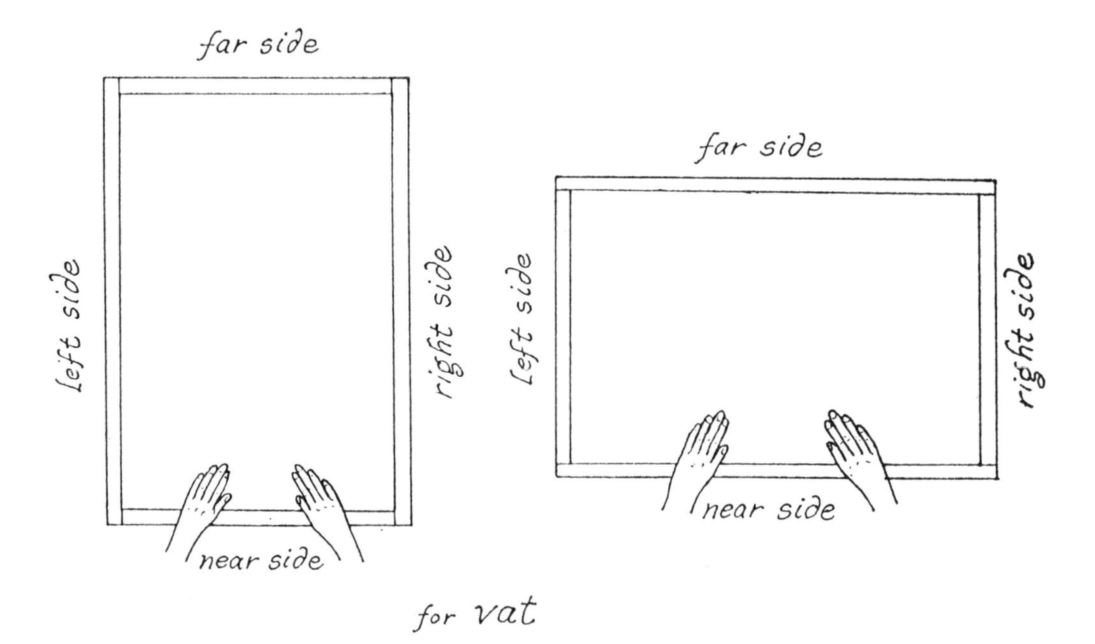

29. Terminology chart

properly constructed, it will perform adequately for limited papermaking. The basis of this *su* is a bamboo placemat purchased at an Oriental import house or second-hand goods shop. Take care to look for a mat free of dye or paint to avoid possible color bleeding. If you are lucky you will be able to find a new or used item with round bamboo splints about 1.5 millimeters (1/16 inch) in diameter (see Fig. 76). Sometimes mats sold in art-supply stores for protecting calligraphy brushes are more carefully made than those sold for use as placemats. Mats with very fine threads are not appropriate since they do not have enough open area to allow proper drainage.

Well-made mats with splints and threads of ideal diameters are rare, and you will probably have to settle for the more common but crudely made "matchstick" placemat. Because of the larger size and diverse diameters of the splints, a matchstick mat must be covered with a mesh of some sort to insure proper release of the sheet during couching. The advantage of the less common, more finely made mat is that it may be used bare, without a covering, requiring less work and yielding finished papers with the often-preferred laid watermark.

To cover a matchstick placemat (or any mat that is too rough and catches fiber during couching), first fit the mat to the mould (see Simple Mould, below). Lay the mat on the mould, untie or loosen the chain-line strings on both ends of the mat, and remove an equal number of sticks from both ends until the mat is approximately 2.5 centimeters (1 inch) shorter than the long dimension of the mould. Tie the strings off, and trim the excess string to 4-millimeter (about 3/16-inch) lengths.

For a covering mesh, synthetic sheer material commonly used for making curtains is recommended. Mesh with about 10 lines to the centimeter (25 lines to the inch) is fine for working with kozo. You should be able to find what you need at a well-stocked fabric or upholstery supply house. Look for sheer material of the proper mesh count that is dimensionally stable in both the warp and woof directions and yet flexible. Write Lee McDonald (see Appendix 2) if proper material is not available locally. Also, refer to Advanced Mesh Covering, below, for a discussion of more-involved mesh coverings.

After you have obtained the proper mesh and fitted the mat to the mould, trim the mesh so that it is just as wide as the mat in the narrow direction and 2 centimeters (3/4 inch) longer than the mat in the long direction. Submerge both the mat and the mesh in a sink or tub filled with 10 to 15 centimeters (4–6 inches) of cool water for at least 15 minutes before proceeding to the next step. Intermittently during soaking, stretch the mat in the long direction and tightly roll and unroll it from both ends to help loosen it. Good flexibility in any *su* is crucial.

Working under water, carefully align one end of the mesh to one end of the mat. Raise the two out of the water vertically so the mesh lies flat against the mat free of bubbles and so the extra 2 centimeters of mesh trails at the bottom. Repeat if necessary. Lay the two on a water-repellent surface (one of your finished press boards, for example) mesh side up. Move the extra-mesh end of the mat to the edge of your working surface so that about 2 centimeters (3/4 inch) of the mat hangs over the edge. Slide a nail file or flat object under the loose mat perpendicular to the edge of the board to hold the mat horizontally on a plane with the portion lying on the board.

Carefully fold the mesh over the extended end of the mat, and with a needle and a single length of synthetic thread, begin sewing the mesh to the mat. Sew around the first two sticks of the mat, stitching every centimeter (3/8 inch) or so. When finished, tie the thread off securely at the corner of the mat. During sewing, keep the mat and the mesh wet, smooth, and in intimate contact with each other. This approach will help insure that the pair act as one when wet during papermaking.

After you have finished sewing the mesh to the mat, you have completed the *su*. See Figure 77. If papermaking is not to follow immediately, hang the *su* up on a line using clothes pins at the sewn end. See Simple Mould, below, for construction of a mould designed for use with this placemat *su*.

Tools and Materials for Making Traditional Su While moulds last about ten years, a Japanese *su* in daily use usually needs attention and repair after only a few years and often requires reweaving shortly thereafter. Thus, although construction of *su* more sophisticated than the placemat *su* is complex, it is the only solution if the Western papermaker is to avoid considerable expense and future dependence on Japanese toolmakers.

There are two main components to a *su*: the splints, or "sticks," and the thread. Although you may want to experiment with native grasses or your own drawn bamboo splints, my own experiments have been mainly with stronger, man-made substitutes. The most promising of these are custom-made glass fiber and polyester or epoxy resin "pull-truded" rods of the appropriate

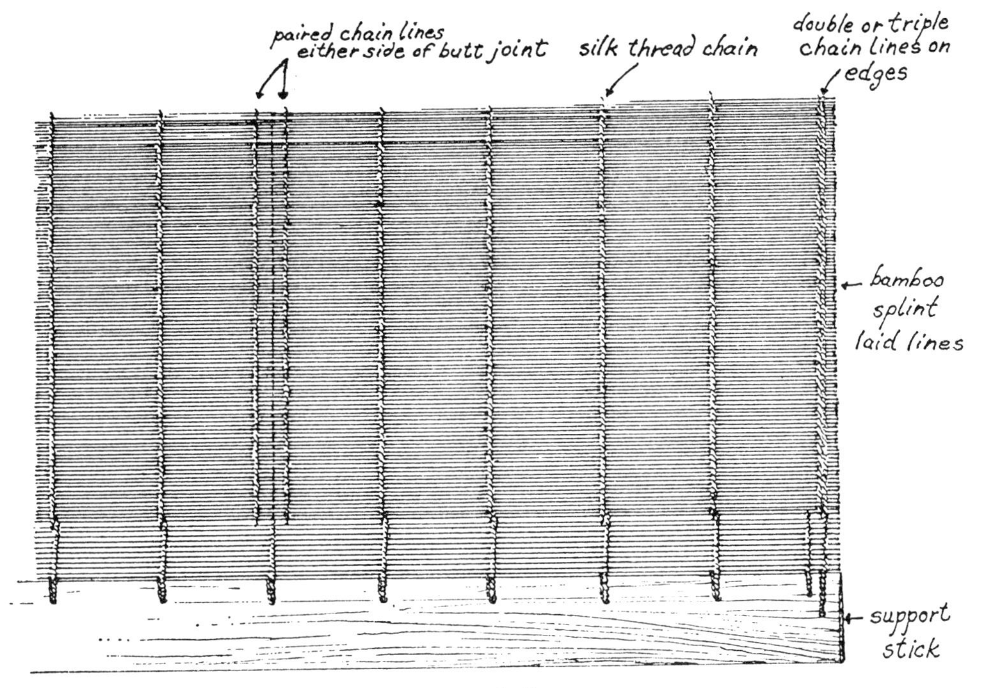

30. *Detail of Japanese su*

diameter (.625–1 millimeter, or .025–.040 inch). At this writing, carbon fiber, an even stronger material, has resisted pull-trusion into the small diameters required. In addition to their indefinite life span, synthetic sticks also have the advantage of availability in coil form, which means they can be cut to the full length of the finished *su,* eliminating the butt splices requisite with bamboo or grasses. (Coated, or anodized, tempered aluminum rod is another yet-unexplored possibility.) See Figure 78 for two versions of home-constructed traditional *su.*

If you decide to work with the fiberglass sticks, calculate the number required, assuming roughly 8 sticks of 1 millimeter (.040 inch) in diameter for each centimeter (.40 inch) of the *su's* width. Closer to 11 sticks per centimeter (27 sticks per inch) will be required if the sticks are of the more standard .625 millimeter (.025 inch) diameter. (The smaller diameters are harder to manufacture but provide a more uniform surface and action in the finished *su.*) Cut the total number of sticks required (plus about 20 extra) to the exact same length one at a time by rolling the material under the blade of a sharp matt knife, so as to cause minimal fraying of the glass at the raw ends.

To reseal the ends, grasp a group of about 20 cut sticks, fan them slightly, and dip both ends in liquid fiberglass resin and catalyst (available at an auto-parts or marine-supply shop). Carefully wipe away any excess with a cotton cloth. Group the sticks in bundles of about 20 sticks each, fanned at both ends with a rubber band at the middle to keep the wet ends from touching. Gather together and re-fan the sticks several times during the next 12 hours to make sure no two stick tips get stuck together. When the resin has hardened, sort all the sticks and eliminate any irregular or defective ones.

For threads, I have used a #69 bonded nylon thread with fair success. This thread is often used by upholsterers and awning and tent manufacturers. Although very water-resistant, it does not retain a round shape where it passes between splints, resulting in insufficient splint spacing. A monofilament fishing line may work better, particularly if Orvis fly-tying bobbins (see Fig. 32 and Appendix 2) are used in lieu of the homemade bobbins described below. Ideal thread diameter is .25 millimeter (.01 inch). Silk thread shrinks more and stretches less when wet than the nylon, yet it is considerably weaker and less resistant to water in the long run. In addition, the very tightly spun silk thread required does not seem to be readily available in the West. When workability and functionality are considered, nylon appears to be the best choice at present, at least for first attempts at *su* making.

Obviously, both of the synthetic components, sticks and thread, will not act exactly as the traditional materials during papermaking. While the traditional *su* is light in weight and remains square even when wet and even though large in size, problems may be encountered when synthetic *su* much larger than 45 by 60 centimeters (about 18 by 24 inches) are attempted. As the size and weight of a *su* increase, the synthetic threads are more prone to distortion. However, the suggested materials, when used with the tools and techniques described below, will yield smaller *su* that can function in daily production. Future experimentation is likely to result in usable larger synthetic *su* as well.

The two major tools used in making *su* are the bobbins and the jig, or weaving stand (see Fig. 31). A suggested method of constructing bobbins is shown in Figure 34. Alternative designs are fine as long as you produce a weighted bobbin that has a soft, or at least resilient, surface. Bobbins for nylon thread should weigh approximately 60 grams (2 ounces) each. To

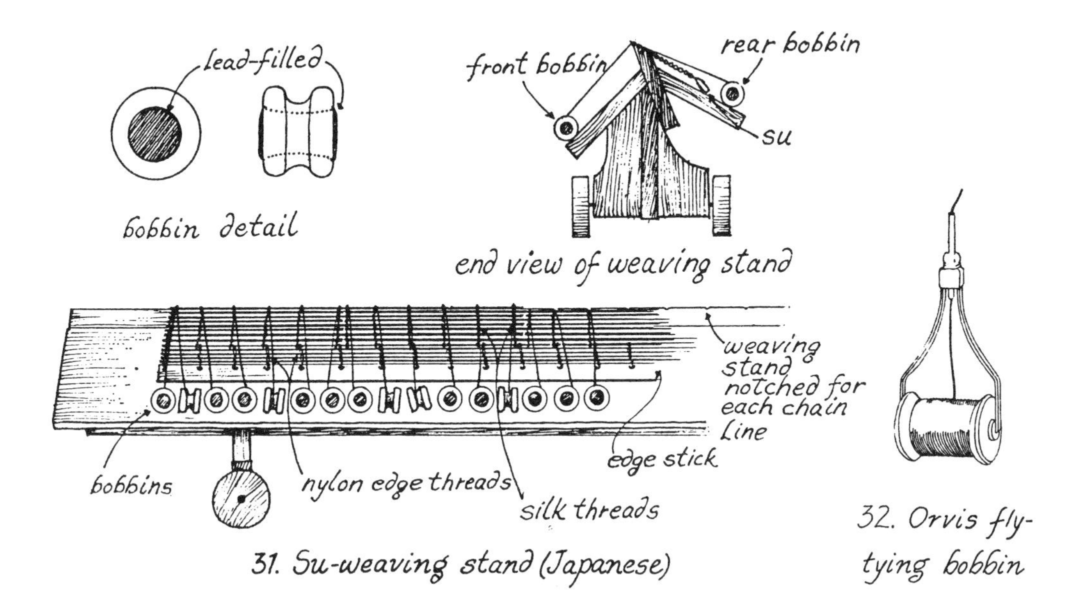

31. Su-weaving stand (Japanese)

32. Orvis fly-tying bobbin

make a set of bobbins, first calculate the total number of bobbins needed to make the size *su* you require. Chain lines run every 2.5 to 3 centimeters (every 1–1 3/16 inches), and each chain line requires two bobbins. Remember that if you intend to have butt splices (required with bamboo) within the surface of the *su,* you must run two chain lines (one on each side) where a line of splices occurs. For each bobbin required, with a matt knife cut two 9-millimeter pieces of 19-millimeter ID (inside diameter) rubber garden hose (two 3/8-inch pieces of 3/4-inch ID hose) and one 19-millimeter length of 19-millimeter OD (outside diameter) plastic plumbing pipe (one 3/4-inch length of 3/4-inch OD pipe). A miter box and saw will prove helpful in cutting the pipe to even lengths. A section of 1.5-centimeter (5/8-inch) OD plastic pipe slid inside the hose will help when cutting the hose. Assemble the bobbins by sliding the hose pieces over the open ends of the pipe. Carefully adjust the hose pieces to overhang the pipe ends about 4 millimeters (about 3/16 inch), leaving a channel about 6 millimeters (1/4 inch) wide in the middle for the thread. Tape one end of each bobbin with a flat piece of wide masking tape, taking care to make a tight seal. Also be sure that you do not alter the position of the hose on either end of the pipe section. Set up your prepared bobbins on newspaper and fill them all with lead buckshot or BBs (both available at a sporting goods shop). Mix up a cup of fiberglass resin by adding the catalyst that comes with it, and with a spoon, begin filling up the insides of the bobbins with the resin. Because the resin is thick and the shot slows down the flow, completely filling all the bobbins may take some time, but keep at it. When they are filled, leave them to harden overnight. The next day remove the tape and sand down both ends of each bobbin so that the plastic and shot are flush with the hose. A face mask and an electric belt or table sander with a vacuum attached are recommended.

When you have completed all the bobbins, wash them free of all dust, and let them dry. Then brush the bottom of the thread channel with rubber cement to provide a nonslip surface. To make bobbin leaders, cut a 20-centimeter (8-inch) piece of cotton string (approximately kite-string weight) for each bobbin. Tie as shown in Figure 33. Trim the short end almost

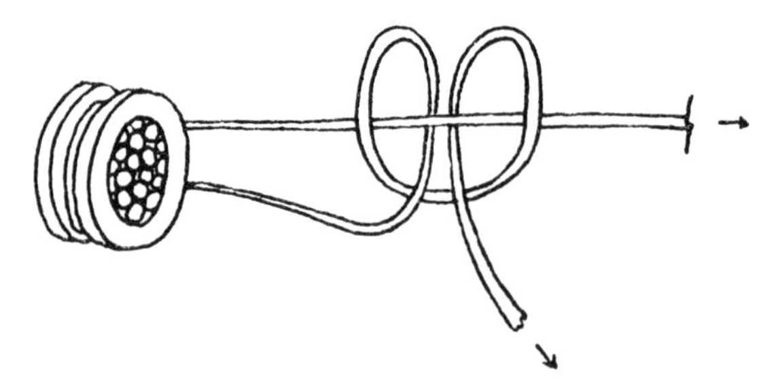

33. *Tying leader to bobbin with two halfhitches*

flush with the knot and the long end to about 10 centimeters (4 inches). These leaders always stay on the bobbins and are used as an anchor to which the nylon chain-line threads are tied prior to weaving.

Figures 35 and 80–82 show one approach to building a *su* jig, or weaving stand. Much simpler tools are possible, of course. You may even be able to make a workable jig from a 2.5-by-15-centimeter (1-by-6-inch) pine board by planing the top edge into a sharp, straight, wedgelike point. Clamp the board in a vise to hold it upright. You will have to do more leaning and stretching without the wheels and track, but setting up this board is a lot quicker than building one of the regular jigs.

Determine the proper spacing for all your chain lines with consideration for where the *su* will fall on the ribs of the mould and where the deckle will close on the *su*. Use a small triangular or knife-edge file to make a *slight* notch on the jig edge at the precise spacing of each chain line. This notch will carry and space each chain line during weaving. Later, when making subsequent *su*, if you decide to change the spacing you can add other notches.

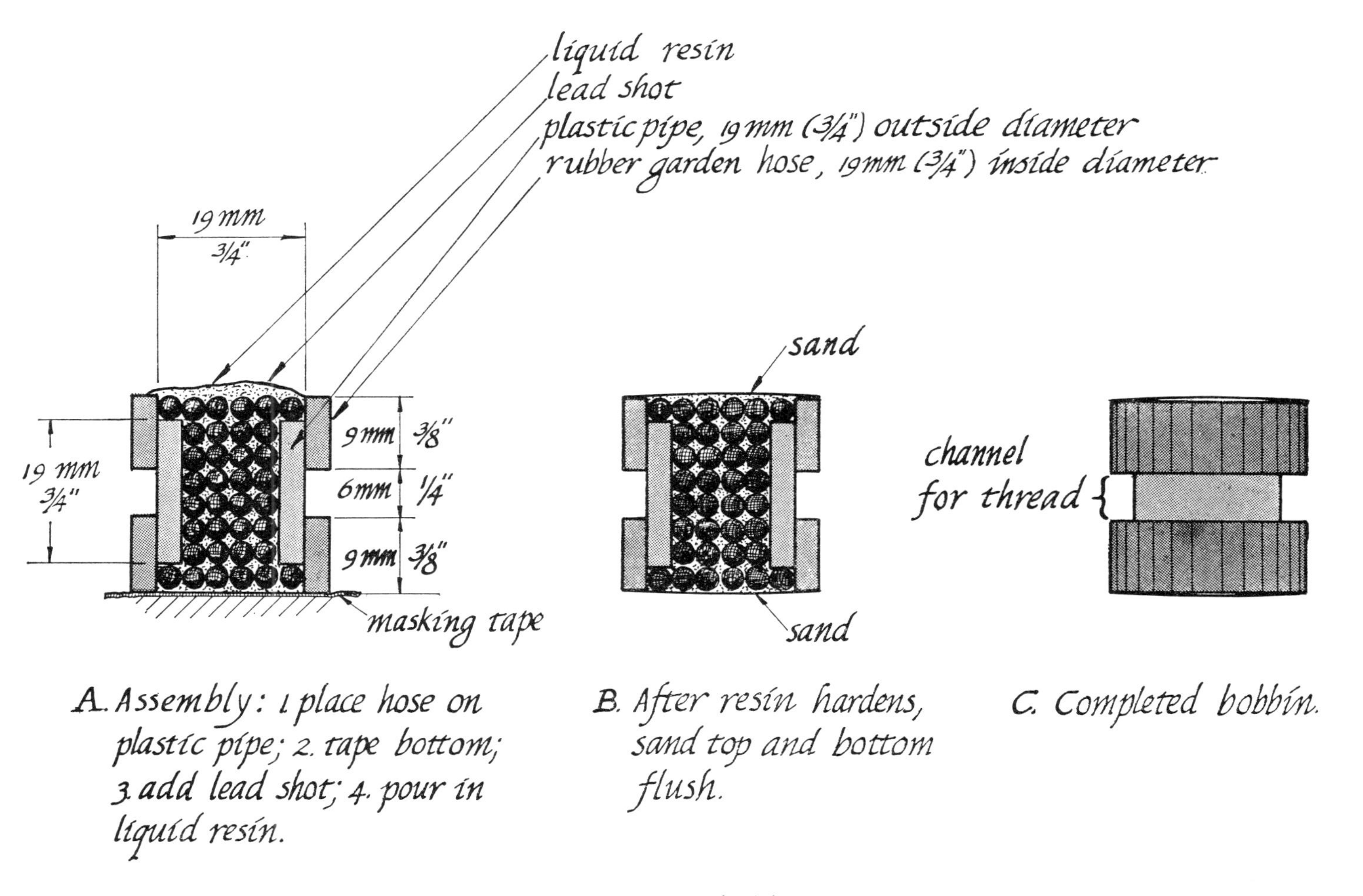
liquid resin
lead shot
plastic pipe, 19mm (3/4") outside diameter
rubber garden hose, 19mm (3/4") inside diameter
19 mm
3/4"
19 mm
3/4"
9mm 3/8"
6mm 1/4"
9mm 3/8"
masking tape
sand
sand
channel
for thread
A. Assembly: 1 place hose on plastic pipe; 2. tape bottom; 3 add lead shot; 4. pour in liquid resin.
B. After resin hardens, sand top and bottom flush.
C. Completed bobbin.

34. **Su bobbin**

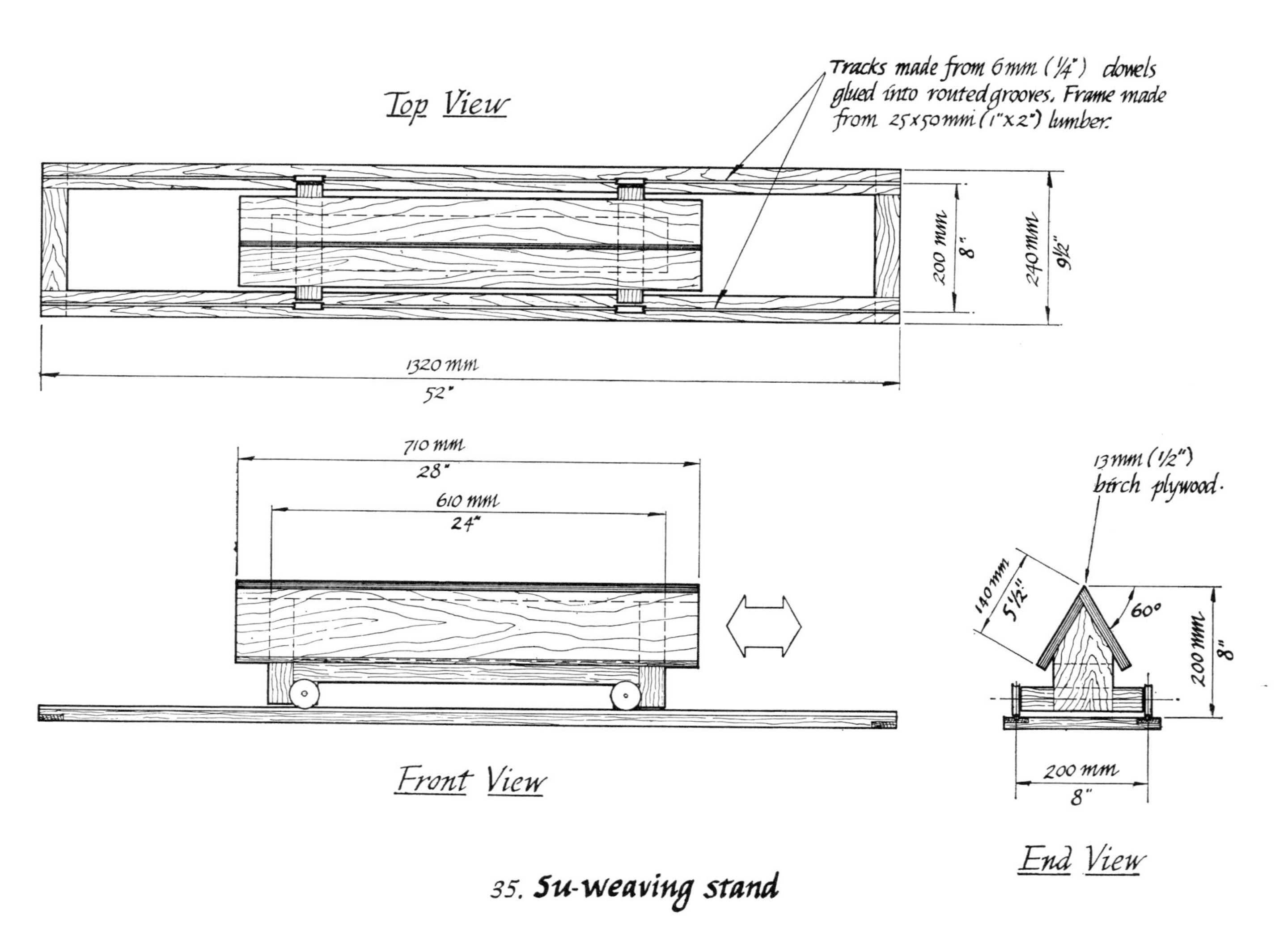

35. **Su-weaving stand**

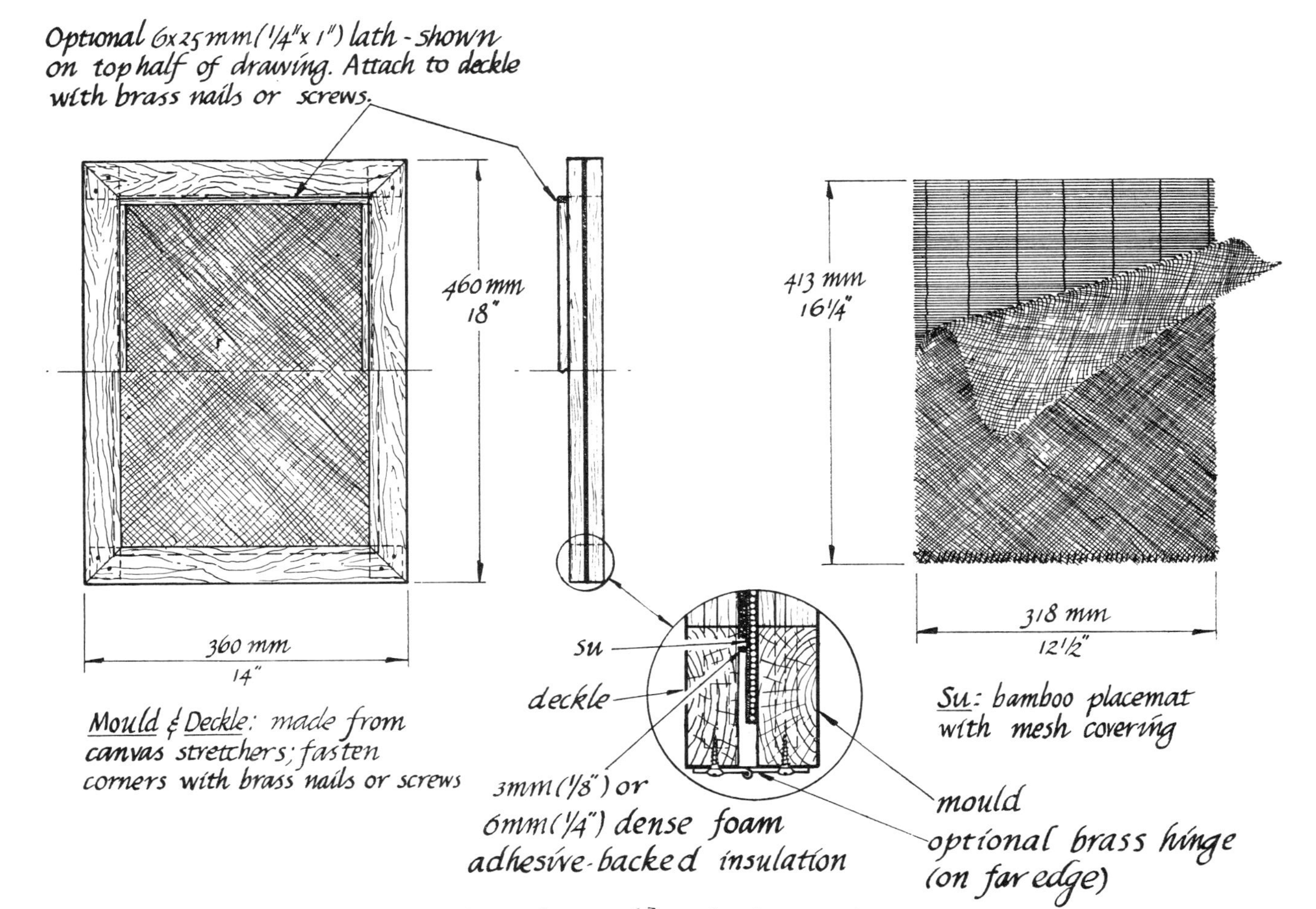

36. **Simple mould and placemat su**

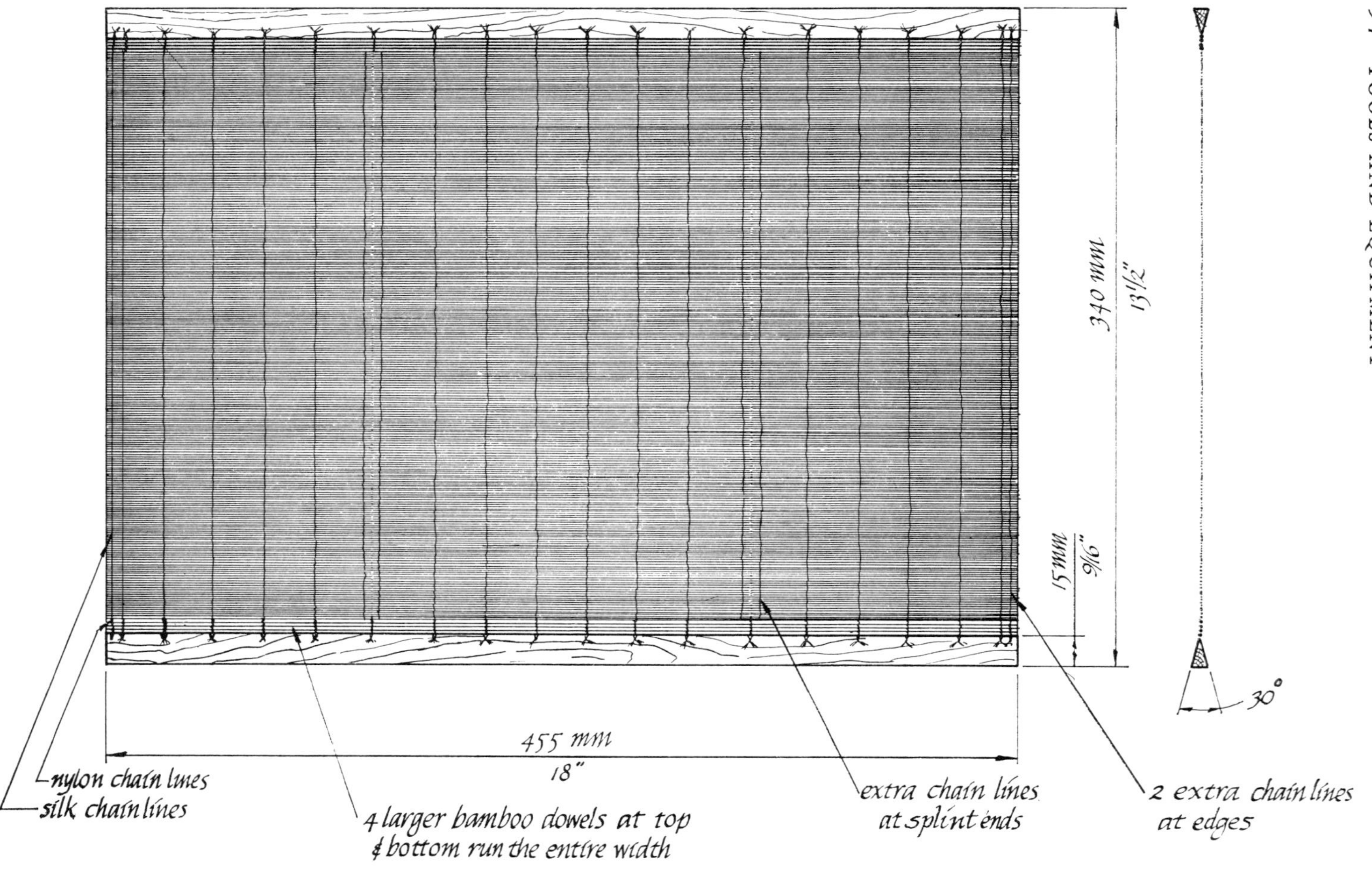

37. ***Su for small traditional mould***

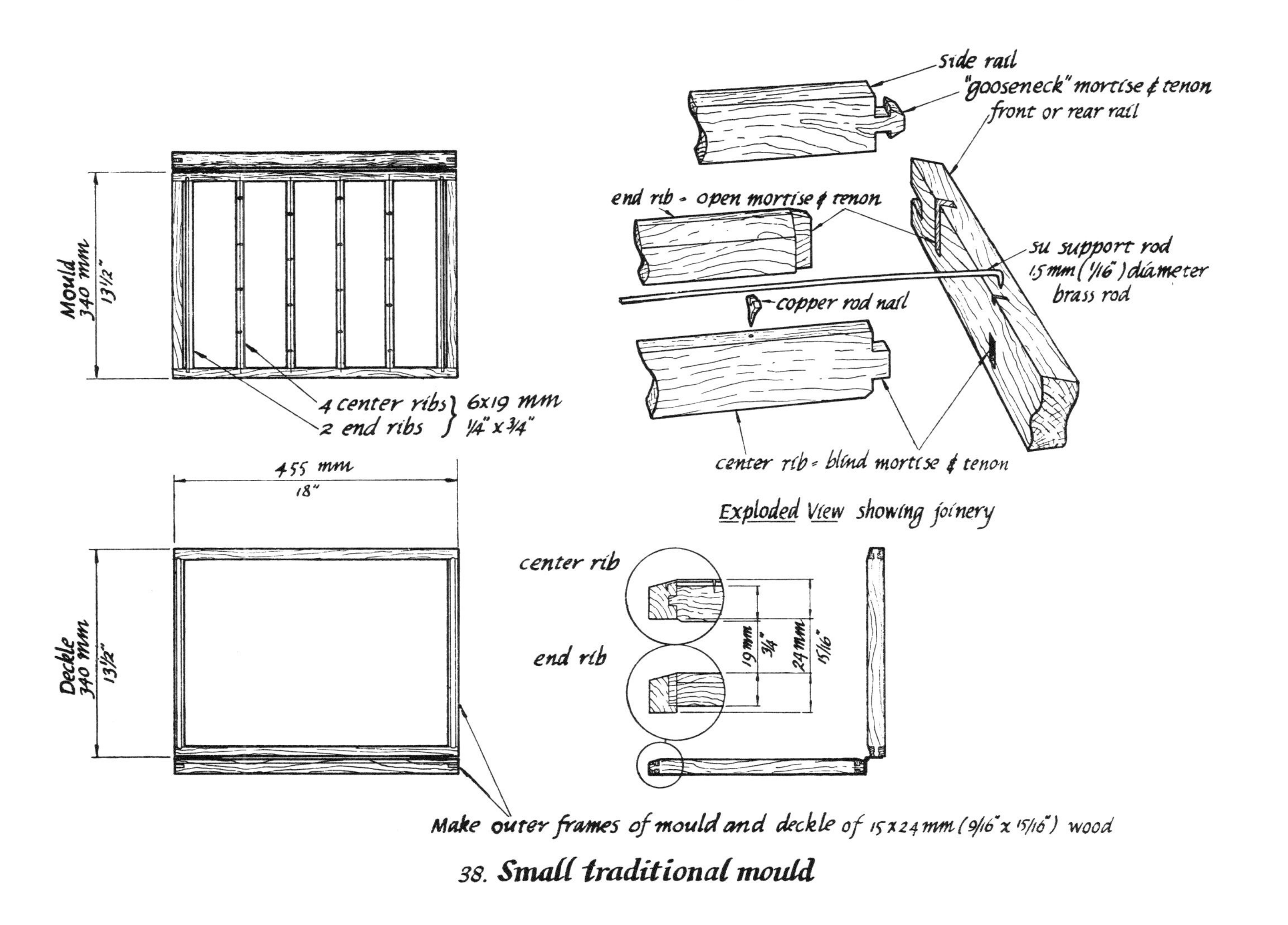

38. **Small traditional mould**

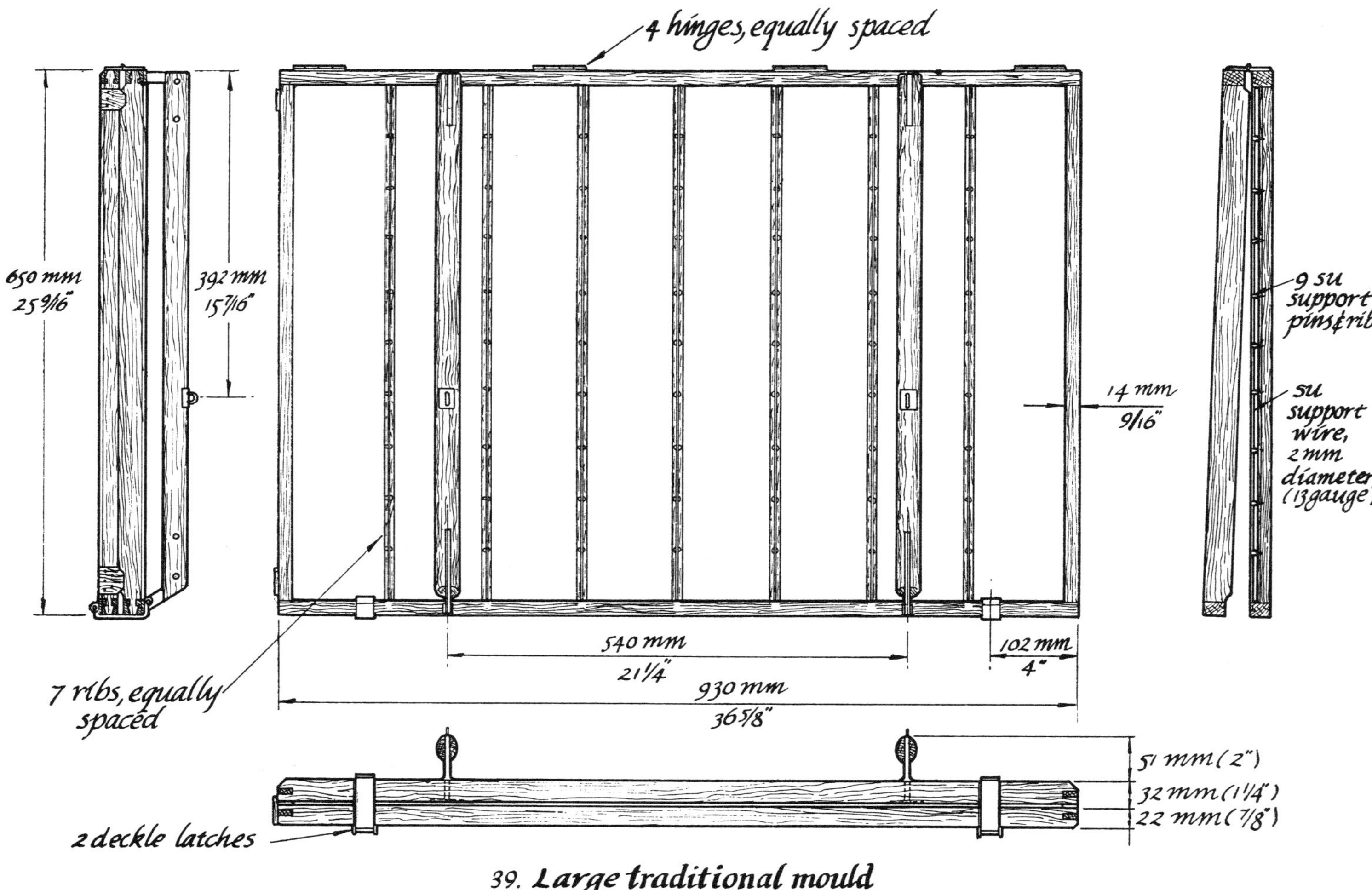

39. **Large traditional mould**

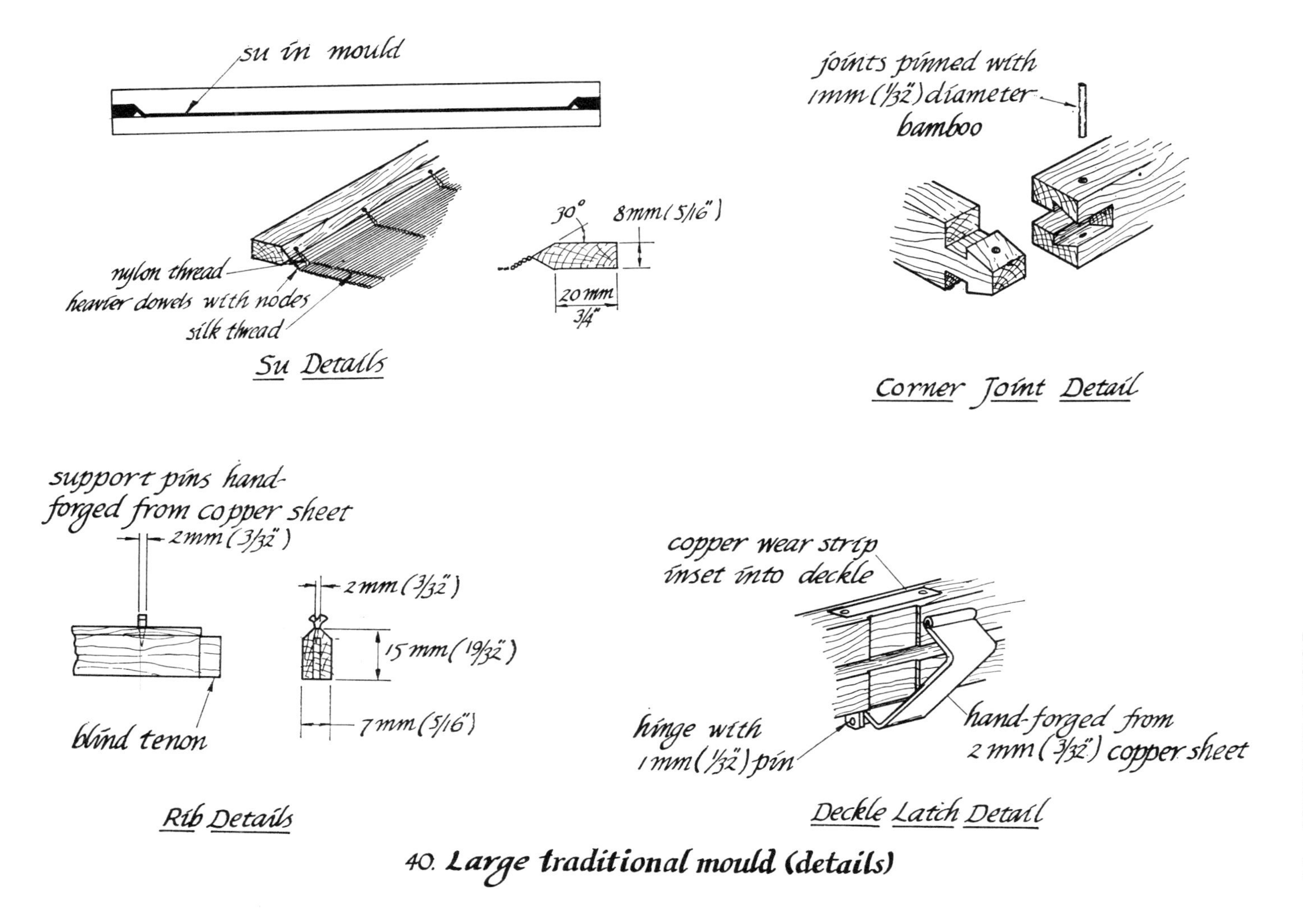

40. **Large traditional mould (details)**

To construct vat, first clamp all four sides together, place on a level surface, and square up the sides. Next drill holes for dowels; then disassemble and glue the dowels into one set of sides. Remember to mark the sides prior to disassembly to ease reassembly.

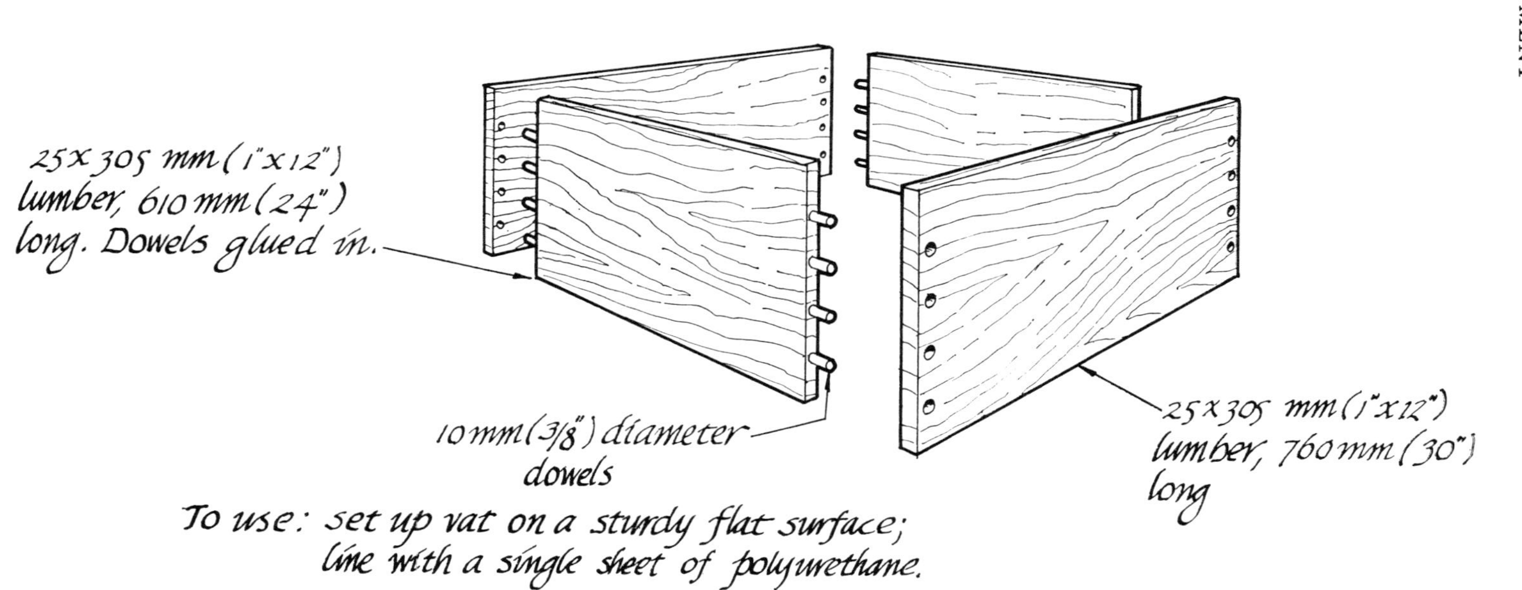

41. **Simple vat**

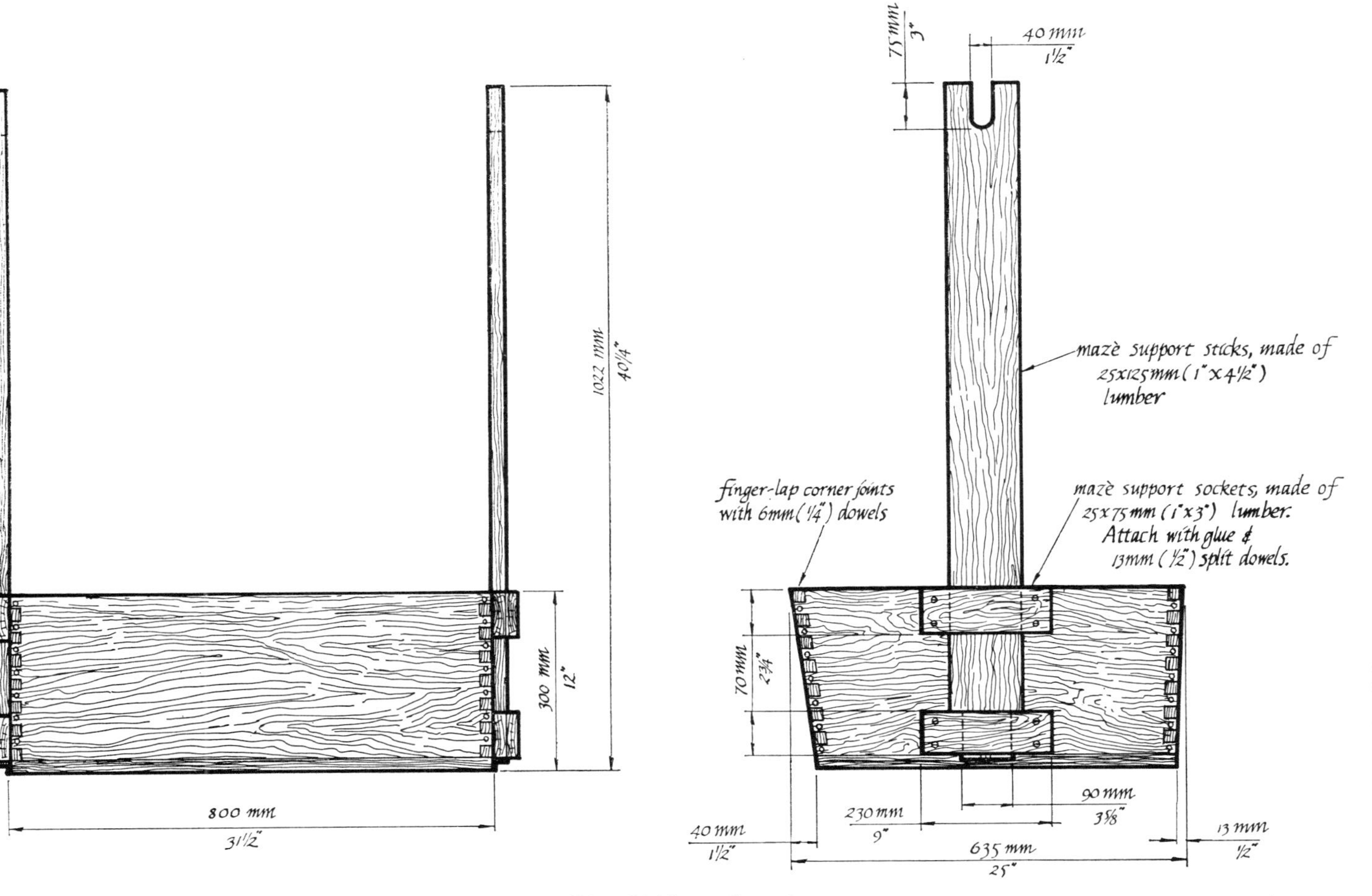

42. Traditional vat

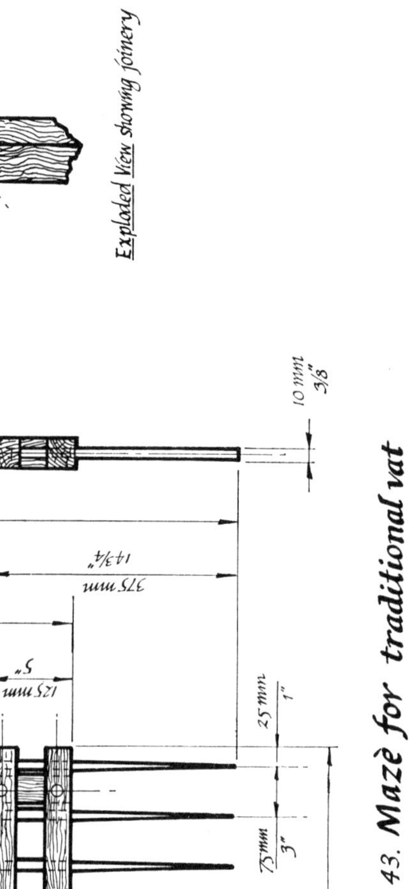

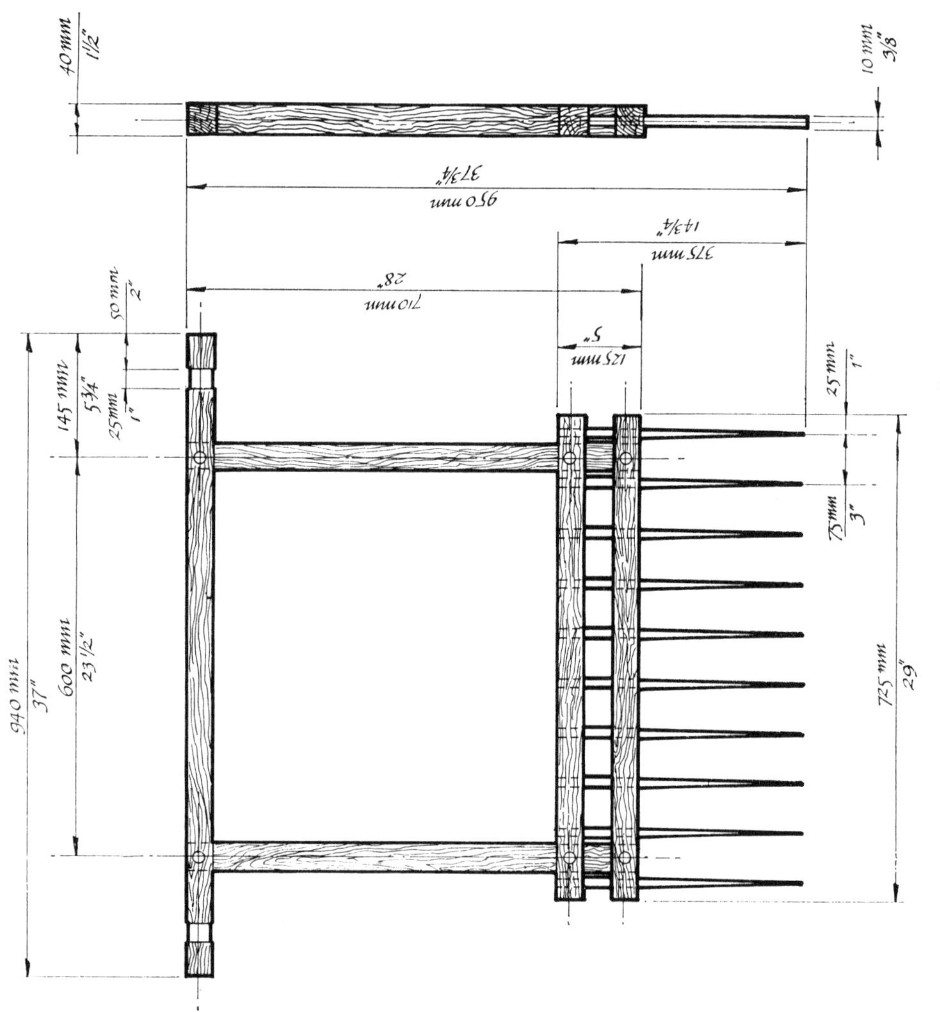

43. Mazè for traditional vat

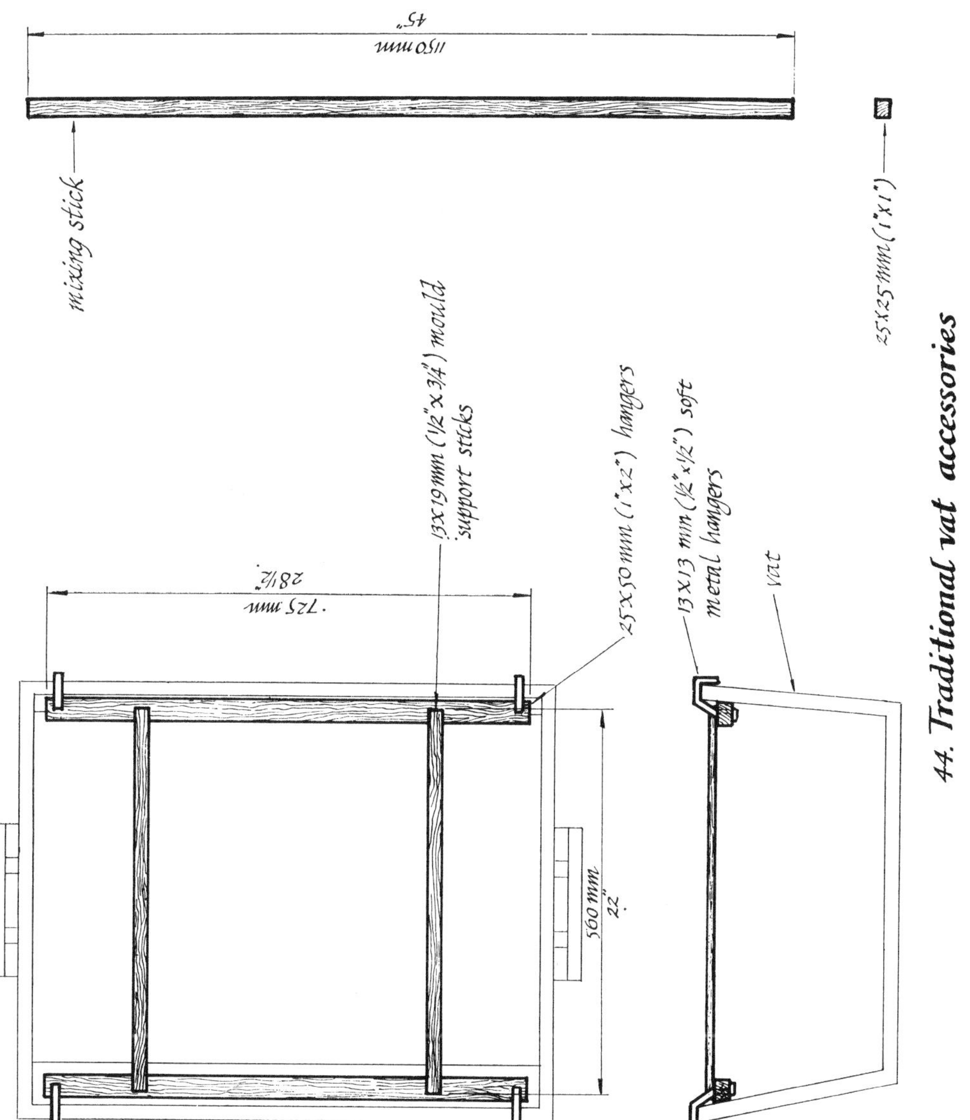

44. Traditional vat accessories

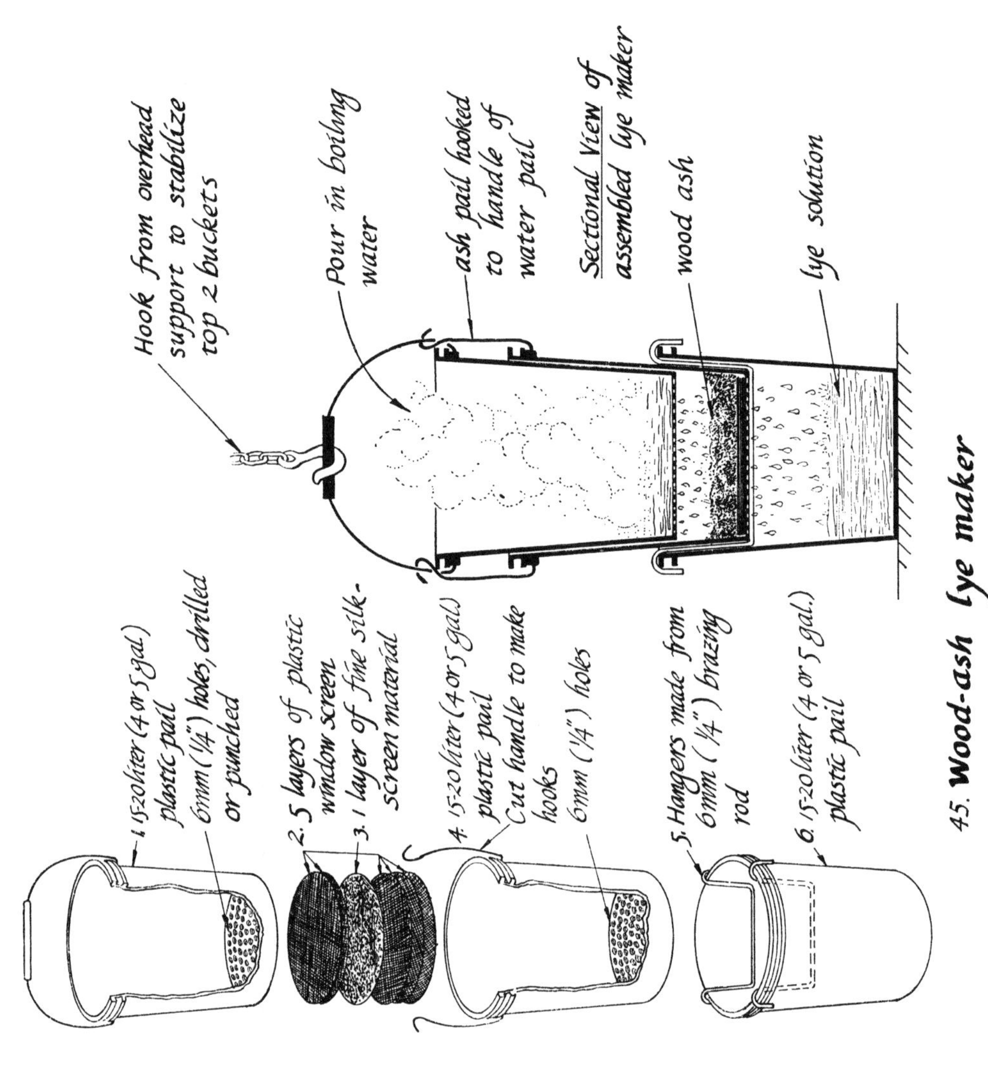

45. **Wood-ash lye maker**

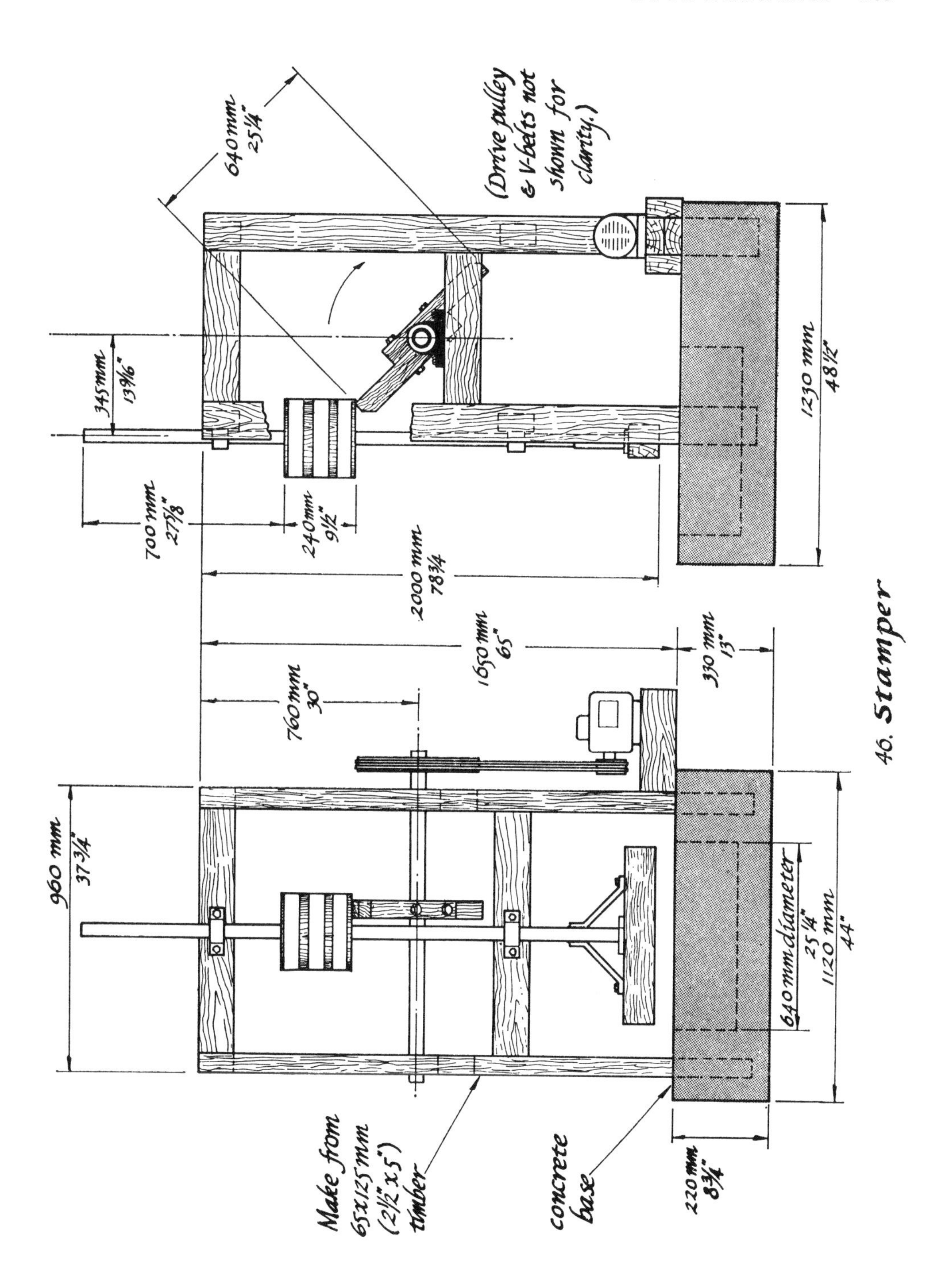
640 mm
25¼"
(Drive pulley & V-belts not shown for clarity.)
345 mm
1230 mm
48½"
700 mm
27⅝"
240 mm
9½"
2000 mm
78¾
1650 mm
65"
330 mm
13"
760 mm
30"
960 mm
37¾"
640 mm diameter
25¼"
1120 mm
44"
Make from 65x125 mm (2½" x 5") timber
concrete base
220 mm
8¾"

46. **Stamper**

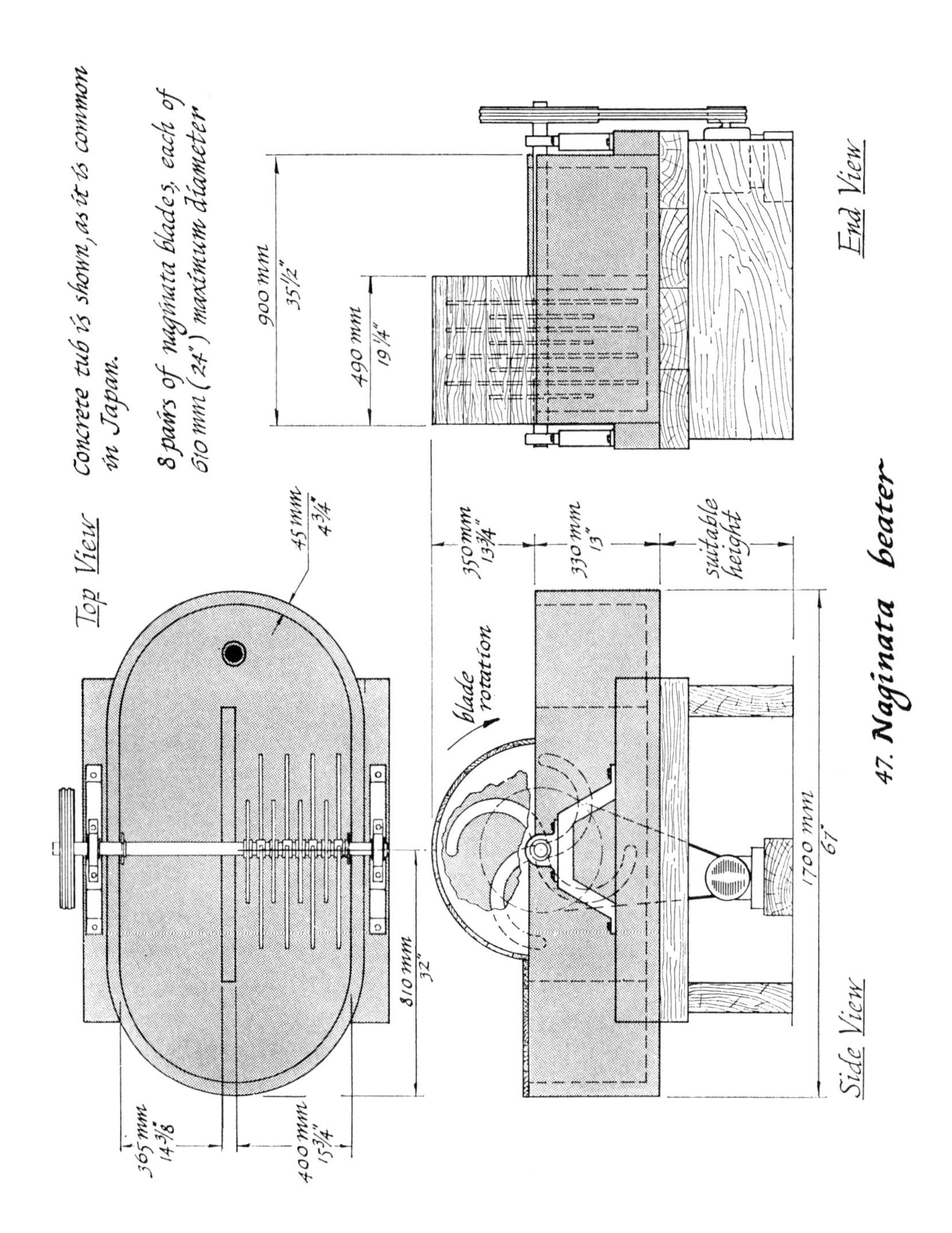

47. Naginata beater

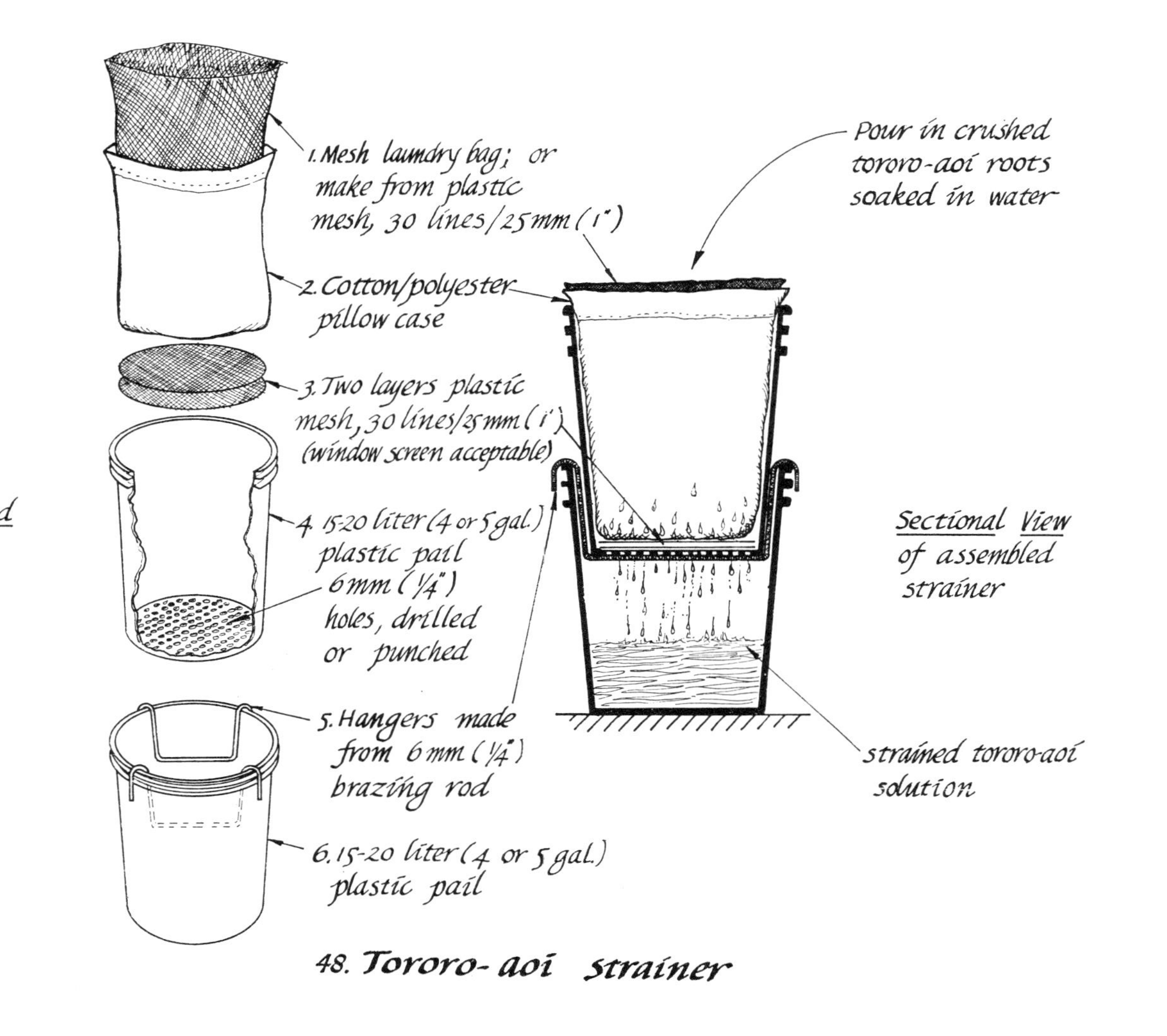

48. Tororo-aoi strainer

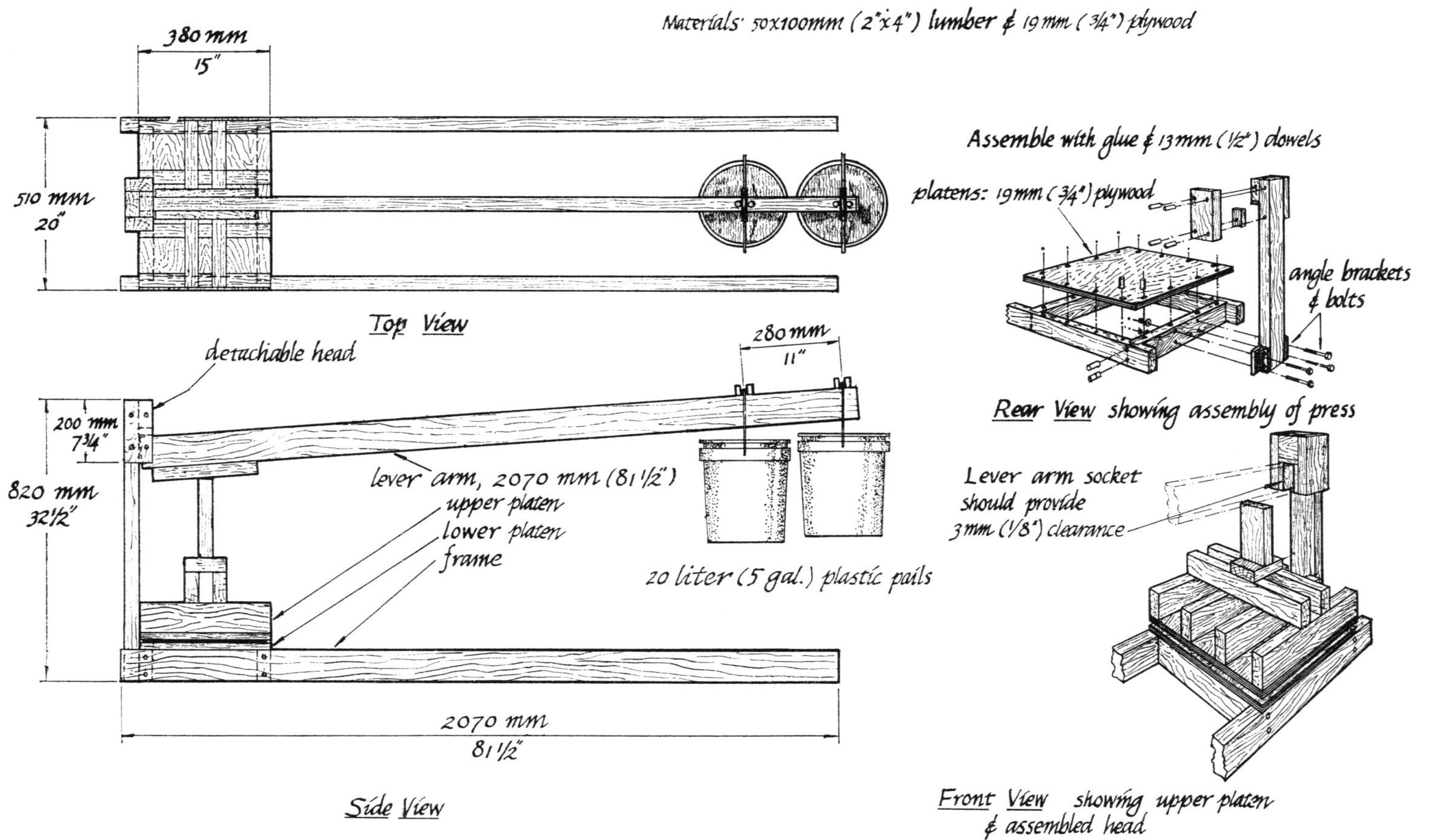

49. Lever press

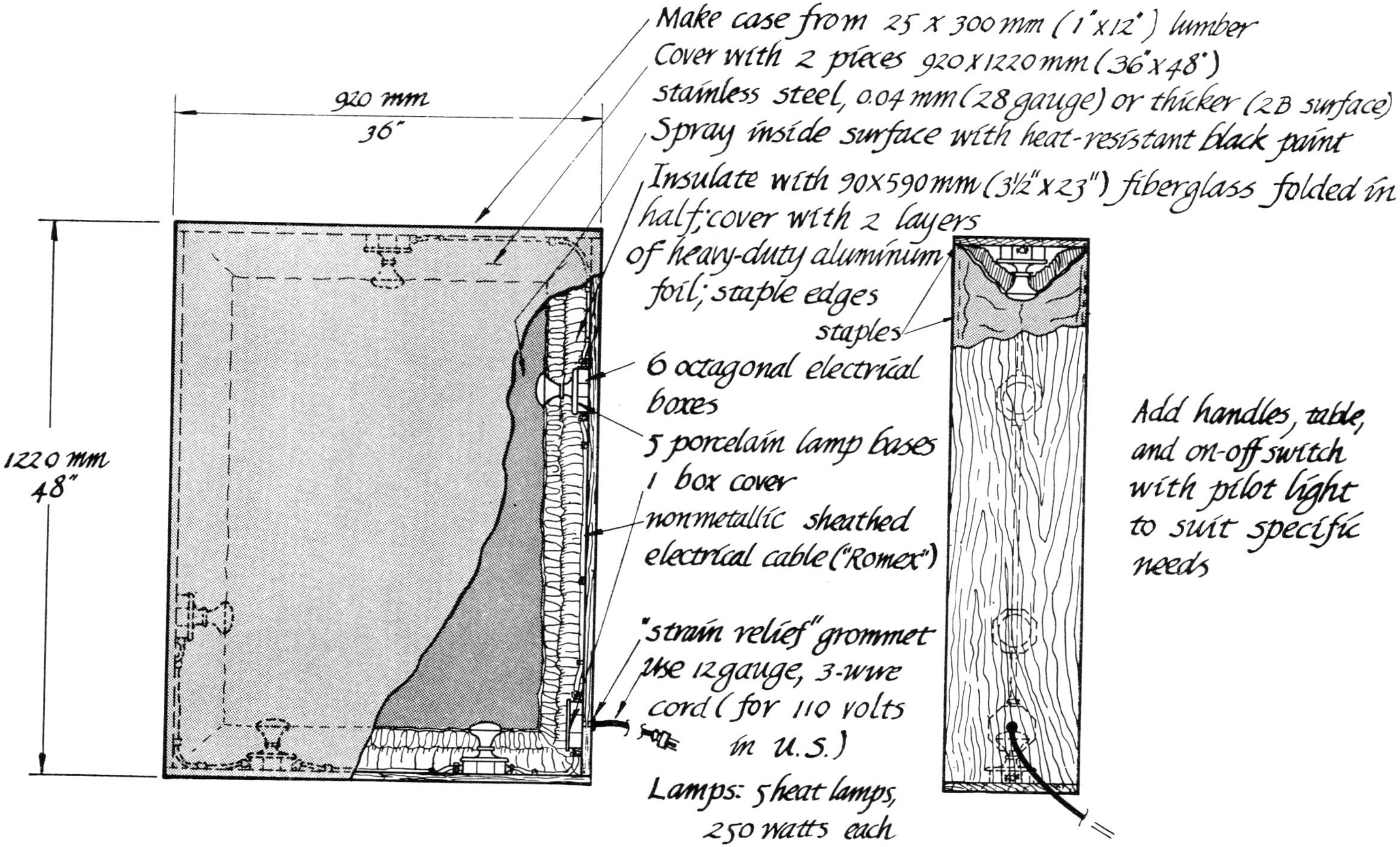

920 mm
36"

1220 mm
48"

Make case from 25 x 300 mm (1" x 12") lumber
Cover with 2 pieces 920 x 1220 mm (36" x 48")
stainless steel, 0.04 mm (28 gauge) or thicker (2B surface)
Spray inside surface with heat-resistant black paint
Insulate with 90 x 590 mm (3½" x 23") fiberglass folded in half; cover with 2 layers of heavy-duty aluminum foil; staple edges
staples
6 octagonal electrical boxes
5 porcelain lamp bases
1 box cover
nonmetallic sheathed electrical cable ("Romex")
"strain relief" grommet
use 12 gauge, 3-wire cord (for 110 volts in U.S.)
Lamps: 5 heat lamps, 250 watts each

Add handles, table, and on-off switch with pilot light to suit specific needs

50. **Heat-lamp dryer**

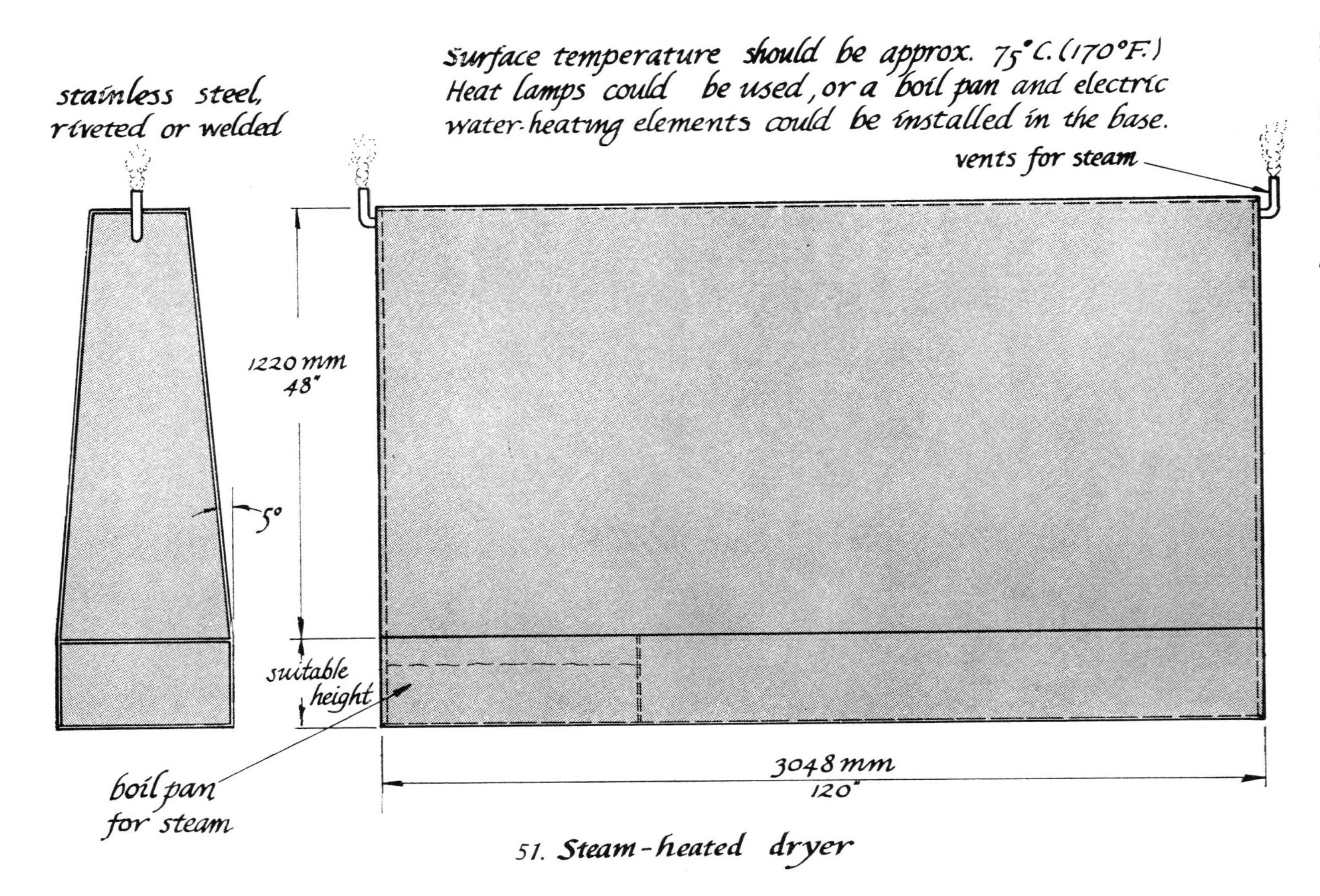

51. Steam-heated dryer

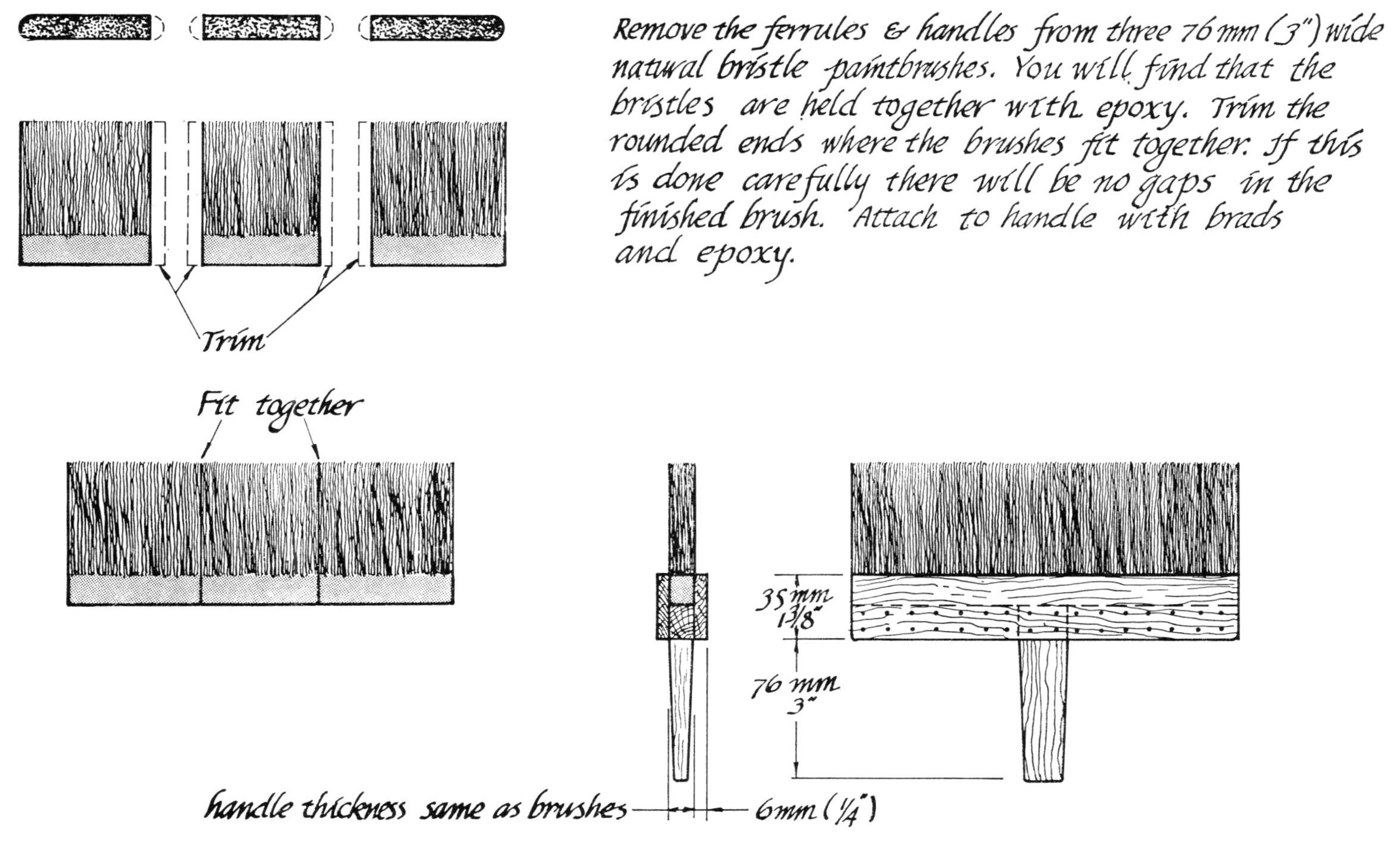

52. Drying brush

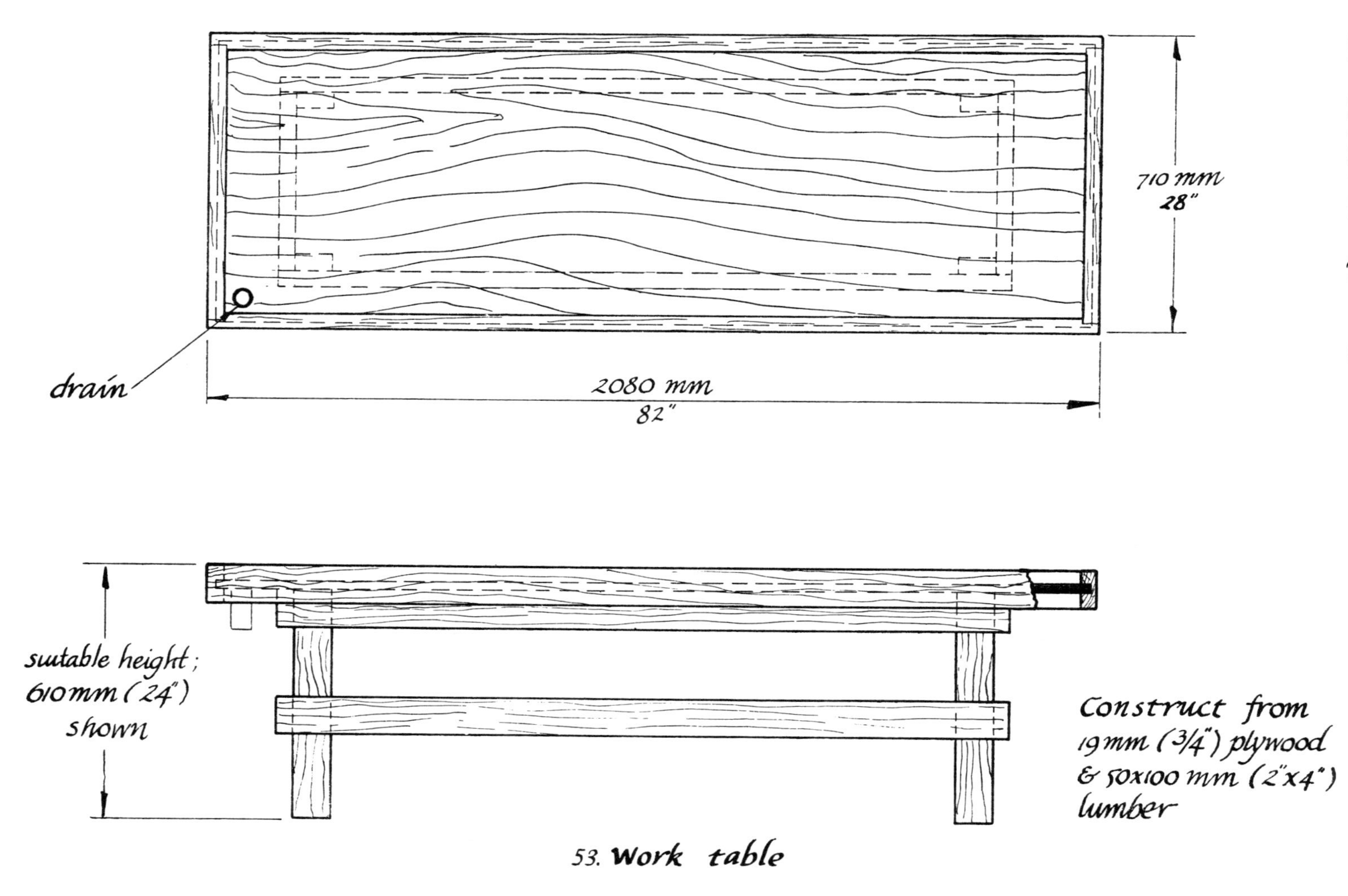

53. **Work table**

If the edge is eventually spoiled with too many notches, it can be planed down to fresh wood. Remember, however, that this working edge must be kept very straight and true.

Setting Up for Su Weaving Generally speaking, each length of thread in a chain needs to be twice as long as the intended finished width of the *su*. Since there are actually two threads in one chain line, the total length of thread required for each pair of bobbins is four times the finished *su* width. The trick is to cut all the required threads to the proper length and mark their midpoints in one operation. To do so, the Japanese use a very simple jig that can be made from a board and two nails. To set it up, double your final *su* width to arrive at a figure and hammer two nails partway into the board that exact distance from each other. To one nail, tape the free end of a spool of the thread you have chosen, and then begin looping the thread around the two nails. When you have passed the first nail the total number of chain lines in the *su,* make a few more loops, stop, cut the thread end, and tie it off at the first nail. Now, at the second nail, mark *all* the threads along the back of the nail with a black magic marker. Go back to the first nail, and, with a pair of scissors, cut through all the threads along the back of the nail, releasing them. This will give you a complete set of cut-to-length threads for all chain lines with their midpoints marked. Set the threads under a weight so they will not get tangled.

Threading the Bobbins Using the knot pictured in Figure 54, tie the leader of a bobbin to one end of a nylon thread. Wind the thread up to within about 10 centimeters (4 inches) of the midpoint mark, and use the bobbin slip knot pictured in Figure 55 to tie it off. Do the same with another bobbin on the other end of the same thread, and hang the pair over the first notch

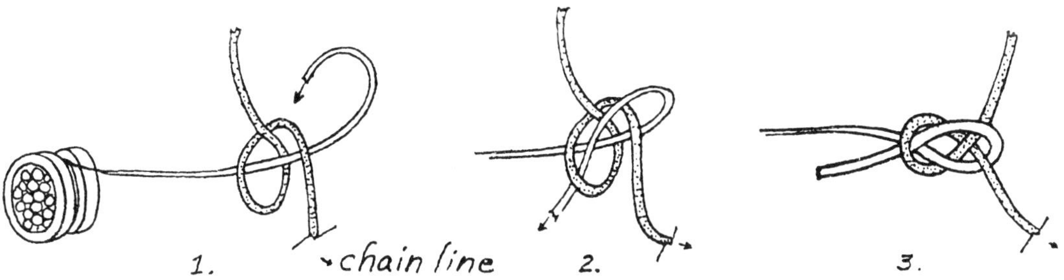

54. Tying bobbin leader to nylon chain line

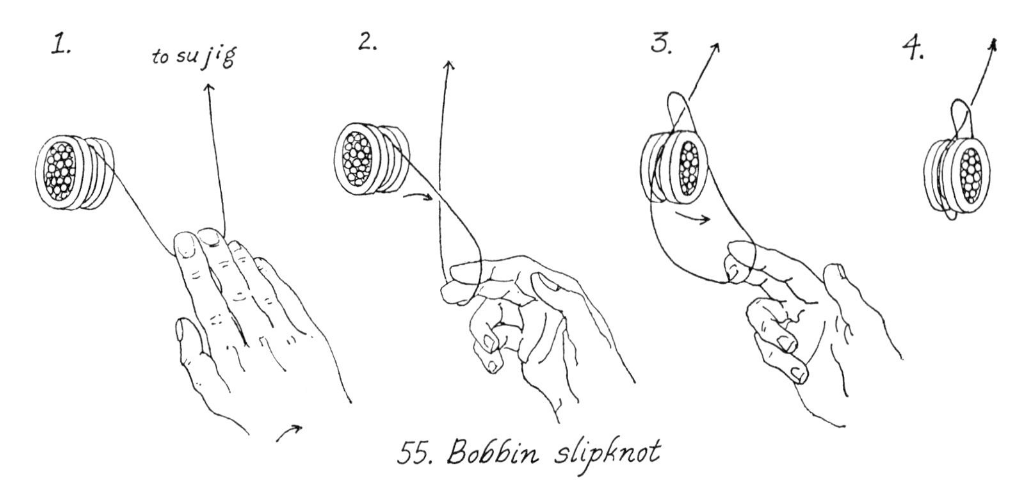

55. *Bobbin slipknot*

on the jig with the midpoint mark riding in the notch. Proceed in a similar fashion with all of the bobbins and threads until you have accounted for all the required chain lines. All bobbins should hang roughly 5 centimeters (2 inches) below the working edge of the jig.

Weaving the Su Establish a mark on the working edge of the jig, just to the left of the first chain-line notch, that corresponds to *exactly* where the finished left end of the *su* should run. Each time you lay down a new stick, you must align its left end with this mark. Pick up your first stick, set it, aligned with the mark, along the working edge of the jig. Now exchange two pairs of bobbins near the center of the stick. (To properly exchange a pair of bobbins, use your right index finger to pick up the front bobbin by the thread, pass it over the splint, drop it and, in the same motion, pick up the rear thread and bobbin with your right middle finger and bring it to the front.) Always work in the same routine to keep the chain progressing in a consistent pattern—i.e., pass the front bobbin to the left of the rear, forward-moving bobbin. Check the stick end to make sure it is still located properly against the left edge mark, and finish exchanging all the bobbins, locking the stick in across its entire length. Lay another stick down, and, following the same procedure, weave it in on top of the first. While your right hand does the actual exchange of bobbins, your left hand should rest on the working edge of the jig. Use your left thumb to hold the new stick snug against the previous one. If you have a long enough nail on your left thumb, you may notch it and use it to hold the splint down as pictured in Figure 56.

Consistency of style is very important as weaving progresses. Work until you have produced about 5 centimeters (2 inches) of *su*. Use a ruler to check the accumulated width at the left, center, and right. If there is more than a 3-millimeter (about 1/8-inch) discrepancy, tighten up your weaving action where the measurement was greatest, and check again after weaving an additional 3 centimeters (about 1 1/8 inches) to see if you are correcting the problem. The spacing of splints (*su* width) should be exactly the same for the full length of the *su*.

If you are working with nylon threads and synthetic sticks you should

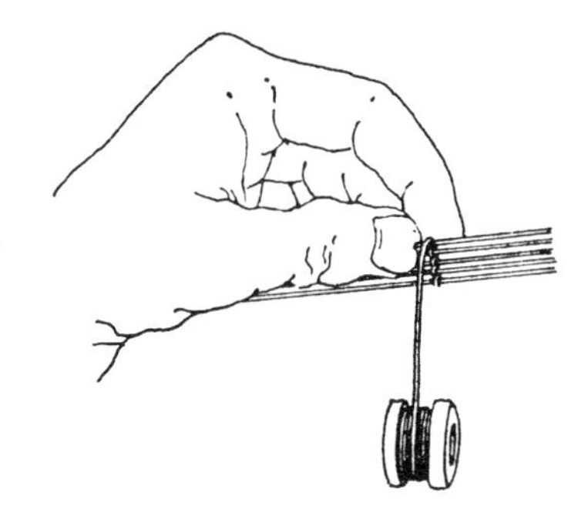

56. *Notched thumbnail used in weaving su*

stop weaving approximately three sticks' width from the inside deckle dimension. Generally speaking, the Japanese *su*-maker working with silk and bamboo figures that every 30 centimeters (12 inches) of new *su* will shrink about 1 centimeter (about 3/8 inch) when first wet, so he weaves extra to compensate. Nylon and synthetic splints, however, retain their finished width in water; if anything, they need to be stretched a bit when finished.

Tying Off the Su Once the proper width has been reached and confirmed, obtain a length of tin foil several centimeters (inches) longer than the length of the *su*. Fold the tin foil widthwise several times until it is several layers thick and presents a straight, clean edge along one side. Place the folded tin foil under the *su*, and slide it, straight edge first, all the way up under the final stick and just a bit more—right over the notches on the working edge of the *su* jig. With bobbins still attached, tie off the *su* using a single overhand knot and let the bobbins dangle on either side of the jig. Make sure the knots, final sticks, and tin foil are all in exactly the right places. Now, with a *minute* amount of a cyanoacrylate glue ("Krazy Glue," "Super Glue," or the equivalent) "touch" the single knot on top of the final stick. The idea is only to secure the knot. Do not apply so much glue that it spreads to the thread and stick below or to the *su* jig. If any glue accidentally spreads to the tin foil, the foil can be removed later with a needle.

Once you have checked the set of the knot and glue by raising the bobbins slightly, cut all the bobbins away, leaving at least 8 centimeters (3 inches) of thread hanging from each knot.

Set aside the bobbins, *su* jig, and track. Finish tying off the *su* using the knot shown in Figure 57. Unless a knot looks especially loose after the final

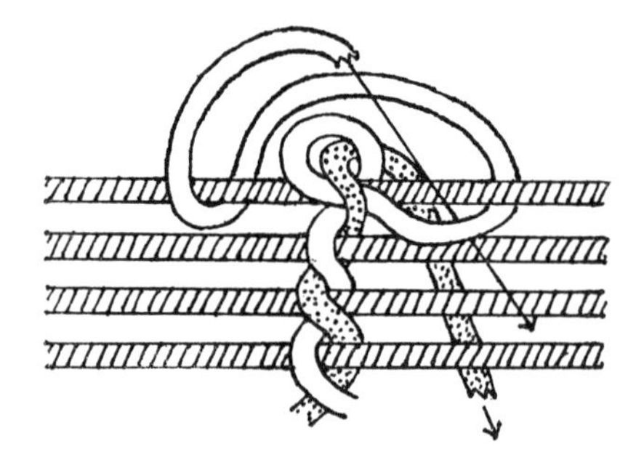

57. Final tie-off knot

tie and trim, do not use any extra glue. Doing so increases the chance of making the *su* inflexible at that location and, thus, less effective at couching.

The edge sticks for the *su* should be cut to fit the mould comfortably with the deckle closed. (Note the different edge stick configurations for the small and the large traditional moulds. Either type is acceptable, but that with a triangular cross section, pictured in Fig. 37, is being discussed here.) Remember that a little extra room will be required for the threads that tie the finished *su* to the edge sticks, especially if a mesh covering is to be added later. White pine is an acceptable wood substitute. (The usual wood, Japanese cypress, *Chamaecyparis obtusa* Endl., is similar to white pine but tighter grained, harder, and more water-resistant.) Lay your completed *su* weaving on a flat table in front of you and set one edge stick at the far edge of the *su*. The unknotted, starting edge of the *su* should be attached to whichever becomes the near-edge stick. Maintain this orientation during papermaking for successful couching with synthetic or traditional *su*. Mark the wood just to the right of the chain lines for the chain lines left of center, and just to the left, for the chain lines right of center. Do this by making slight indentations with a nail or punch 5 millimeters (about 3/16 inch) from the narrow edge of the edge stick. Drill all the marked locations with a 1.5-millimeter (1/16-inch) bit. Treat the sticks with tung oil or an equivalent wood preservative.

Tying on the Edge Sticks Cut a 13-centimeter (5-inch) piece of thread for each hole in the edge sticks. Follow the steps indicated in Figure 58 to attach

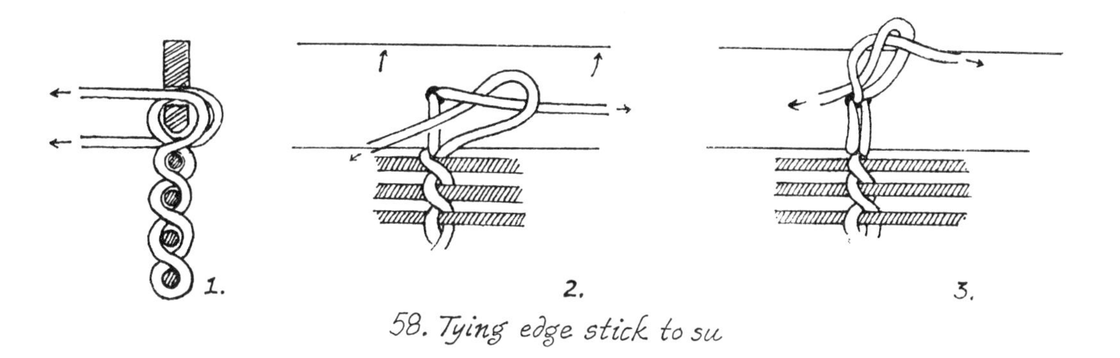

58. *Tying edge stick to su*

the edge sticks to the *su*. If you have trouble getting the thread through the opening between the end splint and the edge stick, use a sewing needle to spread the sticks slightly. Once you have tied off all attaching threads at their respective holes, pull each knot down into the hole, using one of the free ends, and then trim off the threads about 2 millimeters (1/16 inch) from the hole. Mark one edge stick with the maker's name or initials and the date of completion for future reference in measuring longevity.

A thorough understanding of a *su's* function during papermaking is essential to successful construction of a *su* that will perform well at papermaking. Once you develop such a sensitivity and the correlated toolmaking skills, you will be much more capable of implementing the entire *nagashi-zuki* process free of dependence on Eastern suppliers.

At this point, if you have actually made a *su*, give yourself a generous pat on the back. You have accomplished no small deed. If, in addition, your completed *su* functions well at papermaking, you have a right to be even prouder.

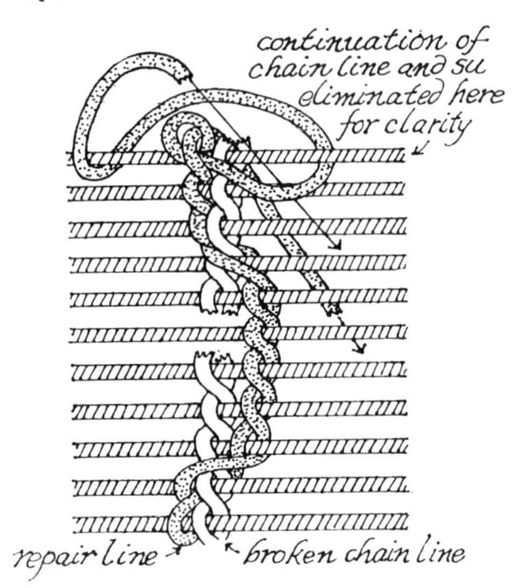

59. Repairing broken chain line

Repairing Su If a chain line breaks while the *su* is in use, it can be repaired as illustrated in Figure 59. A seriously damaged *su* should be cut apart and completely rewoven with new splints and threads.

Advanced Mesh Covering If the sticks of a finished homemade *su* are too large in diameter or too rough for successful papermaking, or if you wish to eliminate the laid and chain-line watermark pattern in your finished sheet, you may attach a refined version of the mesh applied to the placemat *su* described earlier. At this writing the best Western substitute for the Japanese silk *sha* (mesh covering) treated with fermented persimmon juice is real silk mesh (silk screen) 18 lines to the centimeter (40–45 lines to the inch) treated with several coats of diluted exterior polyurethane varnish. Both the persimmon juice and the varnish are required partly to preserve the silk but more to cement the warp and woof threads together at their intersections, giving the mesh the required body.

Proceed as follows to apply the varnish: First cut a rectangle of mesh about 5 to 8 centimeters (several inches) larger in both directions than the full *su* dimension. Draw the mesh flat in a silkscreen stretcher or use a rough wooden frame and pieces of tape to hold the material smooth. Mix the varnish in a ratio of 1: 2 with mineral spirits. Use a piece of soft cotton cloth, folded to form a straight edge (as shown in Figure 61), to carefully apply the first coat. Using long, even strokes, make sure all areas receive an equal coating. Then, working quickly, use a dry cotton cloth, again folded to make a smooth edge, to wipe away *all* excess varnish. Make sure no holes are left plugged. A cloth pad on both sides of the mesh may help to blot out any filled holes. If necessary, use a needle to clear all openings. Let the mesh dry for 30 minutes to 1 hour, and then repeat the application at least two more times. Using a strong light, examine carefully for any clogged areas. After the final application has dried, the mesh can be cut away from the frame. It should now be stiff enough so that the mesh cannot be easily moved on a diagonal to the warp or woof. Take care not to fold or crease the treated mesh.

Attaching the silk mesh to a *su* is basically identical to the placemat procedure, but there are a few refinements. Soak the *su* and mesh in a vat of clear water as before, but do not trim the mesh. After they both have been in the water for about half an hour, adjust the mesh so that it lies over the full *su* area and draw them out by one of the edge sticks held horizontal. Make sure the mesh comes out of the water lying smooth against the *su*. Lay the two

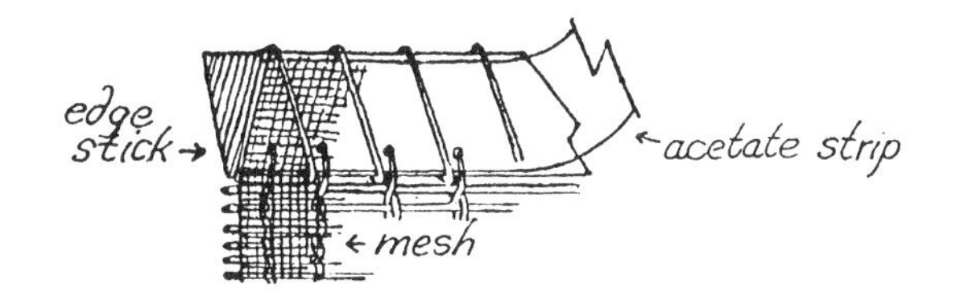

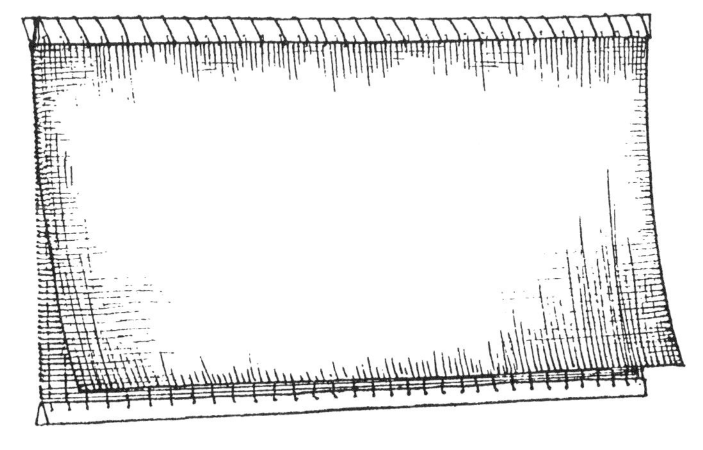

60. *Mesh covering attached to su*

61. *Folded cloth for treating mesh*

on a flat surface without disturbing the mesh. Trim the mesh to the left and right stick ends and to the outer edges of the near and far edge sticks. Cut an acetate holding strip just a bit smaller in size than the face of one of the edge sticks. Lay the strip over the mesh where it lies on top of the edge stick that is sewn to the knot-free edge of the *su*. Now start to sew the acetate and the mesh to the edge stick by inserting the needle down between the edge stick and the first stick in the *su*. Bring it up and continue sewing around the edge stick until the acetate with mesh beneath is neatly attached to the edge stick. Make sure you keep the mesh wet during sewing, and also take care that you do not cause any disruptions of the smooth surface of the mesh while it is being attached. When finished, rinse the *su* and mesh in water, and hang the assembly to dry from the sewn-edge stick using a clothes pin. During papermaking the sewn-edge stick will be at the near edge of the mould.

Production-Level Su If sheet size will be larger than 45 by 60 centimeters (18 by 24 inches), the *su* is probably best ordered from Japan or Korea until Western craftspeople further develop *su*-making materials and techniques. For 45-by-60-centimeter (18-by-24-inch) and smaller *su,* instructions above will yield *su* fully serviceable in daily production.

Moulds

Japanese Moulds Moulds are built in Japan (by approximately ten remaining artisans) of clear-grained Japanese cypress. The Japanese deckle is hinged to the mould and fitted with two handles running front to back. Japanese moulds are surprisingly lightweight, reminding one more of fragile, balsa-wood model airplanes than tools for use in water. There are at least two reasons for this light construction: Japanese moulds are used only to support the *su* during papermaking, so no added strength is required for couching against felts, as is the case in Western papermaking. In addition, lively action and large sheet sizes require an initially light mould if the combination of mould, *su,* and stock is not to become unmanageable during papermaking.

Corner joints on Japanese moulds are impressively intricate, especially considering they have been cut by hand. All ribs are cut straight but set with brass wire runners arched slightly by pin supports in each rib. The curve sags straight as the wooden rib bends under its load at papermaking, resulting in an even flat surface. The wire runners also serve to lessen slightly thicker streaks that would form in the paper if the *su* rested directly on the wooden ribs. The average life span for a Japanese mould is ten years, and it is generally agreed that moulds last longest if they are lacquered before being put into service.

Most moulds used in contemporary paper production are at least 60 by 100 centimeters (24 by 40 inches) except for the longer and narrower moulds used for making scroll-mounting papers. Sizes range up to 100 by 180 centimeters (40 by 71 inches) for one-person moulds, and up to 180 by 300 centimeters (71 by 118 inches) for moulds operated by two people. All are suspended from bamboo poles and/or stationary lines rigged from above. Without light mould construction and the supportive rigging systems, large contemporary *nagashi-zuki* sheets would not be possible.

Ideally, you will eventually undertake building your own mould and *su* following instructions in this chapter. However, you may elect to purchase a small Japanese mould (usually with matching *su*) if you do not feel confident about building the tools yourself. A Japanese-made mould (see Figs. 84, 85) with *su* will be expensive ($375 for a 30-by-40-centimeter, or 12-by-16-inch, model, price subject to change), but since most of the tool craftspeople in

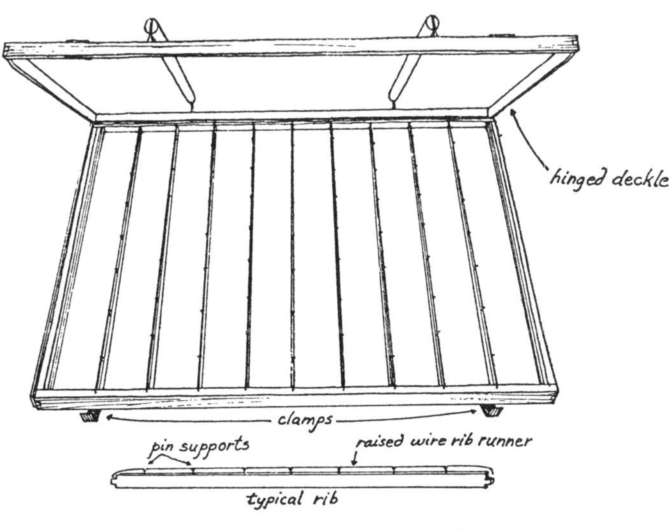

62. *Japanese mould*

Japan are over the age of fifty-five such a tool may not be available at all in the near future, at any price.

For those who decide to purchase a Japanese-made mould, a few notes on proper care are in order. Treating a new, bare Japanese mould with tung oil or a high-quality lacquer will make it last longer than if you leave it untreated. After papermaking each day, rinse the mould thoroughly, and hang or stand it to dry where it will be well exposed to the air.

Simple Mould Store-bought canvas stretchers (four 45-centimeter, or 18-inch, ones and four 36-centimeter, or 14-inch, ones) were used to make the mould and deckle that accompany the placemat *su*. See Figures 36, 63, and 76. To assemble the simple mould, fit the pieces together as shown in the drawings. After checking to make sure corners are square, use 2-centimeter (3/4-inch) brass nails or screws to lock the corners in place. Peen or file down any protruding metal. Use a matt knife to carve down any high ridges on the faces of each canvas stretcher. Round all corners. Pick one frame to be the mould (lower) and one to be the deckle (upper). Carve comfortable handholds on the sides of the mould and deckle.

Next add strips of 3-by-10-millimeter (1/8-by-3/8-inch) foam insulation tape or felt to the underside of the deckle. Sometime before papermaking begins, lay the dry *su* on the mould, center it carefully, and draw a rectangle around the *su* with a waterproof marker. These lines will help keep the *su* properly positioned during papermaking. A light linseed oil finish on the wood is recommended, and hinges may be added at the far

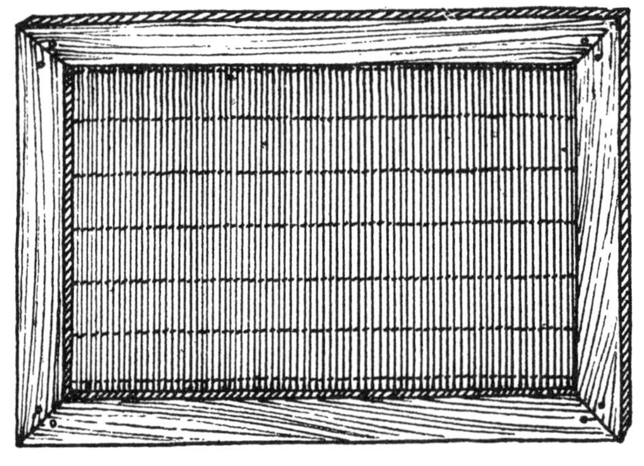

63. Simple mould with su in place

side of the mould once the sandwich is complete. Later, after you see how the mould functions during papermaking, you may elect to add 6-by-25-millimeter (¼-by-1-inch) pine strips to the inside of the deckle. This will decrease the sheet size in both directions by about 13 millimeters (½ inch) but increase the deckle's charge capacity and allow more efficient papermaking. Note the "optional lath" in Figure 36. Be sure to relocate the foam or felt strip if you incorporate the lath.

Advanced Mould A mould very similar to the Japanese item may be constructed by a skilled woodworker, using Figures 38–40, 84, and 85 as guides. Clear-grained white pine is similar to the tight-grained, water-resistant Japanese cypress normally used, but other woods may prove more successful. The finished tool should be treated with tung oil or another water-resistant wood finish. Generally speaking, moulds larger than 30 by 45 centimeters (12 by 18 inches) should be attempted only after smaller moulds and production of smaller papers have been attempted. If you are building a mould to fit an already completed *su,* remember to base your final design measurements on the *wet* dimensions of your *su* (that is, after soaking it for 15 to 20 minutes). The *su* should be just a bit taut when locked in place between the mould and deckle.

Vats and Attachments

Japanese Vats Pine, cedar, concrete, concrete and tiles, or thin stainless steel or copper sheeting and wood, are used to build vats in Japan. Note the drawings and construction procedures below for details.

Simple Vats A functional vat can be fashioned from virtually any container of the appropriate dimensions (50 by 75 by 30 centimeters deep, or 20 by 30 by 12 inches deep). Once lined with sheet plastic (4-mil, or .1 millimeter, polyethylene), even a sturdy cardboard box will suffice if kept out of standing water. The collapsible plastic-lined vat shown in Figures 41 and 89 has the added advantage of being easily stored when not in use. Fold the plastic neatly at the corners. Tie a piece of rope or wire tightly around the outside to keep the vat from falling apart when filled with water. Any vat with a temporary sheet-plastic liner should, of course, be treated with care to prevent puncturing during mixing and papermaking. You may wish to purchase a ready-made container that has the proper dimensions, if such is available, but if you are concerned about permanence, only plastic or stainless containers should be used. The amount of paper-making you intend to do should determine the time and money you put into your vat and other tools.

Traditional Production-Level Vats A real working vat is most easily made of wood. The small traditional vat used in Chapter 7 (see Figs. 42–44, 86–88) requires considerable woodworking skills to build, but it will serve the papermaker indefinitely. It represents, on a small scale, a common Japanese design. A production vat for making 60-by-91-centimeter (24-by-36-inch) sheets is simply a larger version of the same vat. To make the larger vat, refer to Figure 64, but use Figures 42–44 as guides and scale up the (inside) dimensions to 100 by 140 by 35 centimeters deep (40 by 55 by 14 inches deep). *Mazè* supports should be 115 centimeters (45 inches) tall.

If you are going to the trouble to build a good wooden vat, of any size, it stands to reason that a quality lining should be installed. The best alternative is sheet stainless steel if you have the skills to work it yourself or can afford to have it done. If you are reasonably dexterous you can make paper templates for your wooden vat and have a metal shop cut and bend the pieces for you. Once trimmed and fitted, you can solder the pieces yourself. Twenty-eight-gauge sheet stainless steel is recommended for most vat linings. Sheet copper is relatively easier to work but will release harmful copper ions into the water and is therefore not recommended. Fiberglass is probably the easiest, quickest, and least expensive lining material, but over the years it tends to chip, requiring recoating. Fiberglass is recommended only if you cannot afford to go the stainless route. Some Japanese vats are smooth cement, occasionally layered with tile on the inside. If you are familiar with masonry work, and do not plan to move your shop, a cement vat may be both practical and economical.

Attachments and Related Tools Vat attachments, including cross sticks, a *mazè* (mixer), *mazè* supports, mould support sticks, and a mixing stick, are pictured in Figures 42-44 and 88. The *mazè* shown is standard in Japan and can be extremely helpful in producing uniform fiber distribution when working with hand-beaten fiber. The rinse vat, used to keep the

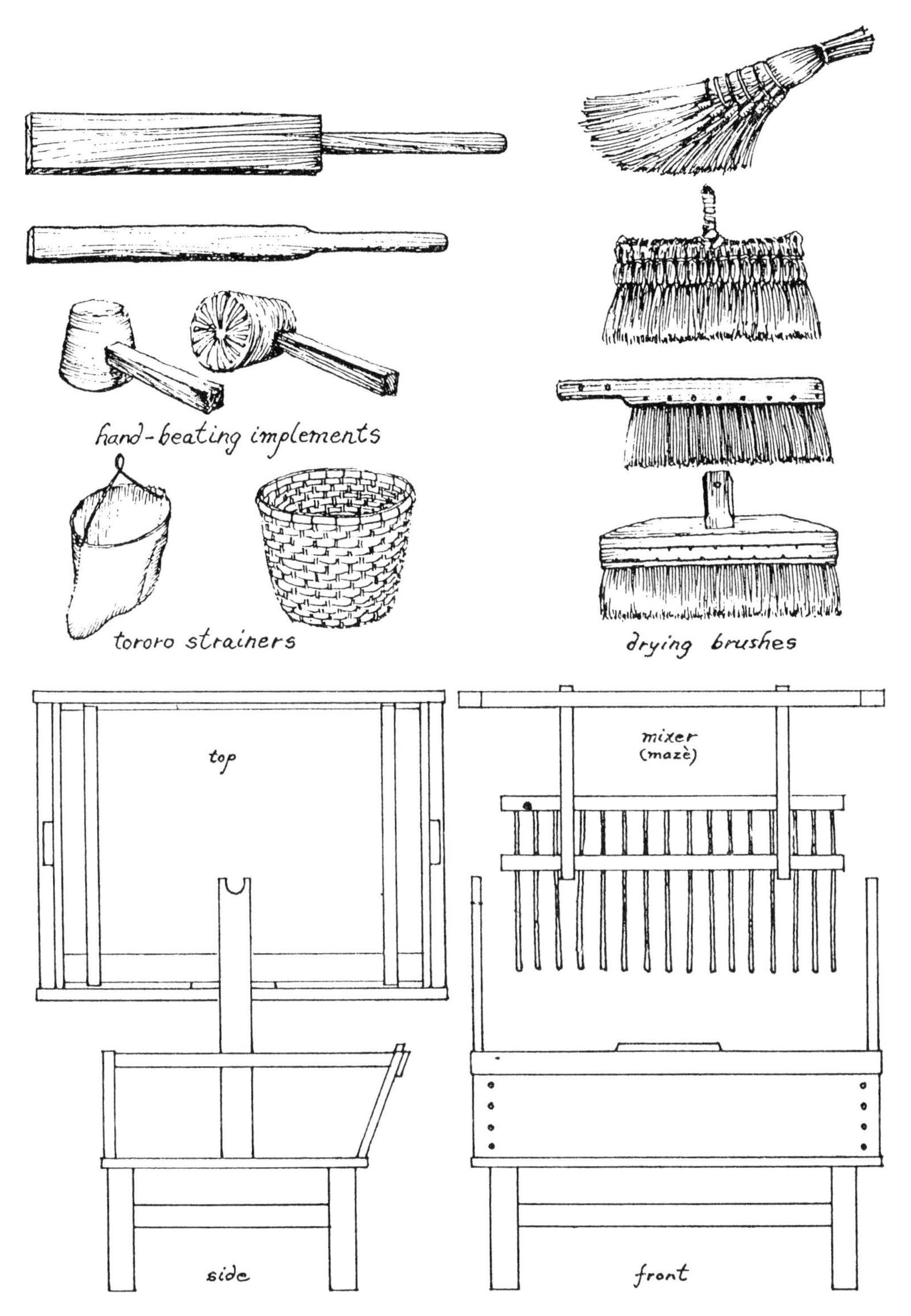

64. Large traditional vat and tools

su clean during papermaking, can be any container, preferably plastic or stainless steel, that is large enough to accept the *su* lengthwise during papermaking. Couching guides are shown in Figure 90 and various other photographs. Note also the holder (stand) for the thread spool, fashioned from a block of wood the size of your hand or smaller; a 5-centimeter (2-inch) nail—or, better yet, brazing rod—4 millimeters (1/8 inch) in diameter has been driven through its center and sawn off flat.

Cooking Equipment

Japanese Cauldrons The standard cooking pot in Japan is a large cast-iron cauldron. (See Figs. 91, 92.) The closest equivalent in America is an old farm cauldron for washing or making apple butter. The alternatives listed below, however, are nonrusting and are therefore recommended.

Simple Pots Small quantities of fiber (250–300 grams, or 9–11 ounces) can be cooked on a household range in a large 8-to-10-liter (8-to-10-quart) pot, preferably of enamelware or stainless steel. Stay away from aluminum, copper, and iron when making any paper intended to be permanent. A lid and stirring stick are also requisite.

Cooking for traditional-method papermaking in Chapter 7 requires a pot with a capacity of about 20 liters (21 quarts). Cooking can still be done in the kitchen, but two burners may be required.

Production-Level Pots For quantities of fiber weighing 1 kilogram (2.2 pounds) or more, a 20-liter (21-quart) capacity or larger cooking vessel is required. If you cannot afford a new or used restaurant cooking pot, check junkyards for any type of stainless steel container that may be serviceable. The level of activity (considerable steam emission, use of two or four burners, accidental overboils, and so on) during a cook of this size strongly recommends the use of an old gas stove or cast-iron burner rings specially installed in a ventilated workshop with floor drains, rather than continued use of a home kitchen.

Drain Basket This tool (see Fig. 93) is fashioned from a laundry basket with a 110-by-110-centimeter (44-by-44-inch) square of plastic window

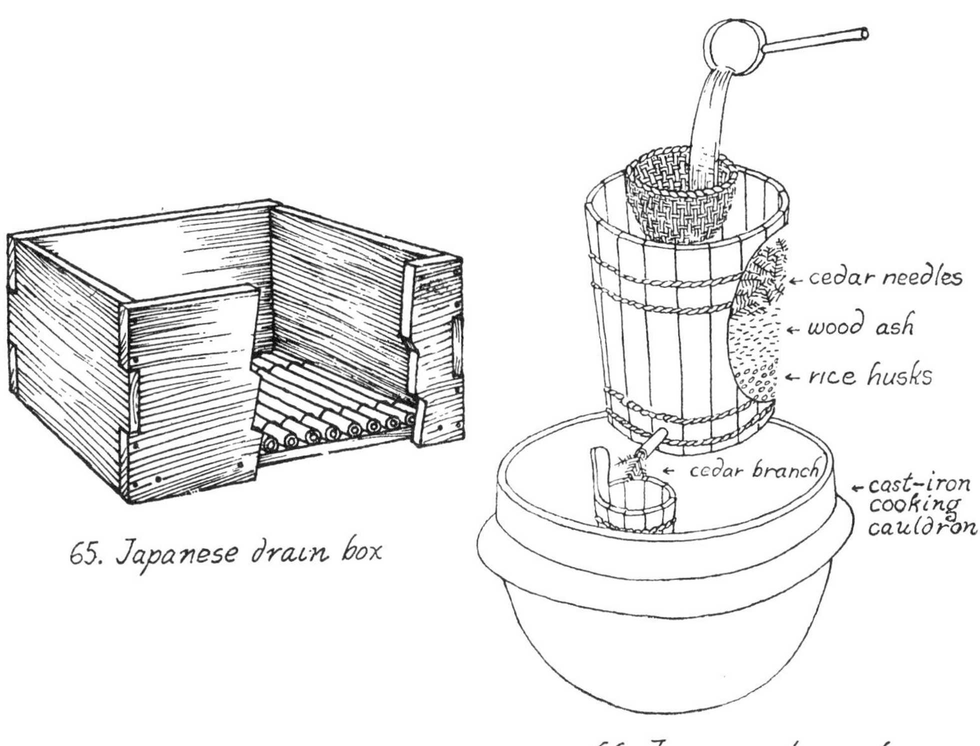

65. *Japanese drain box*

66. *Japanese lye maker*

screen or, preferably, a finer mesh plastic screen (12 lines per centimeter, or 30 lines per inch) draped inside. The drain basket is used to retain fiber when emptying a vat or for rinsing fiber after cooking. Cutting 2-centimeter (1-inch) holes in the bottom of a laundry basket with a matt knife and resting the assembly on several scraps of wood will provide more efficient drainage. Use the drain basket over a sink, in a bathtub or shower, or on a floor with drains. A larger version of the same tool, which is common in Japan, is shown in Figure 65. Built of wood, the drain box has solid sides but an open bottom covered with bamboo slats. Plastic mesh is required as before.

Wood-Ash Lye Maker Figure 45 should provide sufficient data to enable construction of this item. Note the sketch of the old Japanese lye maker in Figure 66. You are free to improvise with other containers if you wish, but remember to stay away from aluminum, copper, galvanized metal, and other materials that may react with strong alkalis to yield unwanted constituents in the final paper.

Washing Equipment While the drain basket and cooking vessel are recommended for most of the washing described in Chapter 7, if your production begins to involve raw fiber amounts larger than 1 kilogram (2.2 pounds), you may want to use a separate large vat for washing. The Japanese often use 1-by-3-meter (about 3-by-10-foot) open, shallow cement outdoor pools for this purpose (see Fig. 94).

Beating Equipment

Japanese Tools Various implements used in Japan are accurately documented in the accompanying tool drawings. Directions for use of stampers, *naginata* beaters, and hollander beaters are presented in Chapter 6.

Beating Sticks Stick configurations vary widely in Korea and Japan without drastically different effects. Tolerable results are possible with a wooden meat-tenderizer, baseball bat, billy club, or the like, but the recommended pattern is shown in Figure 95. Although considerable variation is permissible, this is a composite of the most common traditional Japanese beating utensils. The rounded handle is 30 centimeters (12 inches) long, and the stick's striking surface is 60 to 90 centimeters (24–36 inches) long and 2 to 3 centimeters (¾–1¼ inches) thick. Build from a tight-grained hardwood such as birch or maple. (See also Figs. 64, 121.) Procedures for using beating sticks are described in Chapter 6.

Beating Surfaces Any heavy, tight-surfaced material not prone to shedding color, paint, or other contaminants is acceptable as a beating surface. An area at least 30 by 60 centimeters (1 by 2 feet) is required for the simplified papermaking in Chapter 7; and an area of about 40 by 60 centimeters (16 by 24 inches), for the traditional approach. A smooth stone, hardwood, or laminated cutting block or slab of 60 by 90 centimeters (2 by 3 feet) is ideal. The more solid the support structure under the slab, the better. See Figures 95 and 96.

Stamper Stampers appear to be similar to hand beating in their overall effect on final sheet quality. As is the case with hand beating, however, high-quality original fiber and careful cooking are required to yield very uniform fiber separation.

The stamper pictured in Figures 46 and 97 has a capacity of 2 kilograms (about 4½ pounds) of cooked fiber (4 kilograms, or 9 pounds, before cooking) and requires a one-horsepower electric motor. The motor is geared to produce about 50 strokes per minute. The base is of cast concrete.

Naginata Beater The *naginata* is a very efficient piece of finishing equipment for producing even fiber separation in Japanese bast fiber.

A detailed drawing of a *naginata* is provided in Figure 47, but basic engineering skills and considerable hand-tool experience are required for successful construction. See Figures 98 and 99. Tubs may be built of wood, cement, or shaped foam covered with fiberglass. The shaft speed should be about 300 rpm. The seriously interested reader may wish to consult the papermaking equipment suppliers in Appendix 2 for estimates on a custom-built *naginata* before attempting a home-built machine. The same suggestion applies even more to stampers and hollander beaters.

Hollander Beater Building or purchasing a hollander specially for *nagashi-zuki* is not recommended since other pieces of equipment (i.e., a stamper and *naginata*) are more important and versatile. However, if you already have a hollander on hand, it may prove very helpful with certain fibers. (See Chapter 6, Beating Fiber.) Japanese hollanders are shown in Figures 100 and 101.

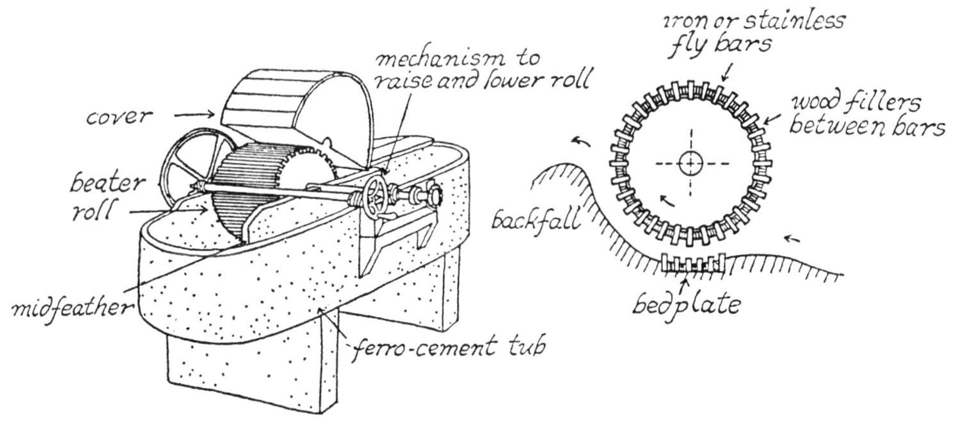

67. *Hollander beater*

Cleaning Equipment

Speck Removal by Hand In Japan most speck removal is done in baskets immersed in gently flowing cold water. A pan of cold water, changed occasionally, will serve the same purpose. A large glass bowl or container backlighted with a strong light will allow more rapid sighting of unwanted specks.

Flat Diaphragm Screen Although common in Japan and very effective for cleaning large amounts of fiber, the flat diaphragm screen is expensive and rare in the West.[2]

Tororo-processing Tools

Mallet Construct a tool similar to the mallet pictured in Figure 124. Use the mallet against a hardwood, smooth cement, or rock surface. Avoid using an iron hammer.

Strainer The tool pictured in Figure 48 is used for the traditional-method papermaking described in Chapter 7. Papermaking with a larger mould of 60 by 90 centimeters (2 by 3 feet) will require additional units of this strainer or a larger version of the same tool. A cotton or cotton-polyester pillowcase must be used inside the strainer. Note the *tororo* preparation procedure described in Chapter 6, Formation Aids.

Presses

Regardless of the hardware, in all *nagashi-zuki* pressing the idea is to remove excess water without disturbing the precise stratification between one sheet and the next. Operationally, this means applying additional weight very gradually over a long period of time. In a production shop the ideal total weight required at the paper's surface is about .73 kilograms per square centimeter (10 pounds per square inch) for most papers. Thinner papers and those of mitsumata or gampi may require 50 percent more pressure. On the other hand, for simplified papermaking, much less pressure will suffice.

Properly pressed, a pack of paper will be compact and damp but not soggy. Procedural details follow in Chapter 7.

Japanese Presses Most presses in contemporary Japanese shops are very simple affairs actuated by a screw or light hydraulic jack (up to 9 metric tons, or 10 tons) capable of delivering pressure of approximately .73 kilograms per square centimeter (10 pounds per square inch) at the paper. The earliest Eastern pressing methods employed direct weight on top of the upper press board or weights added to a lever that, in turn, applied more pressure to the paper. Designs for all of these approaches are outlined below.

Simple Weight System Pressing is most simply accomplished by gradually adding weights directly to the post. Bricks will work, or a large plastic garbage can can be slowly filled with water or sand. The total weight figures mentioned above are ideal but if your paper is small—e.g., the placemat size (25 by 35 centimeters, or about 10 by 14 inches) used in Chapter 7—as little as 100 to 150 kilograms (220–330 pounds) total weight will suffice. Note procedures in Chapter 7.

Lever Press See Figure 102. This press design goes back many centuries. The only change is the use of a gradual flow of water into the buckets to slowly increase the weight on the paper. This saves having to add weight every 20 minutes or so. See Figure 49 and procedures outlined under traditional-method papermaking in Chapter 7.

Screw and Hydraulic Presses While most screw presses can be used without fear of overpressing, heavy hydraulic presses designed for Western *tame-zuki* papermaking can be dangerous. Too much pressure applied too rapidly will make the entire post go fluid, ruining the entire pile. If this happens, soak the damaged sheets in water, remake them, and press more slowly and gently. Follow the pressing guidelines outlined in Chapter 7. See Figures 103 and 104.

Press Boards and Felts Press boards are most easily constructed of 2-centimeter (3/4-inch) plywood. Cut the wood to a size several centimeters (inches) larger than the paper you plan to make and rasp and sand all the edges and corners so there are no rough edges prone to catching and splitting later. Varnish with several coats of a high-quality exterior polyurethane varnish.

Felts for starting a post can be made of old machine felts from a paper mill, old woolen blankets, or old muslin or bed sheets. Many papermakers in Japan use a layer of mesh between the felt and the press board to aid in drainage during pressing, but it is not necessary.

Drying Equipment

Japanese Dryers Although the outdoor drying board is the traditional tool, the vast majority of Japanese papermakers today use heated metal indoor dryers for normal production work. The configuration of the machine and source of heat vary from area to area, but the principle is the same. A large sheet-metal box is heated from within by steam, and the damp paper, brushed onto the outside surface, is dried by the heat of the metal. Compared to outdoor boards, the indoor heated dryers are very fast. One person can brush eight damp sheets onto the metal, and by the time he or she is finished, the first four sheets are dry and ready to be stripped off. In addition, the heated dryers have the added important advantage of being perfectly functional regardless of the weather outside. Their successful operation, however, requires special attention to the interrelationship of moisture content of the paper, dryer temperature (maximum 70° C, or 150° F), fiber type, and paper thickness. Thin papers and papers of gampi and mitsumata generally require very low temperatures and slower drying times. Slow, low-temperature drying is less inclined to cause any type of paper to break away prematurely from the metal.

Boards Note the boards in Figures 105 and 107. Drying can be done on any smooth, tight-surfaced material that is not reactive in the presence of water and mild heat. Thus, glass (preferably in frames for safety's sake), plexiglass, stainless steel, Formica, and smooth, tight-grained wood will all work. Some woods may stain the paper until they are broken in. In Japan, a new board is usually set aside to mature for at least a year. Then the board is washed well and used to dry poor-quality paper in bright sunny weather until the sheets come off with no sign of discoloration. A similar approach should be taken with boards used in the West. If damp paper fails to stick to a board it is probably because the wood is too porous to permit the proper capillary action between the paper and the board surface. Creating a more tightly grained surface with a wood scraper may provide better results.

To dry the paper, the chosen surface with paper applied may be left in a heated room or placed in the sun. An electric hair-dryer can be used to speed up the drying process. A major consideration in choosing a drying surface is the final paper texture that will result. The wood-grain finish imparted by old worn drying boards is considered a definite plus by connoisseurs of Japanese papers.

Heat-Lamp Dryer This is a workable tool for making thinner Japanese papers. If larger or thicker paper is to be produced on a regular basis, a larger, steam-heated device may be in order. The heat-lamp dryer is lightweight and relatively easy to build, but it produces uneven heat and cool areas at the edges. See Figures 50, 108, and 109.

Steam-Heated Dryer The machine shown in Figure 51 very closely approximates the workhorse dryer used in Japan today. To give uniform, consistent heat it is heated from the inside with steam. The water in the reservoir can be heated with an electric water-heating element or with an oil or gas flame. Working temperatures for this dryer and the heat-lamp dryer should range around 75° C (170° F). Although most dryers in Japan (see Fig. 106) are made of sheet steel, stainless steel is recommended for making permanent papers.

Note: Be sure to have your wiring checked by a professional electrician before working with electricity, including the use of this or the heat-lamp dryer.

Drying Brushes See Figures 110 and 111. While a quality paintbrush about 8 centimeters (3 inches) wide will work for limited papermaking, at present there is nothing available off-the-shelf that possesses the proper brush width and stiffness for drying paper on a production level.

Generally speaking, "gentle stiffness" is required of a good drying brush. A very soft brush without body is inappropriate, as is a stiff brush with coarse bristles.

Although you may wish to order drying brushes from Japan for drying very thin, delicate sheets, very serviceable substitutes can be made in the West from several high-quality paintbrushes trimmed and set together in a new handle.

To assemble the brush pictured in Figure 52, purchase three natural-bristle paintbrushes each approximately 8 centimeters (3 inches) wide. Remove their handles, and you will find the bristles set in a plastic material that was poured in around the bristles when the brush was manufactured. Working with a very smooth sanding block, or a table sander, square one edge on each of two brushes and both edges on the remaining brush (which will be sandwiched end to end between the first two brushes). Roughly sand the bottoms of all three. You will lose plastic and bristles doing this, but keep working until the three fit together nicely. Build a new handle to hold the three, glue them in with epoxy, and carefully adjust the brushes to form a straight outer edge and to make the bristles closely mesh where they meet. Clamp, and let the glue dry. Later you can sand down any protrusions of glue or wood.

Other Tools

Below are several optional tools that you may wish to build:

Work Table There is considerable construction time involved here, but once finished you can use this table to make paper anywhere, without risk of spilling water on the floor. This is an especially helpful tool if you plan to work routinely in areas without floor drains. Note Figures 53, 90, and 113. A section of copper pipe with one end flared will work well as a drain. Apply three or four coats of exterior polyurethane varnish to the finished table.

Mould Suspension System If you begin to make paper of 60 by 90 centimeters (2 by 3 feet) or larger, some type of suspension system will be necessary. In Japan one to five lines running to flexible bamboo poles or stationary points on the ceiling are used to carry the weight of the mould. See Figure 68 for one typical setup. When the mould is wet but uncharged, it should hang free at a slight angle over the center of the vat. The near

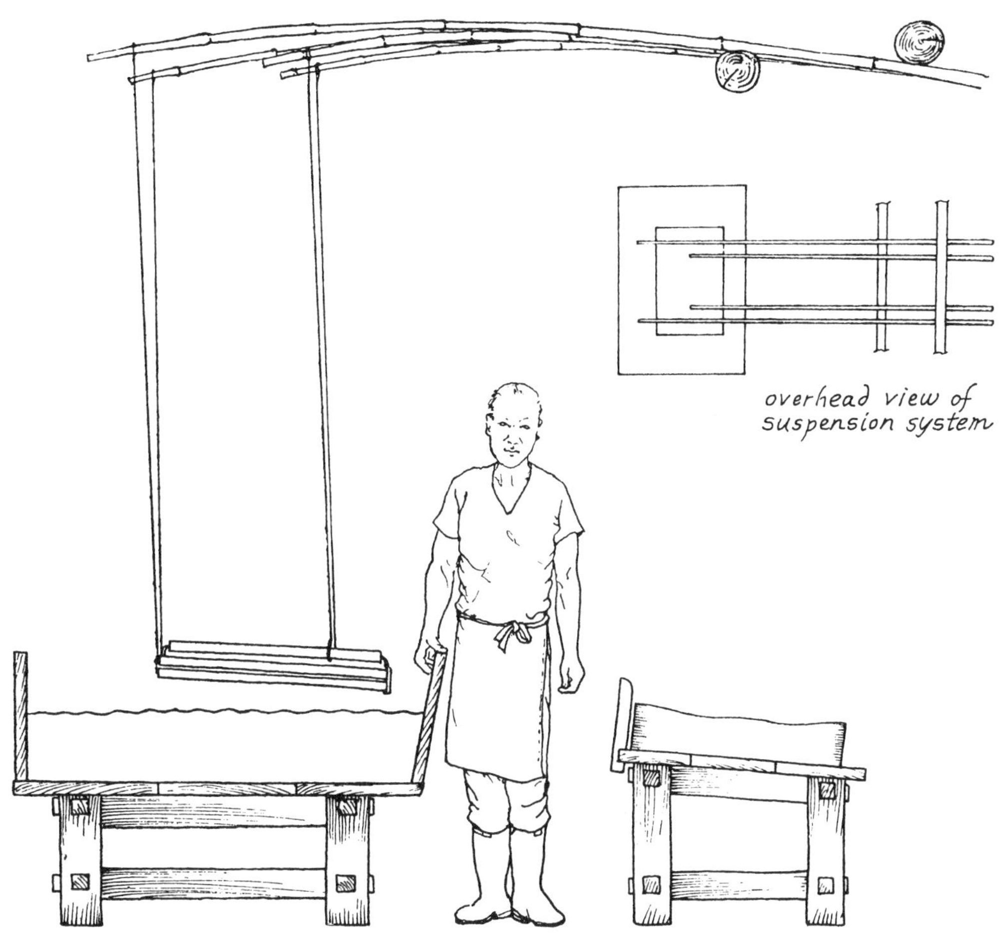

68. Mould suspension system

edge of the mould should be about 4 centimeters (1½ inches) from the charged vat surface; and the far edge, about 10 centimeters (4 inches) away. In action, during papermaking, the mould should act lively and move freely but stay out of the stock. See Figure 112. Surgical tubing or lightweight bungee cords may prove an acceptable substitute for the bamboo poles.

COW
MAN

CHAPTER SIX

Materials and Their Preparation

IN THIS CHAPTER raw materials and preparation processes for proceeding with Japanese papermaking in the West are presented in a step-by-step fashion. Various methods are described progressing from the most simple to production-level approaches. An outline follows below for ease of reference.

- Kozo
  - Cultivating Kozo in America
  - Preferred Climate
  - Diseases and Pests
  - Harvesting Kozo
- Other Fibers
  - Mitsumata, Gampi, and Other Eastern Basts
  - Abaca
  - Dried Abaca, Sisal, and Other Long-Fiber Pulps
  - Cotton Rag, Cotton Linters, Wood Pulp, and Raw Flax
- Cooking and Washing Fiber
  - Water
  - Preliminary Steps
  - Cooking
  - Wood-Ash Lye
  - Other Cooking Alkalis
  - Washing
  - Speck Removal
- Beating Fiber
  - Hand Beating
  - Evaluating Beating Degree
  - Stamper Beating
  - *Naginata* Beating
  - Hollander Beating
  - Storing Beaten Pulps
- Formation Aids
  - *Tororo-aoi* Cultivation
  - *Tororo-aoi* Storage
  - *Tororo-aoi* Formation Aid Preparation
  - Plant Substitutes for *Tororo-aoi*
  - Synthetic Formation Aids

There are many types of fibers, native and imported, that can be used by the Western *nagashi-zuki* papermaker, especially if an artistic or unique effect is the chief goal. The range of available fibers narrows considerably, however, if permanent papers are to be produced, and even more so if they are to be produced for sale in relatively large numbers. I will leave any discussion of North American non-Japanese fiber substitutes to Winifred Lutz's presentation in Appendix 1. What follows is an introduction to the fibers presently available in America (including Japanese fibers) that can be used to make quality *nagashi-zuki* papers. Consult Appendix 2 for sources of these materials.

Kozo

Kozo fiber, usually imported from Japan or Korea, is the best fiber for small-scale *nagashi-zuki* papermaking in the West, in spite of its price. Kozo responds readily to light cooking and hand beating. Large amounts of hemicelluloses, superior fiber length (12 millimeters, or about ½ inch, on the average), and the strength and fineness of its fiber all make kozo perfect for the beginning *nagashi-zuki* student as well as the advanced papermaker interested in achieving quality, permanence, and durability.

Cultivating Kozo in America Between 1950 and 1960, C. H. Dexter and Sons, Inc., a paper manufacturer in Windsor Locks, Connecticut, conducted extensive experiments on the cultivation of kozo in America. At the end of the project, utilizing entirely new propagation and cultivation techniques, Dexter researchers were producing per-acre yields considerably better than those of the Japanese. Although questions may be raised about the effects of non-Japanese agricultural methods, soil, and climatic conditions on the final fiber quality, many of the Dexter findings are unquestionably of great value to the papermaker bent on growing kozo in America. The information presented here is based on discussions with authorities at Dexter and, to a lesser extent, with Japanese authorities. Data from my own experiments with kozo cultivation in Michigan is also included.

The two most common citations for kozo are *Broussonetia kazinoki* Sieb. and *Broussonetia papyrifera* Vent. The former seems to be the preferred species for cultivation of papermaking fiber, although it is not as hardy as the latter. *Broussonetia papyrifera* Vent. can occasionally be found growing wild in America, but its fiber is not the best for quality papermaking. Both of the above species are known to have additional subvarieties, further complicating botanical identification of the most ideal material for papermaking fiber.

Seeds for *Broussonetia papyrifera* Vent. are occasionally available in America. However, starting tree stock from seeds is extremely difficult, and consistent characteristics may not result. Professional assistance and facilities are often required. In addition, the value of any resultant fiber, compared to that of imported Japanese kozo stock, is questionable.

If cultivation is to be seriously undertaken, taking root sections or budded hardwood cuttings from quality Japanese tree stock in the early spring is the most favored approach. Such starting plant material has to be flown in from Japan under a specially requested permit from the United States Department of Agriculture after making arrangements with a Japanese exporter. Write Shimura or Flavin (see Appendix 2) with any inquiry.

The various propagation techniques for the imported Japanese cuttings, or for their offspring, are outlined below:

1. Root cuttings (root suckers). This is the normal Japanese method of cultivation. Once a healthy stand of trees with well-developed root systems has been established (2–3 years), cut roots may be harvested in early spring for cultivation of new trees elsewhere. Healthy root sections 1.5 centimeters (about 5/8 inch) in diameter and 15 to 20 centimeters (6–8 inches) in length are required. The cut sections should be planted in a starting bed at a 45-degree angle with about 2 centimeters (3/4 inch) of the root exposed above the soil. Buds should appear in the early summer months. Suitable media for starting a limited number of sections are sand, vermiculite, or a mixture of one part sand and two parts topsoil. Keep the cuttings moist, warm, and protected from direct sun until leaves are well developed. If many roots are on hand and your location and rainfall ideal, you may elect to plant directly into the field. Exposed root tips should be covered lightly with straw to protect them from the sun and cold. Note other considerations discussed below, such as soil, spacing, weather, water, and so on.

2. Dormant hardwood cuttings. This is the preferred method of establishing a healthy stand of many trees when only a limited number of healthy Japanese trees are on hand to work with. Budded sections of dormant branches (5–10 millimeters, or 3/16–3/8 inch, in diameter) are cut in early

spring and moved to wooden flats or beds partially shaded from the sun. (A slatted covering in place of a roof over the propagation area is recommended. One such covering used by Dexter researchers was 5-centimeter-wide, or 2-inch-wide, aluminum strips or wood laths set parallel and roughly 3.75 centimeters, or 1½ inches, apart.) Sand, vermiculite, or a light sandy loam are all possible media for propagation. Cuttings should be set about 10 centimeters (4 inches) deep and rooting response should be evident in four to six weeks. Working in a greenhouse will generally yield a higher rate of success than working outdoors.

3. Greenwood (emergent) cuttings. If neither rootstock nor hardwood cuttings are available, this method may be used to raise large numbers of trees from limited stock. Using this technique, 150 or more cuttings can be taken from one healthy, established tree. Though more prolific, greenwood cuttings require more attention than hardwood cuttings, and usually greenhouse protection as well. Greenwood cuttings should be taken as the tree enters its active growth stage, i.e., late spring or early summer.

In working with either hardwood or greenwood cuttings, selection of healthy stock and a constantly moist (but not soaked), warm (27° C, or 80° F) bed both appear essential for successful cutting development. To maintain the required temperature, electric heat from below may be necessary at the propagation site. Both hardwood and greenwood cuttings should be slit at the lower end before planting. (All cuttings should be kept in their original root-end-down orientation.) For best results, two slits are made at right angles about 2 centimeters (¾ inch) up from the base. These cuts will improve root development. Commercial hormone root stimulants may add to successful rootings.

Regardless of the type, once cuttings are well established in their protected location, they should be transferred to pots or, if the grower is well-prepared, to the field. Rooted kozo cuttings can usually be successfully transplanted in the field any time from early spring to late August. Success in midsummer transplanting requires sufficient water, a protective mulch, correct fertilizer, and correct soil pH. Proper spacing is staggered rows with plants 1.2 meters (4 feet) apart in every direction. During the growing season, all weeds and vines should be kept off the plants. In Japan, some farmers remove emerging lower branches by breaking them off sideways at the main shaft.

A light loam, if its moisture-holding capacity is high, appears to be the most satisfactory soil for kozo. However, drainage must also be sufficient to prevent any chance of the kozo standing in water. Roots must be in a well-aerated but moist medium at all times. A soil pH in the 5.5 to 6.0 range is required.

While the Japanese have traditionally used natural composts, modern fertilizers are now prevalent. Kozo responds well to a field fertilizer of the 5–10–5 type (5 parts nitrogen, 10 of phosphate, and 5 of potash). Extra nitrogen and phosphate prove beneficial in obtaining maximum yields. The effects of various fertilizers on final fiber *quality,* however, has not been investigated. Fertilizers should be applied in early spring at the start of the growing season and again in early summer.

Preferred Climate Dexter researchers concluded that coastal South Carolina and Georgia and north-central Florida are the areas best adapted to kozo culture in the United States. The Florida location is actually favored slightly over others due to more reliable summer rainfall and less drastic temperature fluctuations during the winter. More limited success may be obtained in other areas of the United States if trees are protected from wind and hard freezes and provided with the other requirements described in this section.

If natural rainfall and soil conditions do not yield a continually moist condition at the roots, irrigation may be needed for maximum yields. Any water tested and shown to be high in bicarbonate alkalinity will cause poor rooting response in kozo cuttings. In one instance, growth problems encountered by Dexter researchers with pH 8.7 water from a 180-meter (600-foot) artesian well were immediately eliminated when pH 7.6 water from a shallow well was substituted.

Diseases and Pests Kozo seems generally resistant to serious infestations and infections. The following notes, however, are worthy of attention:

1. A white scale, *Pseudaulacaspis pentagona,* is sometimes observed on the bark of kozo and should be treated with a commercially available spray. Contact your local agent of the United States Department of Agriculture for advice if this scale appears.
2. Root rot will develop if the roots are injured or if the plant stands in water. In the latter case, the rot may follow death rather than cause it.
3. Deer are fond of young kozo plants, although they will not bother

well-established trees. Fences are in order if deer are prevalent in your area.

4. Wood rats appeared at some of the Dexter research plots and were controlled with poison.

5. Field mice may remove lower bark sections of young trees protected during the winter from freezes with straw. Set out mouse poison, or surround the trees with wire mesh.

At Dexter test sites kozo usually developed maximum production four to six years after being transplanted in the field and lost its vitality after ten years. During ongoing cultivation of kozo, plan for a ten-year tree replacement cycle.

Harvesting Kozo Stripping kozo bark from trees in the West very closely follows the Japanese process. Review the procedure described in Chapter 2. When working with a very small number of trees, you can use a large cooking pot with a tight-fitting lid and 2 or 3 centimeters (1 or 2 inches) of boiling water inside. Cut the tree into lengths short enough to fit, standing upright, inside the pot. The tree sections have steamed sufficiently when the bark has drawn back from the wood for about 1 centimeter (3/8 inch) at the cut ends.

If you want to process a larger number of trees, the next step in the West might be to place a 208-liter (55–gallon) drum over a wood fire outdoors. The trees must be wrapped with a plastic tarp or covered with a second drum to keep the steam in. This is a low-budget way of solving the steaming problem that is occasionally used in South Korea. Any other system you invent that successfully contains both the trees and steam for about 2 hours is quite acceptable.

Stripped bark should be hung up to dry as soon as possible. (See Fig. 118, which shows kozo drying in Japan.) Later, when more time is available, the bark must be soaked and scraped free of the black outer layer.

For black bark removal, a scraping knife and board as pictured in Figures 116 and 117 are required. Soak the stripped bark for at least an hour before beginning the scraping process. Follow the description of Japanese outer bark removal in Chapter 2. Be sure to work in the direction of the tree's growth, i.e., from root end to upper extremities. Figure 69 shows how to distinguish the lower (root) end and upper end of a bark strip. Decide if you are aiming for white or green bark, which will depend primarily on the desired color of your finished paper. After scraping, hang the bark to

69. *Proper scraping direction for removing black bark*

dry completely before storage, preferably outdoors in the sun and breeze. Dried kozo bark is shown in Figure 120.

Other Fibers

Mitsumata, Gampi, and Other Eastern Basts Generally these materials yield papers that are crisper and more translucent than kozo paper. Shorter fiber lengths and higher hemicellulose contents often leave papers made from these fibers more difficult to part after pressing. And once parted, the finished sheets are more inclined to pull away from drying surfaces before they are completely dry. As a result of these potential problems, in spite of their very distinctive character, non-kozo Eastern basts should be avoided until a basic familiarity with kozo has been developed.

Abaca Also known as Manila hemp, abaca may represent the best alternative to Japanese fiber when the production of larger quantities of less expensive papers is being considered. Cooking takes considerably longer due to larger amounts of lignin and other encrusting matter, and for any degree of control, a hollander beater is required to properly separate and manipulate the fibers. Parting abaca sheets can be difficult. Generally speaking, however, with careful selection of a high-quality raw fiber at the outset, and with proper cooking and beating, a wide variety of high-quality papers can be made from abaca. Note the discussion of various treatments under the headings Cooking and Beating Fiber below.

My one reservation about abaca concerns its higher lignin content. Lignin is generally considered an undesirable constituent in paper since Western machine-made papers high in lignin are known to discolor rapidly. However, all three of the Japanese fibers retain varied amounts of lignin in the finished papers without apparent harmful effect in old, traditionally made sheets. Abaca, as well, if properly cooked and well washed, should also yield sound papers. Eventually, thorough testing will be required if abaca, a relatively new fiber in papermaking, is to be used with the same degree of trust kozo has long since earned. The type and degree of processing are likely to be the determining factors in this regard.

As for selection of raw fiber, for optimal quality in the finished paper, grade A-D Philippine abaca, Ecuadorian abaca of grade 1, 2, or 3, or any abaca very light in color normally used for textile production is recommended.

Dried Abaca, Sisal, and Other Long-Fiber Pulps Dry sheets of pulped (cooked and usually bleached) fibers are available from various suppliers and can be used to dilute the more expensive and troublesome basts. Although they are relatively inexpensive and ready for papermaking after only brief mixing, these fibers are less than ideal for several reasons. First, the quality of the water used by the manufacturer, the type and condition of their cooking equipment, the quality and type of chemicals and bleaches used, and the degree of washing employed are all unknown. Unless the manufacturer can supply an analysis of the pulp, the possibility remains of there being residual chemicals or metals in the finished pulp. Crucial decisions regarding water and fiber quality as well as cooking, bleaching, and washing degrees have all been relinquished to an outside source (the manufacturer), compromising the papermaker's control of subtleties of character and quality. Also, once-dried fiber will never form bonds as strong as those occurring between freshly processed still-damp fibers, and parting of sheets made from these fibers, without a kozo additive, is likely to be difficult.

In summation, when and if necessary, these commercial pulps can be tested and perhaps proved perfectly acceptable from the standpoint of permanence and durability. However, the *character* of the final paper is largely predetermined when such materials are used. The only fiber that makes a traditional handmade paper is that selected and prepared by the papermaker himself, with water, equipment, and alkali known to him. Even then the artisan must remain constantly aware of slight changes in processing, which may have an affect on the permanence, durability, and/or character of the finished paper.

Cotton Rag, Cotton Linters, Wood Pulp, and Raw Flax Because of its lack of hemicelluloses and its springy contorted fiber structure, cotton fiber does not work well in the Japanese papermaking process. In order to produce strong papers, cotton must be beaten thoroughly, resulting in stock with a reduced freeness that, in combination with the viscous formation aid, does not drain efficiently. Abaca or kozo concentrations can be diluted with cotton rag or linter fiber that has been beaten only slightly and, perhaps, cleaned with a flat diaphragm screen to remove knots. The resulting paper, however, lacks strength, and at the present writing I do not believe *nagashi-zuki* papers of combined cotton fiber and bast prove attractive or viable beyond experimental usage. Please note, however, Winifred Lutz's significant work with fermented and stamped Belgian flax for *nagashi-zuki* papermaking (see Appendix 1).

Wood pulps, most notably bleached and unbleached kraft pulps, are used commonly in Japan today to dilute the much more expensive native bast fibers. Wood pulps have the same disadvantages as the commercial long-fiber pulps mentioned above. Generally, papers made with wood-pulp additives turn out softer and weaker than their pure-bast counterparts. The use of wood pulps is not recommended for anything beyond experimentation or practice.

Cooking and Washing Fiber

Review Chapter 3 before reading this and the following section on fiber preparation.

Water Of all the materials required in making a superior paper perhaps none is as important, yet often neglected, as high-quality water. Because even small amounts of unwanted constituents in a water supply actually accumulate in the paper during sheet forming, water quality plays a crucial role in the permanence of the finished sheet. Ideally, water should be checked for pH and calcium, magnesium, iron, and copper content. Businesses that sell water-softening equipment will usually test water for basic impurities at no charge. The services of a commercial testing lab, however, may be necessary to learn the actual parts-per-million for elements present. If your water has a neutral or slightly alkaline pH (higher than 7) and some magnesium or calcium content, but negligible amounts of pollution, particulate matter, microbes, chlorine, iron, and copper, the water is at least acceptable if not very good for high-quality papermaking. The finished *paper* should contain less than 300 parts per million of iron and 30 parts per million of copper if future foxing or premature aging is to be avoided. Some conservators prefer even lower figures. Excessive levels of iron and copper can usually be traced to the water, iron or copper equipment, or cooking chemicals. Remember that without quality water a lasting, superior-quality paper is not possible.

Preliminary Steps The major activity prior to the actual cooking of the fiber is soaking the dry bark in clear, cool water so that it will more readily react to the hot alkali solution at the cooking step. If you have access to a mountain stream or river, you may elect to soak and sun-bleach the fiber in the traditional manner. Wall off an area with rocks to make a pool of slightly moving water about 25 centimeters (10 inches) deep, and then submerge your raw bark so that all strands are well exposed to the water and sunlight for about two days. Natural bleaching techniques should be used where a quality paper of very light color is required.

The more water, and the fresher, cleaner, and colder the water you use during soaking, the better the final quality of the paper. However, if nothing more is available, tap water in a bathtub, sink, or bucket will suffice. Two hours are required for minimum soaking.

At some point during the soaking step, you may want to clean the bark of black flecks and other defects by repeating the black bark removal process (see Harvesting Kozo, above). With thorough cleaning at this stage, only limited final picking will be required to yield very clean fiber. Unless your work will be interrupted for several days, proceed directly to cooking without again drying your bleached and soaked fiber. If you must stop, dry the fiber at this point by hanging it outdoors. Do not forget to soak it again before cooking.

Cooking The cooking step should be done only immediately prior to papermaking. The quicker the fiber is made into paper after cooking, the "fresher" the final paper—that is, the less chance of fiber spoilage, which can dull luster and crispness and leave an unpleasant odor in the paper. Plan to cook and beat on the day before you are ready to continue with the rest of the process.

The average cook in Japan requires 200 grams (7 ounces) of soda ash (Na_2CO_3) and 15 liters (4 gallons) of water for every 1000 grams (2¼ pounds) of dry bark. Cooks are described by stating the amount of chemical added as a percentage of the total fiber weight. Thus the recipe above is a "20 percent cook." A 15 percent cook would require 150 grams (about 5 ounces) of soda ash; a 12 percent cook, 120 grams (about 4 ounces) of soda ash; and so on. This system works fine until you begin cooking very small quantities of fiber, for the 15 liters/1000 grams (4 gallons/2¼ pounds) ratio of water to dry fiber does not provide enough liquid to cover the fiber and somewhat more water is required. This of course dilutes the concentration of the soda ash (or whatever other alkali you may be using) and means your small-scale cook will not necessarily give a proper indication of what will result if you cook larger amounts of fiber. However, this is a problem one has to live with. The total amount of alkali available to chemically react with the various constituents in a given amount of fiber is usually considered the primary relationship. Go ahead and add more water when and if you need it, but keep a close record of your work. (Note: Most barks, stiff at first, will loosen up considerably after 10 to 15 minutes of cooking and sink below the cooking solution's surface.) Typical volumes required with small amounts of fiber are 12 liters/750 grams, 10 liters/500 grams, 8 liters/250 grams, and 4 liters/100 grams (or 12½ quarts/1½ pounds, 10½ quarts/1 pound, 8 quarts/½ pound, or 4 quarts/3½ ounces). In all cases, add the water to the cooking vessel, and when the water is almost boiling stir the alkali in and then add the soaked fiber. Cover the pot and cook at a steady gentle boil for 2 hours, stirring and turning the fiber every 30 minutes. When the fiber is fully cooked, all strands, large and small, thick and thin, should part easily with and against the grain. See Figures 70 and 71.

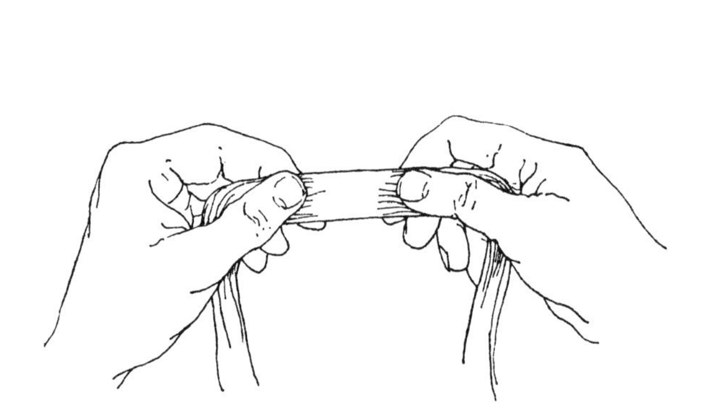

70. Testing fiber for sufficient cooking, with the grain

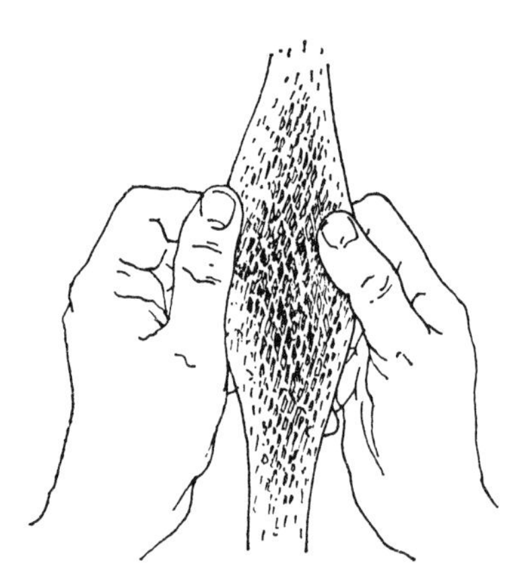

71. Testing fiber for sufficient cooking, against the grain

Cooking is a very important step and should not be regarded lightly. Many subsequent problems with fiber beating, formation quality, hardness or softness of the paper, and the like can be traced to cooking. Keep a careful record of your cooking, assigning numbers to each batch of fiber and attaching correlated paper samples so that you eventually develop a sensitivity to the effects of cooking. Variations on the average *nagashi-zuki* cook for specific fibers follow:

1. Kozo. If a Japanese papermaker knows his kozo fiber has been harvested within the last year and is of very high quality, he will often cook it for about 1½ hours in only a 12 percent cook. This lighter treatment goes back to a hidden but pervading sense of duty in traditional Japanese papermaking that embodies great respect for the integrity and natural character of the fiber. Thus, the traditional papermaker cooks with the minimal amount of alkali and for the minimal time necessary to yield good fiber separation. As a result of this approach he ends up with a stronger, more reliable paper, possessed of natural color, warmth, and luster. Overprocessing would lessen these qualities and result in an inferior paper.

If kozo fiber is more than one year old or of rough quality, try a surer 18 to 20 percent soda ash cook. If any residual toughness in the fiber is detected after 2 hours of cooking, more time may be required.

2. Mitsumata and gampi. Both of these fibers are usually processed in 15 to 20 percent soda ash cooks with the same consideration for age and quality

as that given kozo. To gain a pleasing darker color, gampi is sometimes cooked with the black bark adhering even though picking time will be greatly prolonged. Mitsumata is almost always cooked as white bark. Since both mitsumata and gampi trees change radically in diameter and bark thickness from trunk to outer branches, very often Japanese papermakers add the thicker bark strands from the lower third of the tree to the cooking vessel about 20 minutes before the rest of the bark. This tends to give the thicker sections the extra action they need to end up with treatment similar to that received by the thinner, smaller sections. Cooking time averages about 2½ hours for both mitsumata and gampi.

3. Foreign and native basts. Any inner bark fiber from Korea, Taiwan, China, Nepal, or Mexico, as well as any native North American type, is often more resistant to cooking than new Japanese kozo and should be treated initially with a 20 percent cook for at least 2 hours for the best chance of success.

4. Abaca (Manila hemp). Because of its resistance to a basic 20 percent soda ash cook, abaca, when used in Japan, is normally cooked in caustic soda, usually in a 20 to 25 percent solution. Even with the use of such a strong chemical, cooking usually takes 4 or 5 hours, and the cooked fiber is often left to sit covered but unwashed in a cool area for a week or two to let any residual chemicals continue to act on remaining unwanted constituents. CAUTION: Caustic soda is very dangerous to work with; the use of rubber gloves and a face shield is strongly advised.

Much longer cooks (8 to 12 hours) in soda ash rather than caustic soda may leave more natural color and character in the fiber. Whatever the cooking method, sufficient treatment has been accomplished if a single strand of the abaca comes apart against the grain with little or no resistance.

Wood-Ash Lye Traditional wood-ash alkali is a very promising alternative to soda ash because it is regarded as a gentle cooking agent. But, if it is not thoroughly rinsed out after cooking, wood-ash alkali can leave residual potassium in the fiber, which is just as likely to cause premature oxidation of the cellulose as the sodium residue remaining after a soda ash cook. The basic procedure for making 14 liters (about 15 quarts) of the alkali is as follows:

Set up the wood-ash lye maker and add 1200 grams (about 2½ pounds) ash as indicated in Figure 45. (One-hundred-percent hardwood ashes are recommended, but the Japanese have used rice straw, rice chaff, and/or various grasses to produce the required ash. Feel free to experiment, but avoid ash from high-resin woods—e.g., pine—or any ash containing iron scraps or coal or oil residue.) Use fresh ash for the most effective cooking.

Heat 15 liters (about 16 quarts) of water to near boiling, and pour it into the top bucket. Let all the drainable water pass through the ashes into the lower collection bucket. Do not worry about the change in water color. You should end up with about 14 liters (about 15 quarts) of wood-ash lye, sufficient for cooking 750 to 1000 grams (about 1¾–2¼ pounds) of kozo fiber.

Generally, in working with wood-ash lye you should use 100 grams (3½ ounces) of ash to make each liter (quart) of cooking solution and plan on 1 to 2 more hours of cooking time than the 1 to 1½ hours required with soda ash. Remember that roughly 15 liters (about 16 quarts) of cooking solution are required for each kilogram (2¼ pounds) of fiber.

Increase the ratio of ash to water if you do not obtain effective cooking action with the 100 grams/liter ratio. Wood-ash lye is harder to work with, less predictable, and more time-consuming, but more traditional and perhaps better for the paper's luster and crispness. In addition, wood ash may yield more permanent papers than chemical cooks due to its more gentle action and possibly a tendency to rinse out more readily than soda ash.

Other Cooking Alkalis In addition to ash lyes, lime also has a reputation as a traditional alkali. Moreover, it is especially attractive from a standpoint of paper permanence since the calcium carbonate residue remaining in the paper acts as an alkaline reserve to counteract possible future environmental acidity. The proper material, commonly referred to as hydrated or slaked lime, $Ca(OH)_2$, can be obtained from suppliers of industrial chemicals and is usually used as a 25 percent cook (250 grams lime/1000 grams fiber/15 liters water, or 9 ounces lime/2¼ pounds fiber/4 gallons water). Total cooking time is usually about 5 hours. Make sure you use fresh lime, as lime readily carbonates in a humid atmosphere, which renders it less effective at cooking.

Sodium hydroxide, mentioned above, known also as lye or caustic soda ($NaOH$), is a very strong chemical that should be used only when necessary. Not only is it dangerous, but from a traditional standpoint, any fiber that is really appropriate for making *nagashi-zuki* papers of quality and character will not require the stronger caustic action of NaOH.

Soda ash surfaces, in the end, as the best alkali for beginners, combining convenience, versatility, and reliability. Moreover, properly executed, a soda-ash cook followed by a lime-water wash (i.e., .75 grams lime/1 liter water, or 1/4 teaspoon lime/1 quart water), which facilitates removal of the sodium, is likely to yield a very permanent finished paper.

Immediately following cooking, many papermakers add a little water to the pot to cover any strands that tend to stick up above the solution's surface, and then they leave the fiber in the hot solution to stand until the next morning. Some Japanese papermakers believe there is an important advantage in this continued subtle treatment during the overnight steeping. However, if necessary, you can immediately proceed to the washing step.

Washing Dispense with the majority of the spent cooking solution by dumping the cooked strands into a drain basket (described in Chapter 5). To wash the fiber, add fresh water to the cooking vessel, and then add the bark strands. Slowly move the bark about in the water for a few moments; then dump the lot into the drain basket again and repeat the process two more times. Eventually the water passing through the mesh will become fairly clear. You may stop here or, if you are especially concerned about permanence, you may give your fiber a final lime-water rinse (made up as described above).

During washing, you can monitor the progress of chemical removal by testing the wash water with pH strips until it drops close to or equal to the pH of your source water. In any case, remember that thorough washing after cooking is crucial to the permanence of the finished paper. See Appendix 1 (p. 252) for more on washing.

Larger vessels are required for washing quantities of fiber larger than 1 to 2 kilograms (about 2–5 pounds). Note the Japanese washing pool described in Chapter 5. To use this piece of equipment, or any very large wash vessel, after the fiber has been washed, drain off the discolored water through a strainer, refill the tank, and repeat the process two or three more times. Whatever the equipment and procedure, treat the bark strands with care during washing. After cooking they have lost their binding materials and will easily shed precious fibers with rough treatment. Remember, too, that limited washing yields darker, crisper paper, while continued or extended washing yields softer, lighter-colored papers.

Speck Removal Very high quality traditionally-made Japanese paper is completely free of foreign matter. Left in, specks may add a certain visual interest, but they seriously harm the paper's respectability as a finely made sheet.

Foreign matter can also cause problems for the user, particularly the fine-art or letterpress printer, and can affect the permanence and durability of the paper as well.

There are two methods of locating specks while picking by hand. The first, and more common in Japan, is to gently pass the individual strands through the hands in a large bowl or pan of water—carefully inspecting the strip for any attached foreign matter. (See Fig. 119.) The backlighted glass bowl suggested in Chapter 5 can be of tremendous help here. In addition to black flecks, watch for discolored areas (usually brownish or reddish), which, if they seem tough and stringy compared to the rest of the strand, indicate a diseased or wounded area that did not respond to cooking. Remove these and any additional defects that could interfere with consistent quality in the finished sheets, but leave any soft greenish matter (the cooked green middle layer). Change the water in the bowl periodically during picking. (In Japan this work is often done in fine mesh baskets partially submerged in gently flowing water.)

The second technique for speck removal allows you to work "dry" and avoid having your hands in water constantly. Working on a water-resistant surface, remove one strand at a time from the group of cooked and washed bark strips, and pull it apart several times along its full length, thereby exposing any defects or foreign particles. As strands are picked clean, keep them damp by packing them into a pile or ball or, if necessary, cover them with plastic.

Working alone, picking all specks from 1000 grams (about 2¼ pounds)—roughly 500 grams (about 1 pound) after cooking—will take about 5 hours depending on the quality of the original fiber and your work rate. Invite curious friends, stray neighborhood children, or anyone else available to help. (Explain that this is a unique learning experience.) Persevere and do not be disheartened.

Foreign matter may also be removed with a flat diaphragm screen.[1]

Beating Fiber

Careful beating can make the difference between a permanent but stringy sheet and a sheet that is not only long-lasting but extremely well formed with very pleasing, uniform fiber distribution.

Absolute minimal beating necessary for good formation is the overriding rule of thumb in beating for Japanese papermaking due to the easily shortened fiber and rapidly lowered freeness.

Hand Beating Hand beating has at least the one definite advantage of rarely resulting in overly shortened slow-draining fiber. Because of this, the low cost of the hardware required, and the traditional respect for the fiber inherent in hand beating, it is the recommended procedure to follow when attempting the best-quality papers. See Figure 121, which shows hand beating in Japan. It is important to note here, however, that superb fiber distribution is very difficult to obtain with hand beating. Fiber selection and cooking must be very carefully executed. If the fiber is of only fair quality, or if the degree of cooking was not adequate, no amount of hand beating will properly disperse the fibers. Often, the papermaker has to accept a slightly stringier quality in the hand-beaten sheet, although some strength characteristics may be superior to those of a paper made with machine-beaten fibers.

Kozo, mitsumata, gampi, and any foreign or native bast fibers that respond readily to cooking can be hand beaten effectively. Two approaches to hand beating, simplified and traditional, are outlined below.

Simplified hand beating is a basic procedure for beating approximately 250 grams (9 ounces) of kozo (125 grams, or 4.5 ounces, after cooking). Be sure your beating surface has been washed clean with water.

Squeeze most of the excess water from the fiber with your hands. Arrange the fiber strands along roughly the same axis and perpendicular to the line of your beating-stick strike, filling a rectangle approximately 10 by 30 centimeters (4 by 12 inches). Use the beating stick as pictured in Figure 121. Strike the pile three times in the same location (smartly on the last blow) before moving half a beating stick's width across the pile. Continue beating, passing back and forth across the pile until the fiber has spread out considerably; then stop and fold the fiber mass in on top of itself from the front and back to the center. Fold the ends in about 8 centimeters (3 inches). Turn the folded wad upside down on the beating surface, and begin the routine again. Repeat until approximately 25 minutes have elapsed, add the fiber to 3 liters (3 quarts) of cold water, mix well, and refrigerate no more than a few days if sheet forming does not begin immediately.

Traditional hand beating is a slightly more serious approach to hand beating starting with 750 grams (1 3/4 pounds) of dry kozo white bark that has been cooked 3 to 4 hours in wood-ash lye.

Squeeze the fiber very "dry" with your hands until little or no more water can be expelled. Arrange the fiber for beating as outlined under the simplified procedure above, noting, however, that your starting pile will be larger, perhaps 10 by 45 centimeters (4 by 18 inches). Beat the fiber, with periodic folding, for 45 minutes. Stop with the fiber well spread out on the beating surface just before you are about to fold in again. Sprinkle 300 milliliters (1 cup) of cool water over the fiber, fold in, and continue beating. After 15 minutes, stop, add another 300 milliliters (cup) of water, fold in, and continue. Repeat again, adding a total of 900 milliliters (3 cups) of water and beating an additional 45 minutes for a total of 1 hour and 45 minutes. When finished, add the fiber to 12 liters (3 gallons) of cold water, mix well with one hand, and store in a cold location until papermaking the next day.

Note: This procedure constitutes more prolonged treatment than that usually employed by Japanese papermakers, but as noted earlier, hand beating is no longer routinely practiced in Japan today and well-developed technique was not encountered during my research. When used today, hand beating is often followed by brief *naginata* treatment. In the author's experience, the described procedure and longer times are necessary when beating by hand only and when seeking excellent formation quality.

Evaluating Beating Degree During hand or stamper beating some indication of the fibers' beaten state may be obtained through use of a water-filled glass jar. Add several pinches of the beaten fiber to the jar, and shake it. If large strands or clumps remain, continue beating. Very well distributed fiber should be in evidence before you stop beating, although thorough mixing with a *mazè* at the vat in the presence of *tororo-aoi* will help improve final fiber separation.

Stamper Beating In Japan, most papermakers use a stamper as a substitute for hand beating for anywhere from 30 to 60 minutes and then follow with brief hollander or *naginata* treatment to separate remaining attached fibers. Follow the same guidelines for adding water during stamper beating as for traditional hand beating. Use a stick to keep the fiber down inside the cement pot as stamping continues. Be sure to keep your head clear of the falling shaft weight. If strands or clumps persist in a glass-jar sample after an hour of treatment, they are likely to remain regardless of continued stamping. Additional treatment of the fiber in a *naginata* or hollander may help, however.

Naginata Beating As mentioned earlier, *naginata* usage generally follows fairly thorough hand or stamper beating. The *naginata's* job is only to tease the fibers apart, and it is much more successful at this than the hollander, particularly with kozo. If the fiber is high in quality, and if cooking and preliminary hand or stamper beating are properly undertaken, then the action required in the *naginata* will be very minimal, usually between 2 and 7 minutes. Again, use the glass jar to judge, but stop as soon as possible.

To start a load, fill the oblong tub with water to within 10 centimeters (3 inches) of the shaft. Without turning the power on, add all the stamped or hand-beaten fiber and disperse it in the tub by hand. Turn the power on, and use a clean dowel to keep fiber moving through any noncirculating areas. When treatment is finished, turn the motor off and dump the load into the drain basket or a wooden drain box. Be sure to collect any stray clumps of fiber from the tub after it has drained; then rinse it clean with a hose.

Note: *Naginata* or hollander beating constitutes an additional washing step that leaves the finished paper lighter in color and somewhat softer than hand beating does. Because of this, wash your fiber less after cooking if you plan on the additional "wash" from a *naginata* or hollander.

Hollander Beating Generally, hollanders can be used effectively with mitsumata, gampi, abaca, or any foreign or native bast on the short end of the fiber-length scale, i.e., 3 to 6 millimeters (about 1/8–1/4 inch) long. However, longer fiber types, such as kozo or anything resembling kozo in length (12 millimeters, or 1/2 inch), tend to knot or lose freeness before dispersing when treated in a hollander.

When using a hollander with bast, remember to avoid any cutting or pounding action. The idea is only to loosen the fibers from one another. If any direct action takes place on the fiber, it should be light and occur only for 60 seconds or so as the strands are added to the beater, to help break up the long lengths. Adjust the beater shortly thereafter so a clearance of about 5 to 10 millimeters ($\frac{3}{16}$–$\frac{3}{8}$ inch) exists between the roll and bed plate. Beating time for mitsumata, gampi, and similar fibers is roughly 20 minutes, but use the glass jar to help evaluate beating degree.

Proper beating has been attained *as soon as* all fibers are well separated from each other. If even fiber distribution is slow in coming, remember that continued beating aimed at eliminating strands or clumps can quickly push the fiber *below* the minimum allowable freeness. You will know you have overdone the hollander beating if the fiber drains too slowly even when mixed with small quantities of formation aid at the vat. Problems at parting and drying can also be traced to overbeating. Be very cautious and gentle when using a hollander with bast fiber.

When finished, dump the load into the drain basket. Thoroughly clean the inside of the beater of any remaining usable fiber, and then rinse the machine with clear water.

Abaca, because of its slightly higher resistance to cooking and larger amounts of encrusting matter, usually requires slightly more aggressive beating action and time than do Japanese fibers (perhaps 30 minutes). Again, however, be conservative. Getting abaca started in the beater can be a problem due to its very stringy nature, even after thorough cooking. One solution to this problem is cutting the abaca before cooking or before it is added to the beater. More extended cooking will also facilitate ready fiber separation.

Any fiber will yield denser, crisper paper the longer beating is continued. Usually, in an effort to maintain maximum freeness and fiber length, this effect is not sought in working with fibers for *nagashi-zuki*. Abaca fiber, however, can be altered during beating to yield very different papers. Very light, minimal beating will yield a paper similar to kozo, while slightly extended beating will yield a paper more like mitsumata, and a bit more again (assuming proper cooking and fiber quality) will yield a crisp, translucent paper similar to gampi. Do not forget that, much as it is an important control factor, such extended beating can again easily result in overly lowered freeness and shortened fiber. Prolong beating of abaca with great reservation.[2]

Storing Beaten Pulps Although the Japanese did not recommend it, I have frozen cooked-and-beaten kozo fiber, as well as fiber mixed with formation aids left over from draining vats, and later thawed the fiber for papermaking with no *apparent* deleterious effects. This procedure is not recommended, however, unless the fiber must be kept well beyond the allowable several weeks in a refrigerator. Freezing is not recommended during the production of archival papers.

Formation Aids

My first choice for a formation aid in the West is *tororo-aoi* grown at your own location and stored without the agricultural disinfectants commonly used in Japan. *Tororo* works exceptionally well in Japanese papermaking, appears to yield a permanent sheet, and enhances the naturally occurring luster in many bast fibers. See Figure 123, which shows Japanese *tororo-aoi* in bales.

Tororo-aoi Cultivation *Tororo* can be successfully cultivated in most areas of the United States. The following suggestions incorporate my personal experience with growing *tororo* in Michigan, the advice of Japanese *tororo* farmers, and data from Winifred Lutz. (See Figure 122.)

Quality root development requires an even temperature of 25° C (77° F) for at least three months with little fluctuation during the day and night. The soil should be fertilized prior to planting and again two months after growth has begun. Any of the three following commercial fertilizers is acceptable: 5–6–6, 5–8–5, or 5–10–5 (nitrogen, phosphate, and potash). I have obtained good results using green sheep manure as a substitute fertilizer.

Planting should be done immediately following the last frost. Set the seeds in groups of three, staggered 10 centimeters (4 inches) apart in rows roughly 50 centimeters (20 inches) apart. After the first leaves appear, thin the weakest of the three plants; then after each plant has developed three leaves, remove the weakest of the remaining two plants. (If only a small amount of seed is on hand you can eliminate these thinning steps and try for all possible plants by planting single seeds only.) The soil should be kept moist until the seeds sprout. Thereafter, only sufficient rainfall or watering to keeps the plants healthy is required. Overwatering can harm *tororo*.

One problem with growing *tororo* is getting a healthy plot started. The tender emerging *tororo* plants are slow to establish themselves and appear to be a favorite delicacy of certain creatures and insects that come out at night. Once well established, and with reasonable moisture and warmth, *tororo* remains a hearty plant.

To encourage maximum root development, the tops of all plants should be kept trimmed back to a roughly 35-centimeter (14-inch) height throughout the growing season. If the tops are not trimmed, the roots tend to develop a woody core and only a thin fleshy outer layer, which contains the majority of the formation aid. You may want to let several of your plants go to flower and seed for the following year's crop. In the fall, do not pick the seed pods until they have fully dried on the plant.

Tororo-aoi Storage When the first frost kills the leaves on the *tororo,* you can harvest your crop. Bring all the roots in, and wash off the dirt. Let the surfaces of the roots dry. If you have the space, freezing is the best method of storing the roots. As a second choice, you can bury the roots in sand and store them in a cool root-cellar-like atmosphere for up to a month, or leave the roots exposed to the air for storage in a cool dry area. In all cases, however, it is important to soak the roots in cold water overnight *prior to* beating and rendering formation aid. The ideal approach is to use your roots fresh from the ground and plan your papermaking for very late summer, fall, and early winter. Approximately 500 to 750 grams (1–1½ pounds) of fresh roots (30–40 roots averaging 1 centimeter, or ⅜ inch, in diameter) are required to make 120–80 sheets of 30-by-40-centimeter (12-by-16-inch) medium-thin paper as described under traditional-method papermaking in Chapter 7. This quantity of roots will yield some leftover secretion for future papermaking. See Appendix 2 for suppliers of seeds.

Tororo-aoi Formation Aid Preparation Wash all of the roots, and thoroughly beat them as shown in Figure 124. Pound all areas of each root, including the small roots branching from the main root. Once the roots are broken open, add them to a 16-liter (17-quart) bucket and fill it with fresh cold water. Mix up the roots and water and set the bucket aside in a cold spot until papermaking the next morning. See Figure 125. (If the work space is warm, refrigerate the *tororo* until papermaking begins. Temporarily adding the roots to a smaller volume of water is acceptable if refrigerator space is limited.)

Just before papermaking pour the 16 liters (17 quarts) of roots and secretion into the top section of the *tororo* strainer (see Chapter 5, *Tororo*-processing Tools), and let the solution drain into the lower bucket. If the thicker lot of the secretion is slow to pass, draw the pillowcase together at the open end and suspend it above the bucket from a rope. Or, you may force the *tororo* through by twisting the pillowcase to push the solution into a constricted area. When the *tororo* has drained or been expelled, return the roots to the 16-liter (17-quart) bucket, add cold water, mix well with your hand, and store in a cool or cold spot until a new bucket of *tororo* is required. When the *tororo* becomes less viscous, pound all the roots again to render any remaining secretion from the roots. Pounded roots will last several days before spoiling if kept cold. When papermaking is finished be sure to wash all components of the strainer thoroughly in clear, cold water.

Plant Substitutes for Tororo-aoi If you would like to experiment with native American substitutes for *tororo-aoi,* there are several possibilities, but bear in mind that even if a new material performs as well as *tororo* at the vat, it will not necessarily yield papers with the same qualities of strength, character, and permanence. Use substitutes for *tororo* with caution. Note Winifred Lutz's suggestions concerning Siberian elm bark and okra roots in Appendix 1 (especially Note 8).

Synthetic Formation Aids When *tororo,* or a suitable natural substitute is not available, certain synthetic materials or a commercially processed natural gum may prove an acceptable formation aid.

A substitute formation aid should not be sticky nor should it leave a noticeable residue in the paper after drying. Although viscous stringy qualities are required, solutions of materials like gum arabic, sodium silicate, gelatin, carboxymethyl cellulose, and corn starch are all off the mark. An ideal formation aid for Japanese papermaking changes the character of the water, giving it a distinctive slithery, ropy quality.

The synthetic I can recommend most highly is a Japanese product called Acryperse. A polyacrylamide, Acryperse is manufactured as white, sugarlike granules. Use type ACP–PNS when making Japanese papers containing no size or other additives. When and if additives are present, use type ACP–PMP. See Appendix 2 for sources.

To prepare the synthetic, measure out 1 gram (1/4 teaspoon) of powder for each liter (quart) of formation aid required. When mixing the powder into the water it is important to introduce the granules slowly so that each particle is encapsulated with water. If the powder is added all at once it will form a thick globular mass resistant to further dissolution.

The most effective mixing procedure is to add the amount of powder to a continuous strong stream or spray of cold water until the full required volume is attained. Hand mixing the powder directly into the full volume of water is a less desirable alternative, but it can be accomplished if the powder is added quite slowly. In either case, as soon as all of the powder has been added, mix well with a stick. Rub any accumulation from the vessel walls or mixing stick. Every 5 minutes for the next 20 minutes, mix the formation aid again to raise any heavier particles that have settled to the bottom. Use an erratic mixing pattern to avoid encouraging concentration of heavier or thicker particles in the center of the mixing vessel.

Prepare the formation aid at least one day before papermaking is planned. A uniform, stringy, clear solution, free of specks or visible inconsistencies should be the final result. If any globular concentrations persist, pass the lot through the *tororo* strainer. Do not use a high-speed mechanical mixer for preparing the formation aid since shear action will lessen its viscous ropy quality.

The mixed solution keeps indefinitely, but prompt use is recommended. The original white powder has at least a one-year shelf life when tightly sealed against humidity.

The Japanese manufacturer claims their polyacrylamide is nontoxic but American manufacturers of similar products suggest avoiding prolonged contact with the skin. Thus, if daily production-level papermaking with the synthetic is planned, use rubber gloves.

Although this polyacrylamide formation aid gives indications of being a benign component in a handmade paper, its effects on the long-term permanence and durability of a paper have not been tested. Therefore, when available, *tororo* is preferred if papers are being made for archival uses. Note that parting, particularly of thin sheets, may be more difficult when the synthetic formation aid is used.

Among the commercial gums that may prove appropriate in Japanese papermaking are kirari, deacetelated karaya, tragacanth, and guar gum.

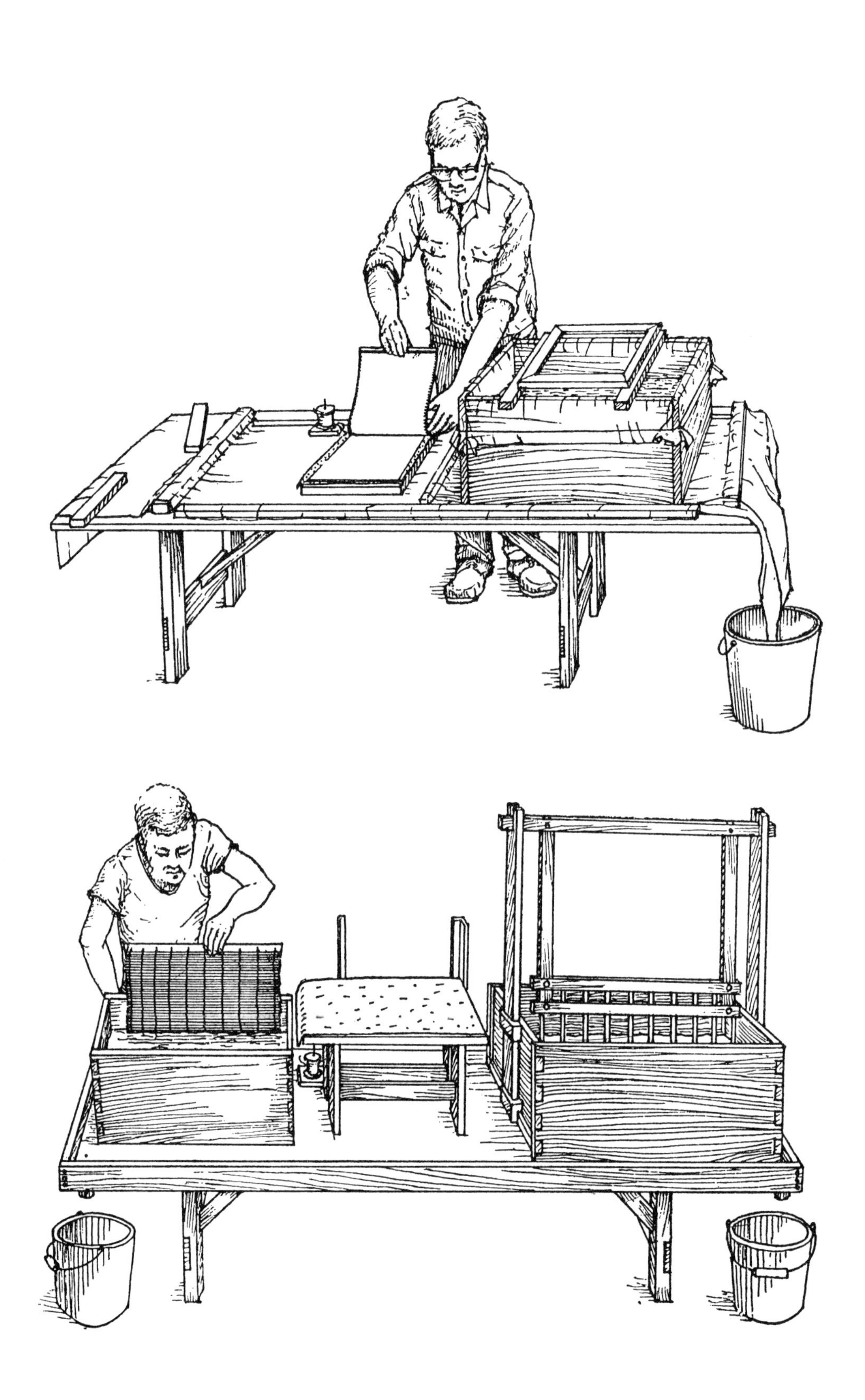

CHAPTER SEVEN

Papermaking: Simplified and Traditional Methods

IN THIS CHAPTER, you will find instructions for making Japanese paper both on a very simplified level and on a much more involved, more serious, traditional level. The facilities, tools, equipment, and raw material preparation procedures required for each approach are outlined with references made to detailed explanations in earlier chapters. Instructions for sheet forming, pressing, and drying follow. An alternating format is used throughout: first the simplified method for a given step appears, set off by lines, then the traditional method follows. You may read through only the simplified entries if you wish to try just the simplified method, but you should feel free to intermix the two approaches as your commitment of time and funds begins to increase. Moving beyond the traditional approach is possible by employing even more sophisticated tools described in Chapter 5.

The Two Methods

SIMPLIFIED

Set aside a day to list and purchase the necessary materials, make the required tools, and decide on the best available work area. Required items not available locally should be mail-ordered from suppliers as soon as you make the decision to undertake papermaking. The time required for papermaking, itself, is about two days, and the amount of paper yielded is twenty-five to forty-five sheets. Figure 130 shows the simplified method in action. The materials and tools cost between $40 and $120 depending on how much you economize and how much you build yourself (versus purchase new).

TRADITIONAL

Under this heading, traditional techniques and hand tools of intermediate sophistication are used to produce 120 to 180 sheets of high-quality permanent paper.[1] This approach not only may be difficult for the beginner fresh from completing the simplified method but represents a fairly high-level goal for the more serious student of Japanese papermaking as well.

Use the master tool list and its references to build or acquire all the necessary tools. Allow three or four weeks' time and at least $650 if you are constructing everything from the ground up. Once you have accounted for all the tools, the time required for papermaking, working alone, will be approximately four days. Figure 133 shows one step of the traditional method.

Facilities Required

SIMPLIFIED

An area with a cement floor and floor drains is ideal, particularly if there is also a sink nearby with running water. However, you may work very comfortably in a kitchen or basement using the plastic-covered table set-up shown in Figure 89. The tabletop should measure roughly 80 by 180 centimeters (2½ by 6 feet), and the table should be between 60 and 80 centimeters (2–2½ feet) high. Access to a gram (or ounce) scale is necessary (perhaps you can borrow one briefly from a potter friend).

TRADITIONAL

Unless you elect to build the draining work table pictured in Figure 113, a work area with floor drains is in order. A cooking stove and a source of cold, high-quality water should be immediately on hand. Cool or cold workshop conditions (about 4°–12° C, or 40°–55° F) should prevail, or else all raw materials must be maintained at similar temperatures in a refrigerator. (Warm working water and air temperature hasten fiber spoilage, weaken the effectiveness of *tororo-aoi* and generally lower the quality of the paper produced.)

Raw Materials

SIMPLIFIED

Dry Japanese kozo, white or green bark: 250 grams (9 ounces)
Soda ash (Na_2CO_3): 50 grams (about 2 ounces)
Polyacrylamide synthetic formation aid: 8 grams (about 1/4 ounce)

TRADITIONAL

Japanese kozo, white or green bark: 750 grams (about 1 1/2 pounds)
Hardwood ashes: 1200 grams (about 2 1/2 pounds)
Home-grown *tororo-aoi* roots: about 35 roots, each at least 1 to 1.5 centimeters (3/8–5/8 inch) in diameter, total weight about 650 grams (1 1/2 pounds)

Tool and Equipment List

SIMPLIFIED

Tool Required	**Specifications**
Cooking vessel	10- or 12-liter (11- or 13-quart) pot and lid
Mixing stick	90-by-2-centimeter (36-by-3/4-inch) birch dowel, ends rounded
Press boards	2 boards, each approximately 37 by 50 centimeters (15 by 20 inches), p. 129
Felts	4 felts, each approximately 37 by 50 centimeters (15 by 20 inches), p. 129
Vat	Collapsible plastic-lined vat, p. 121, or any watertight container approximately 50 by 75 by 25 centimeters deep (20 by 30 by 10 inches)
Mould support sticks	2 pieces of 90-by-1.5-by-2-centimeter (36-by-1/2-by-3/4-inch) pine "stop" stock

	or equivalent (standard item at U.S. lumberyards)
Mould and deckle	Simple mould, p. 120
Su	Placemat *su* and mesh, p. 83
Press	Large plastic garbage can
Large plastic buckets	3 buckets, each of 16-liter (4-gallon) capacity; institutional-use mayonnaise buckets with lids are ideal and usually cheap, if not free
Small plastic container	Any plastic bucket or container of 6-liter (6½-quart) capacity, graduated in liters (quarts)
Drying surfaces	Boards, p. 130
Drying brush	8-centimeter-wide (3-inch-wide) paint-brush, new or very clean
Drain basket	See p. 124
Thread spool and stand	Size 50 white cotton thread; for stand, see p. 122 (Attachments and Related Tools)
Plastic sheet for table cover	90-by-200-centimeter (3-by-6½-foot) plastic sheet, 4 to 6 mil (.1–.15 millimeter) thick (see Fig. 89)
Scrap wood for tabletop water dams	"One-by-two" (about 2.5-by-5-centimeter, or 1-by-2-inch) number 4 pine stock. Two at 90 centimeters (3 feet), two at 120 centimeters (2 feet); see Fig. 89
Beating stick and surface	See p. 126

TRADITIONAL

Tool Required	**Specifications**
Large plastic buckets for *tororo,* lye maker, and work table	Seven 16-liter (4-gallon) mayonnaise buckets or the equivalent, four with lids
Plastic pails	2 store-bought 10-liter (10-quart) pails, graduated in liters (quarts)

Wood-ash lye maker	See p. 125
Liter (quart) measure	4-liter (1-gallon) plastic jug with mouth cut wider, graduated in liters (quarts)
Cook pot	20-liter (21-quart) or larger stainless-steel or enamelware pot with lid, p. 124 (Simple Pots)
Mixing stick for cook pot	90-by-2-centimeter (36-by-$\frac{3}{4}$-inch) birch dowel or piece of bamboo, ends rounded
Glass bowl or pan for speck removal	Large mixing bowl or other glass kitchenware, store-bought
Drain basket	See p. 124
Beating stick and surface	See p. 126
Glass jar	Clear-glass mayonnaise jar or equivalent
Work table with drains	See p. 132
Rinse vat	See p. 122 (Attachments and Related Tools)
Mixing stick for vat	90-by-2-centimeter (36-by-$\frac{3}{4}$-inch) birch dowel, ends rounded, or equivalent
Vat	Traditional production-level vat, p. 122
Mazè and mould support sticks	See p. 122 (Attachments and Related Tools)
Mallet for *tororo*	See p. 128
Strainer for *tororo*	See p. 128
Mould	30-by-40-centimeter (12-by-16-inch) imported Japanese mould, p. 118, or advanced mould, p. 121
Su	Imported Japanese *su*, p. 83, or traditional *su*, pp. 86–115
Couch stand	See photograph (Fig. 90) and build or improvise
Thread spool and stand	Size 50 white cotton thread; for stand, see p. 122 (Attachments and Related Tools)
Couching guides	See couching photographs (Figs. 137–47) and build or improvise
Couching-guide clamps	2 store-bought C-clamps
Felts	2 felts, each approximately 37 by 50 centimeters (15 by 20 inches), p. 129

Press boards	2 boards, each approximately 37 by 50 centimeters (15 by 20 inches), p. 129
Press	Lever press, p. 129
Drying brush	See p. 131
Water sprayer or mister	Store-bought
Dryer	Heat-lamp dryer, p. 131
Gram (ounce) scale	Store-bought or borrowed

Work Outline

SIMPLIFIED

A rough plan for the two days required for papermaking follows:

Day			Hours
One	Morning:	cook and wash fiber	3
	Afternoon:	speck removal	2+
		beating	.5
		sheet forming	3+
		Day One Total	8.5 or more hours
Two	Morning:	pressing	4+
	Afternoon:	parting and drying the sheets	1+
		Day Two Total	5 or more hours

Note: It is not absolutely necessary that you work for two days straight. If you keep the partially processed fiber cold in a refrigerator you may add additional breaks in the schedule following cooking and washing, speck removal, or beating. You may also proceed directly from sheet forming to the remainder of the process if time permits.

TRADITIONAL

The times listed below are approximations only and subject to change based on the extent of your experience and your own attention to detail. If you cannot afford four days' time in one stretch, there are two points at which you may break and postpone the subsequent activity for as long as a week or two. In both cases the fiber must be stored in a refrigerator and in a sealed container to prevent drying. The first possible break occurs after the completion of the first day's activities. The second break may occur during Day Two, after beating but prior to *tororo* preparation. If you break at the latter time, be sure to prepare your *tororo* the day before papermaking begins.

Day	**Step**	**Hours**	**Equipment Required**
One	cook and wash fiber begin speck removal	5 1.5	cook pot and lid, mixing stick, stove, lye maker, 4-liter (1-gallon) measure, drain basket, water and drain, glass bowl
Two	finish speck removal beating *tororo* preparation	4 1 .5	glass bowl, beating table and stick, clear-glass jar, *tororo* mallet and bucket, water and drain
Three	vat mixing sheet forming clean-up	.5 7.5 1	all equipment pictured on the work table (Fig. 90), water and drain, *tororo* strainer
Four	pressing parting and drying the sheets	4 3	lever press, dryer, brush, sprayer
	Total	28 hours	

Before Starting

SIMPLIFIED

On the night before papermaking, submerge the 250 grams (9 ounces) of kozo fiber in a bucket full of cold water. At least one night before papermaking, mix the synthetic formation aid as described on page 158.

TRADITIONAL

See that you have the proper facilities in which to work. Check the master tool and equipment and raw materials lists to make sure you have everything on hand. Soak the 750 grams (about 1½ pounds) of kozo in clear, cold water the night before the first day of work.

Preparing the Fiber

SIMPLIFIED

On the morning of the first day, cook the kozo in a 20 percent soda-ash solution (50 grams soda ash/6 liters water, or 1¾ ounces soda ash/6 quarts water) as described on page 145.

While the fiber is cooking, cover your work table with the sheet plastic, and use the scrap wood to raise the plastic around the edges so any spilled water will run into a bucket placed appropriately. (See Fig. 89.) Set up the vat bearing in mind that you will be working from one of its short edges. Add about 44 liters (46 quarts) of cold water, and place the mould support sticks near the vat. Make sure you have all other required tools on hand. Follow cooking with washing, speck removal, and simplified hand beating as explained in Chapter 6.

TRADITIONAL

Proceed with cooking, washing, speck removal, and beating as described in Chapter 6. Cook as for kozo, making and using wood-ash lye; remove specks in water; and beat using the traditional method. Prepare the *tororo-aoi* formation aid as described in the same chapter.

Mixing the Stock

SIMPLIFIED

Refer to the terminology chart on page 84 for mould and vat descriptions below. Soak the *su* (with mesh attached) in a bucket filled with cold, fresh water. Center one of the felts on a press board and thoroughly wet it down with cold water, taking care to keep it perfectly smooth and in close contact with the board surface. Make sure the near (short) edge of the felt is in line with the near edge of the board. Now lay the *su*, mesh side down, on top of the felt so that its near (sewn) edge is also in line with the near edge of the board. The center of the *su's* near edge should be aligned with the center of the board's near edge. Slide a toothpick or broom straw under the felt, directly in line with the left side of the *su,* leaving about 5 millimeters (¼ inch) protruding to act as a guide during the couching step. Add 2 liters (2 quarts) of your 3 liters (3 quarts) of beaten fiber to the vat. Use the mixing stick to mix the fiber into the water until no large clumps or strands are evident.

Now add 3 liters (3 quarts) of the formation aid. Mix the formation aid thoroughly into the water and fiber with the mixing stick by using a lively circular motion and reaching all four corners of the vat. Continue mixing until fiber dispersion is uniform (about 5 minutes). Let the vat stand for several minutes while you read (and take a dry run through) the next step—sheet forming.

TRADITIONAL

Fill the wash vat with cold water. Presoak the *su* in the wash vat by immersing it as shown in Figure 72. Make sure all areas of the *su* get thoroughly wet. Shim the press board on the couch stand under the near edge at a slight angle for better drainage. Attach the couch guides to the press board using the C-clamps. Spread the bottom felt on the press board and wet it thoroughly. See Figure 126.

Fill the vat with cold water until about 10 centimeters (4 inches) deep. Add 2 liters (2 quarts) of your (well-mixed) beaten fiber. Use the vat mixing stick to give the vat a preliminary stir. Set the *mazè* in its hangers and move it vigorously back and forth 125 times. See Figure 127. The *mazè* should

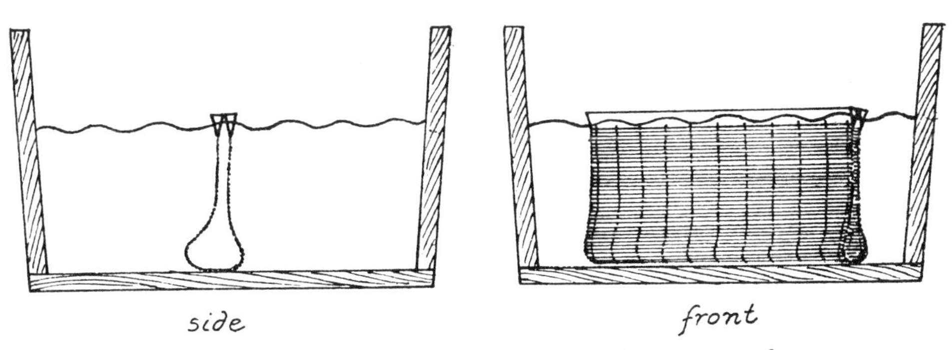

72. Soaking su in rinse vat prior to papermaking

do a good job of breaking apart any final lumps or strands. If lumps remain after 125 strokes, continue working with the *mazè* in hopes of eliminating them. Add approximately half of the bucket of strained *tororo* to the vat, and mix it ten or fifteen strokes with the *mazè*. Remove the *mazè,* wipe any accumulated fiber from the *mazè* fingers, and toss the fiber back into the vat. Stir the vat vigorously with the vat stick until no clumps of fiber or concentrations of *tororo* remain.

If fiber selection, cooking, beating, and mixing and *tororo* addition were perfectly executed, no strands of fiber should be visible in the final vat mixture.

Due to the highly dispersive nature of *tororo,* if you do not pause more than a minute or two during sheet forming, no additional mixing will be necessary until new fiber and *tororo* are required (i.e., after ten or fifteen sheets are made).

Note: The exact volume of *tororo* required at the vat cannot be determined with a formula since *tororo's* consistency varies with the age and size of the roots, the air and water temperature, the amount of mixing, and other factors as well. The best indicator of proper concentration, even for the longtime professional in Japan, is the action of the stock on the mould during papermaking. There is no foolproof way of deciding whether you have added enough without making a sheet. It stands to reason that you should always start with a conservative amount of *tororo* for the first sheet and let poor formation, overly thick sheets, or excessively rapid drainage confirm your suspicion that a bit more is needed. If you have added too much *tororo* and drainage is too slow, you can mix the vat violently for a minute or two and usually decrease the viscosity of the *tororo.* Acryperse synthetic and some of the commercial gums, however, resist such breakdown and should be added slowly until the right concentration is obtained. Generally kozo, and particularly well-washed kozo, requires more formation aid than the shorter, finer fibers (such as mitsumata, gampi, and abaca), which are usually higher in self-dispersive hemicellulose content. Also, as will become apparent with experience, less formation aid is necessary when thicker papers are being made, while relatively more formation aid is in order when thin papers are being produced. Additional instructions for correcting *tororo* concentration are interspersed with the instructions on sheet-forming techniques.

Review the discussions of sheet forming and couching below before proceeding with papermaking.

Sheet Forming

SIMPLIFIED

As mentioned previously, the specific actions required for uniform, quality sheet formation in Japanese papermaking are extremely difficult to describe with the written word. In principle, however, the idea is to keep the surface of the *su* awash with stock that is constantly in motion. A description of the basic technique for making a beginner's sheet follows.

Arrange the two mould support sticks across the vat, front to back, so that the mould will rest on the sticks. Arrange the wet *su* on top of the mould (sewn edge near, mesh side up) using the magic-marker lines as a guide. Add the deckle on top of the *su,* align its edges with the mould below, and grasp the entire assembly (henceforth termed the "mould") at the middle of the long sides. Without releasing your hold on the mould, use two or three free fingers to grasp and move both mould support sticks to the sides of the vat.

Raise the mould until it is almost perpendicular to the water's surface. Slide the near edge of the mould into the stock about 15 centimeters (6 inches) from the near side of the vat and *in the same movement* lower your hands and twist your wrists to scoop a charge (a load of stock) up and out of the vat. Continuing to twist your wrists, tip the mould forward to send the charge rushing across the *su* and off the far edge of the mould. Repeat a total of three times in immediate, but relaxed, succession. (Note: Only the near *one third* of the mould should enter the vat solution whenever you pick up stock from the vat.) Always manipulate the mould so that you are pulling the front of the *su* surface against the stock in the vat; never lower the mould into the vat so that stock is forced through the *su* from the back. Refer to Figure 73.

After the three rapid charge and dumps (roughly 10 seconds' elapsed time), immediately charge the mould in the same fashion but *do not*

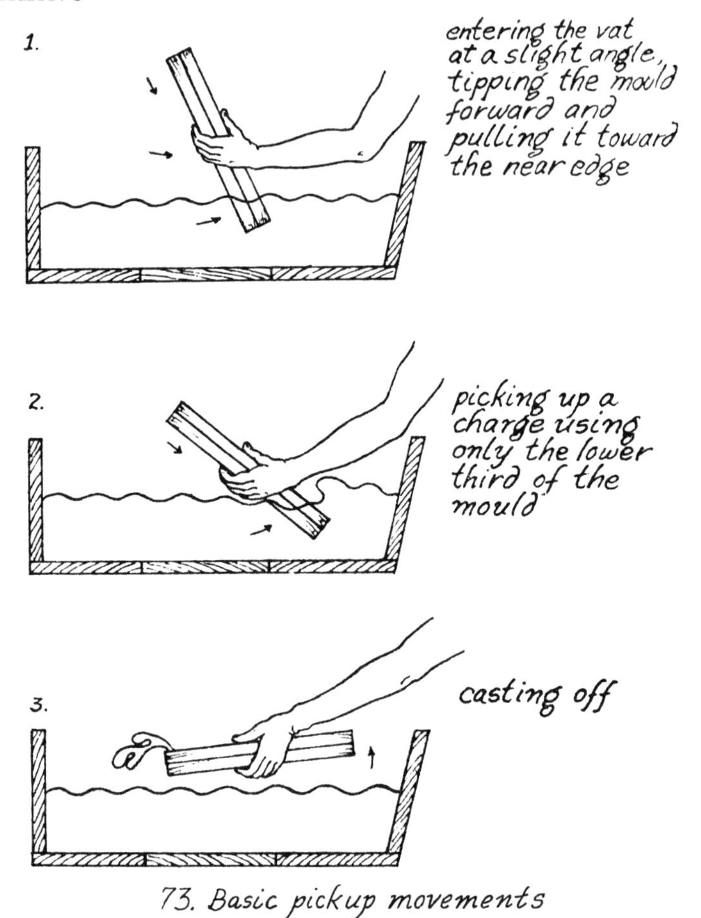

73. Basic pickup movements

cast off any of the solution; rather, fall immediately into a rhythmic rolling of the stock, front to back (near edge to far edge), on the *su*. Try to keep the motion consistent and lively. Before all the water drains from this fourth charge, recharge the mould again from the near edge. This time, if you have mastered the near-to-far-edge roll, work the charge in a side-to-side fashion to even out the grain. Near-to-far action should be used to accumulate the final thickness. Remember that "thick" in Japanese papermaking is generally "thin" by Western papermaking standards. A thick Japanese sheet appears to stand 2 millimeters (1/16 inch) on the surface of the *su* after the deckle is removed.

Determining proper thickness as a result of the gradual change in opacity during papermaking is fairly easily learned from experience. If you are just beginning, however, try for consistency from one sheet to the next and work only until the threads of the *su* start to become hard to see. Generally speaking, forming medium-thick sheets is much safer than forming thinner ones for the beginner because subsequent parting and drying is usually easier.

When a suitable thickness is attained, quickly tilt the mould so the remaining solution flows to the far edge of the mould, and pour the excess off one of the far corners of the mould. Do not tip the mould past perpendicular (to the horizontal plane of the vat stock), or you may see the new fragile sheet slide off the *su* and into the vat.

Returning the mould to a horizontal position, use several free fingers on each hand under the mould to bring the mould support sticks in from the sides of the vat. Set the mould to drain on the support sticks. Carefully remove the deckle, and set it aside.

TRADITIONAL

Open the mould and set it on the two mould support sticks at the vat, hinges at the far side of the vat. Take the *su* from the wash vat, and place it in the mould with the tie-off knots at the mould's far edge. See Figure 79. (Note: If you are working with a Western-made *su,* the tie-off knots should also be at the far edge of the mould. A mesh-covered *su* should have the sewn edge stick at the near edge of the mould.) If the *su* is properly positioned, the hinged deckle should close tightly over the *su* with no resistance. Close the deckle clamps, if your mould is so equipped. Grasp the mould on the sides, thumbs on top of the deckle. Using a few free fingers underneath the mould, move the mould support sticks to the sides of the vat.

To form a sheet, dip the mould into and out of the stock using a scooping action and immersing only the near one third of the mould. See Figure 131. Quickly and immediately, tilt the mould away from you causing most of the charge to rush across the *su* surface and *off* the far edge of the mould. In a smooth continuation of the same motion pick up another charge in the same manner as the first but do not cast it off; instead, begin working it immediately back and forth (near to far edge) across the mould surface. See Figure 133. Handle the mould gingerly, and do not let any stock spill out. The idea is to work quickly yet still *control* the stock. If you do not feel in comfortable control, you are working too fast.

Before the charge drains much more than halfway, cast off the excess as the stock makes one of its trips to the far edge of the mould, and immediately pick up a third charge at the near side of the vat. Work this last charge initially side to side to even the grain a bit (see Fig. 135), but soon thereafter work it near to far edge as above. Again, after about half the charge drains, toss the excess off the far edge. This will complete the formation of the first sheet.

The thickness of the paper you are making is affected by several interrelated factors: (1) the consistency and concentration of *tororo* in the stock, (2) the concentration of fiber in the stock (which changes as each fifteen or more sheets are made), and (3) the sheet-forming action and style. More about sheet-forming action, thickness, and related factors follows.

Couching

SIMPLIFIED

Pick the *su* up with the left hand at the middle of the near (sewn) edge and raise it from the mould. The *su* should be dangling from the left hand, with the new sheet of paper attached to the surface of the *su* facing away from you. With the right hand, grasp the free, lower (far) edge of the *su* by the sticks only (fingertips under the mesh). Now invert the *su* so the left hand becomes the lower hand; and the right hand, the upper. Move the loaded *su* to the press board previously set up with a damp felt.

Align the left side of the *su* with the toothpick or broom-straw marker under the near edge of the felt while at the same time lining up the lower (near) edge of the *su* along the near edge of the couch board. When all alignments are set, lower the *su* gradually across the felt, carefully maintaining a constant tight curl in the *su* where it meets the damp felt. See Figures 137–39, which show proper traditional couching.

When the entire *su* is horizontal, smooth the back side of the *su* along the splints with the flat of the hands from the center out to create intimate contact between the first sheet and the felt. Note that this is done only for the first sheet; successive sheets should receive no pressure other than the weight of the damp *su*.

Once the *su* is smoothed, release the first sheet by gently pressing the back of the *su* along the near edge of the paper beneath. Carefully roll the *su* back 1 centimeter (3/8 inch) to see if the paper is properly adhering to the felt rather than to the *su*. If the paper refuses to come away from the *su,* pour about 150 millimeters (1/2 cup) of cool water along the back of the *su* in the troublesome area. Immediately, before the water drains away, quickly and repeatedly try to curl the first centimeter (3/8 inch) of the *su* away from the paper. Eventually you will succeed. The first sheet often causes problems.

Once the *su* is properly released along the near edge, draw the rest of the *su* away, leaving the paper (if all goes well) smooth and unwrinkled on top of the felt. Return the *su* to the mould in the same position as before. (If you are working with a well-made, fine-splinted, uncovered placemat *su,* you should return the *su* to the mould unused side up. In other words, the same edge of the uncovered *su* should always be the near edge, but the *su* should be inverted from one sheet to the next, presenting a fresh surface to each successive sheet of paper. This alteration keeps stray fiber from building up on one side of the *su*.)

Repeat the sheet formation steps for the second sheet, aiming for consistency and lively, but controlled, action. Try to keep the mould from running "dry" during the formation of the sheet. Before couching and while the finished sheet is draining, lay a length of thread parallel to and about 5 millimeters (1/4 inch) inside the near edge of the first couched sheet.

Stretch the thread taut as you set it into place, but take care not to disturb the damp paper. Leave the thread feeding from the spool stand. Couch the second sheet exactly as before. Remember to use the toothpick and near edge of the board as couching guides. Take care to create a continuous radical curl in the *su* as it is lowered down and across the previously couched sheet. This is an important step since an incorrect curl during couching can leave bubbles between sheets that are likely to increase in size and number as couching continues and cause problems during eventual parting of the sheets. As you lower the *su,* let the weight and natural fall of the su direct the couching. Do not exert any pressure from behind the *su*.

Once the *su* is flat, draw it away from the stack (called a "post") by carefully using the near edge of the *su* folded back a bit to press the near edge of the paper lightly. Work gently or you may distort the paper and weld it to the sheet(s) below. Just as you press the edge of the folded *su* down slightly, you will notice a slight flow of water released from the paper beneath. *At this instant* quickly draw the *su* back and away from the paper about a centimeter (3/8 inch). Try again if you were not successful the first time. Keep trying until you get the near edge of the *su* away from the post. Then continue drawing the *su* away from the full sheet, and return it to the mould.

Learning to depress the *su* and draw it back at the right moment, leaving the near edge of the new sheet clean against the sheet below is not easy, but it must be learned. It is one of the most elusive but essential ingredients in successful implementation of the Japanese papermaking process. If successive sheets do not come away cleanly from the *su,* contributing to a consistent and tight near edge on the post, successive couching becomes more and more difficult. The near edge of the post *must* remain uniform and solid as couching proceeds.

During couching and removal of the *su* from the growing post, a fingernail occasionally comes in handy in separating the wet paper from the *su*. You may use a fingernail during couching of the first several sheets, but later it should not be necessary, nor should it become habit.

Take care during papermaking to return the *su* to exactly the same position in the mould and to continue to align the *su* with the guides during couching as described for the first sheets. Attending to both will help assure a post with one sheet stacked exactly on top of the next. Not watching these details will allow the pile to become irregular, causing problems later at parting.

Continue to make and couch about ten more sheets. Remember to pause immediately after the formation of each sheet to lay a new length of thread along the near edge of the previous sheet. Keep taking the thread off the spool in a continuous strand. If you continue working with no pauses longer than a few moments you should not have to stir the vat. As the concentration of fiber in the vat mix decreases, additional time at sheet forming will be required for each successive sheet to maintain the same thickness as those made before it.

TRADITIONAL

Rest the mould on the support sticks (use your fingers underneath as before). Open the deckle, and lay it back against the far edge of the vat.

Now grasp the near edge stick of the *su* with your left hand and raise it completely into the air. Grasp the loose edge stick with the right hand, and invert the *su,* exchanging the position of left hand for right, and right for left. The new sheet of paper should be on the *su* surface facing *away* from you. As you do this, move to the couch stand.

Keep the *su* hanging straight up and down as you gradually place the lower edge stick along the couch guides. See Figure 137. Once the *su* is properly positioned, start (and maintain) a radical curl in the *su* as you gently lower it down and across the felt. See Figures 138 and 139. Remember that improper couching (Fig. 140) can contribute to bubbles and other inconsistencies between successive sheets, which, in turn, will contribute to more problems at sheet parting after pressing.

Once the *su* is laid flat against the felt, rub it from the center out with the flat of your hands to force intimate contact between the first sheet and the felt. This should eliminate or greatly reduce the number of bubbles under the first sheet.

Release the sheet of paper from the *su* by folding the near edge stick back against the near edge of the *su,* gently pushing down, and immediately drawing the *su* back 5 millimeters (1/4 inch) as in Figure 141. (When working with a *sha*-covered *su,* do not fold the edge stick back against the near edge of the *su*. Rather, press down lightly along the full length of the near edge stick and proceed as before. See Figures 144 and 145.) If the paper clings to the *su* at any spot, lay the edge stick back down against the felt and use the water wash described in the simplified method. Once couching is properly started, draw the remainder of the *su* away from the sheet in one continuous movement with your right hand (see Figs. 142, 143). Return the *su* to the mould with your right hand (just-used side down and unused side up, with tie-off knots again placed along the far edge of the mould). The hand movements may seem confusing at first, but once learned they serve to keep the *su* flipping automatically from one side to the next, preventing excess wear and the gradual accumulation of fiber on a single side. The tie-off knots on the Japanese *su* always stay on the far edge, which Japanese papermakers claim will alleviate some problems during parting of the sheets after pressing.

On this and successive sheets pay close attention to the very near edge during couching. As mentioned in the simplified method, well-couched first sheets are essential to continued smooth couching as the post grows.

Effective release of the near edge of successive sheets is accomplished by gentle pressure and manipulation of the *su's* near edge stick folded back and against the nearest splints in the *su*. Practice, and be stout of heart.

If the first sheet has bubbles beneath it larger than a dime, either use the *su* to push them out toward an edge or deflate them by drawing the air out with a drinking straw.

Sheet Forming (continued)

TRADITIONAL

Return to the vat and prepare to make the second sheet. Keep in mind the following two generalized but important rules about Japanese-style sheet forming.

1. Fast action retards drainage, while slow action encourages drainage. Keeping the stock in motion prevents the settling of thicker strands or clumps and yields a thinner sheet. On the other hand, working slowly permits faster drainage, allows more stray clumps and strands to form into the sheet, and yields a thicker sheet. Aim for a slow or fast style, depending on the thickness of the paper you wish to make. (Additional charges may also be used to increase thickness.)

2. Keep the sheet awash with stock at all times during its formation. Since the Japanese sheet is, in essence, a gradual lamination, the mould must usually be recharged repeatedly during the formation of a sheet. The idea is to toss off most of the excess stock as one charge nears depletion and recharge the mould in essentially the same movement. If you are working correctly, you will plan to dump the remains of each charge so it corresponds to your established rhythm—that is, to dump and then re-enter the vat stock with the remaining ripple of the old charge running back across the surface of the *su* as you pick up the next. See Figures 131–35. The point is to keep the surface of the gradually accumulating sheet awash with stock—*from somewhere*—at all times. Pausing during the formation of a sheet or letting the mould run "dry" during the formation of a sheet breaks up the consistent tight lamination of a sheet and may contribute to sheet delamination problems after pressing.

With these two rules and the basic sheet-forming instructions in mind, you should be able to develop a routine and action that feel comfortable. If your paper parts easily and is of a uniform required thickness, your action is sufficiently correct for the time being. Keep the basic style and further modify it only on advice from a professional or to make papermaking more relaxed.

Although more advanced action is possible, only limited instructions for sheet-forming action are offered here. Note Figures 74 and 136. This is not only because additional written explanation is futile but because I am convinced that once the principles are understood, with time and papermaking experience a successful personal style will develop. In

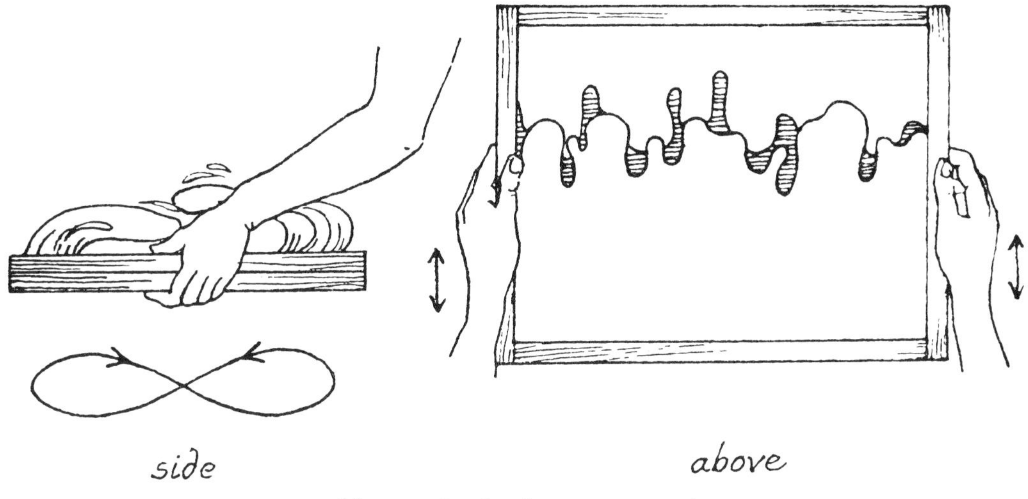

74. *Advanced sheet-forming action*

Japan, there are virtually as many sheet-forming styles as there are papermakers. And so much of it is a matter of developing a routine that *feels* comfortable. Unfortunately, there are no pros in the West to watch. Practicing and learning how to form good sheets by experience is our only choice.

If you spoil a sheet at the vat and do not want to couch it on top of earlier successful sheets (a wise decision), you can save the fiber by folding the *su* against itself, edge stick to edge stick, patting it a bit, and then drawing the *su* back leaving the spoiled sheet folded against itself. Repeating the step with one half of the *su* will fold the sheet into a narrow wad that can be picked up from the *su*. (Slight pressure with the hand against the wad will remove a bit more water and make removing the wad easier.) You may add such a spoiled sheet to the beaten fiber supply, but do not return it immediately to the vat unless you take the time to thoroughly mix it in.

Judging thickness, like adding *tororo,* is also largely a question of experience. Eventually you will be able to sense the thickness of the sheet you are making by watching the gradual change in opacity of the damp fiber mat forming on the *su*. Try to maintain a consistent thickness from one sheet to the next during an entire papermaking session. You will gradually learn what a given dry thickness looks like when the sheet is still wet on the *su*.

In Japanese papermaking you can actually see the *su* through the wet finished sheet. In fact, in Japan a very lightweight tissue is so thin you seem to see *only* the *su*. Remember, too, that the initial charge of fiber added to the vat is generally enough to make approximately fifteen sheets and that because the concentration of fiber in the vat is slowly changing, your sheet-forming action must be shortened when making the first sheets and then gradually extended to compensate for the disappearing fiber supply as papermaking continues.

The concentration of fiber in the vat depends on the thickness of the sheets in production and is also best evaluated by experience. For reference, however, approximate consistency figures for typical Japanese paper-making stocks are as follows:

Dry paper weight (grams/meter^2)	Stock consistency (percent fiber)	Dry fiber weight (grams/liter water)
40–50	.29%–.32%	2.9–3.2
32–37	.22%–.24%	2.2–2.4
11–12 (very delicate tissue)	.05%–.07%	0.5–0.7

Position the *su* in the mould, think briefly about the routine and sheet-forming action you plan to use on the next sheet, and proceed. When you finish the second sheet, open the deckle as before, but before you touch the *su,* move to the couching stand to lay a thread on the first sheet. Pull a length from the spool and stretch it between your hands using your thumbs and forefingers. Lay the thread down approximately 5 millimeters (1/4 inch) from the near edge of the first sheet. See Figure 146.

Couching (continued)

TRADITIONAL

Proceed to couch the second sheet as the first, being especially careful to generate the radical curl discussed earlier. From the second sheet until pressing begins, *do not* press or otherwise add additional weight to the back of the *su*. To do so would risk disturbing the slight, but crucial, stratification between separate sheet faces and guarantee problems at parting. Be *gentle* at all stages of couching, use consistent motions, and, other steps correctly executed, you will be rewarded with smooth parting later.

Remember also to exercise a light touch when drawing the *su* from the second sheet's near edge. If necessary, use a water wash on back of the *su* as described earlier. Subsequent sheets should cause less trouble.

Bubbles under the second sheet should be minimal. In fact, bubbles should diminish in number and size as new sheets are couched. If they do not, you are not couching with the proper curl, or you are failing to pass the *su* from mould to post and back again with the proper hand exchanges. (Incorrect hand exchanges cause the *su* to rotate laterally, near edge changing to far edge, so different *su* areas are presented to the post with each new sheet.)

Return to the vat and form the third sheet. Remember to lay another length of thread on the edge of the second sheet while the third drains a bit. (Pinch the thread where it comes off the first sheet, take up the slack with your other hand, and lay the fresh length of thread on top of the second sheet's edge.) Couch the third sheet. Take care that you use the couch guides and that each new sheet falls squarely on the post.

Continue making paper, couching, and laying threads in this fashion until you notice fiber concentration dropping off. You should be able to make twelve to fifteen sheets before the time required to make a standard sheet increases by a factor of three. When it does, it is time to stop and add more fiber.

Replenishing Fiber and Formation Aid

SIMPLIFIED

After you have made ten to fifteen sheets, concentration of fiber in the vat will have thinned considerably. At this point, set the mould aside, put the *su* in the 16-liter (4-gallon) bucket of clear water, and add the remaining liter (quart) of prepared fiber to the vat. Stir it well with the mixing stick. Because of the viscous character of the formation aid in the water, breaking apart all of the last lumps may take some time, but be persistent. You may find that stirring with both hands, fingers outstretched, in the fashion of an egg beater, works more effectively than the stick alone. Five to ten minutes of consistent mixing should yield a finished mix similar to the starting mix with no large lumps or strands (although strands may be left in for effect).

Add another liter (quart) of formation aid to the vat and mix it in well for about a minute. You are now ready to make another ten or fifteen sheets.

Continue the routine outlined above until you have exhausted the supply of beaten fiber, or your available time for the day. (Whatever fiber remains in the vat mixture can be strained out by dumping everything into the drain basket. Once concentrated, the fiber can be kept in a plastic bag or another container in a refrigerator for up to about two weeks, or it can be frozen indefinitely.) Break the thread from the spool. This should leave you with between twenty-five and forty-five sheets of paper depending on the thickness of the paper you have made and the time you have devoted to papermaking. Cover the paper with a dry felt and the second press board. Leave the assembly undisturbed until pressing.

TRADITIONAL

Pick any major accumulations of fiber from the mould, and set it aside. Rinse the *su* off in the rinse vat, and place it on top of the last sheet made. This protects the post from splash damage from above and prohibits drainage, keeping the post damp and thereby aiding successful bubble-free couching after resumption of sheet forming. Later, if you break for lunch,

75. Japanese su *during couching*

76. Placemat su *(no mesh attached) in a simple mould*

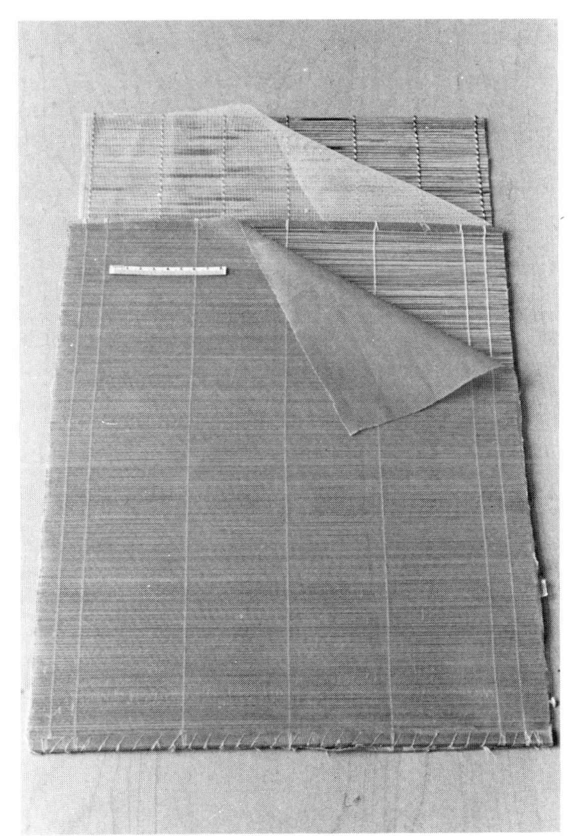

77. Two placemat su *with synthetic mesh attached.* Top: *made from "matchstick" placemat.* Bottom: *made from mat for storing brushes.*

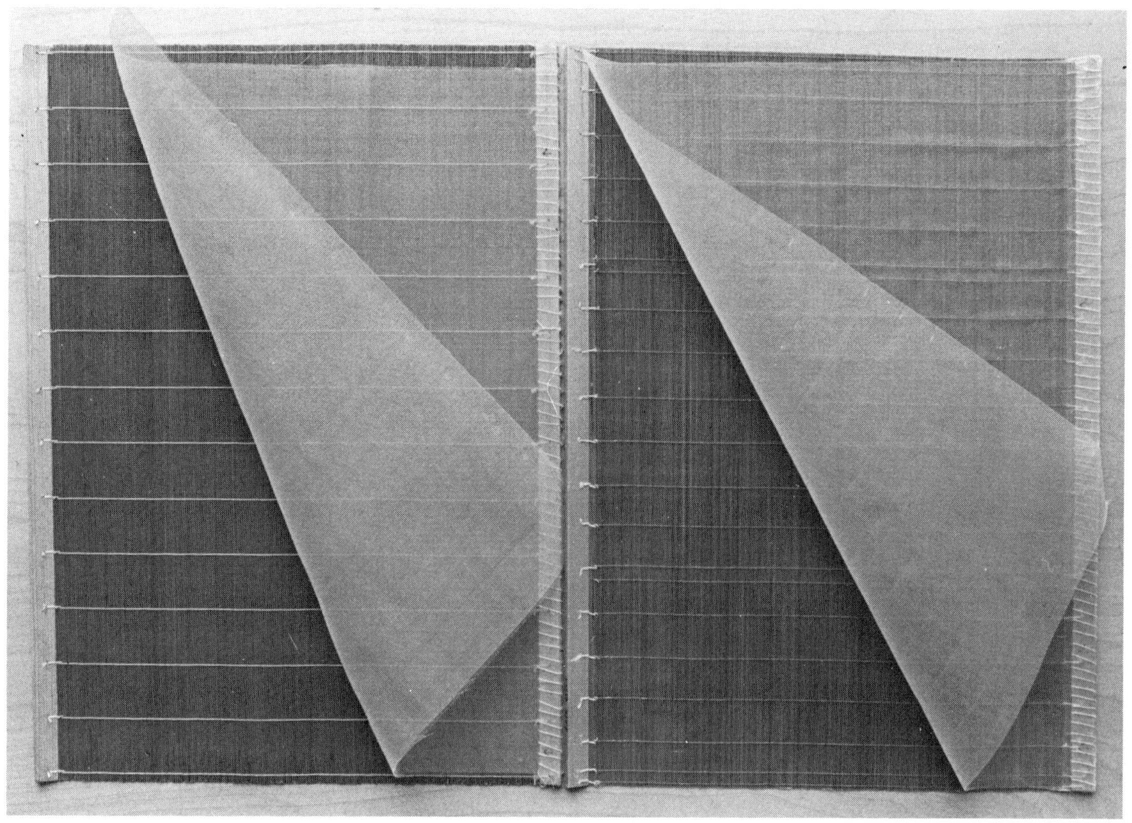

78. *Traditional* su *with treated silkscreen mesh attached.* Left: *made from fiberglass splints and nylon threads.* Right: *made from bamboo splints and silk threads.*

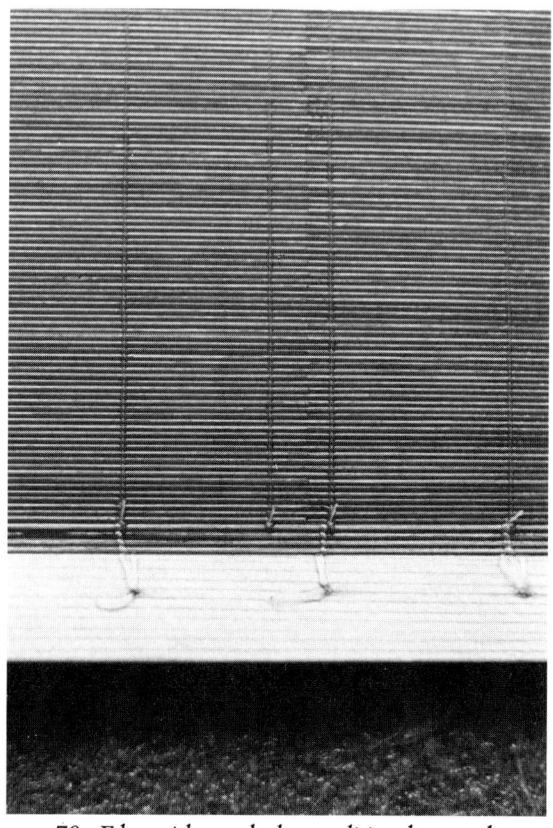

79. *Edge stick attached to traditional* su *made from bamboo splints and silk threads (nylon threads were used to attach edge sticks)*

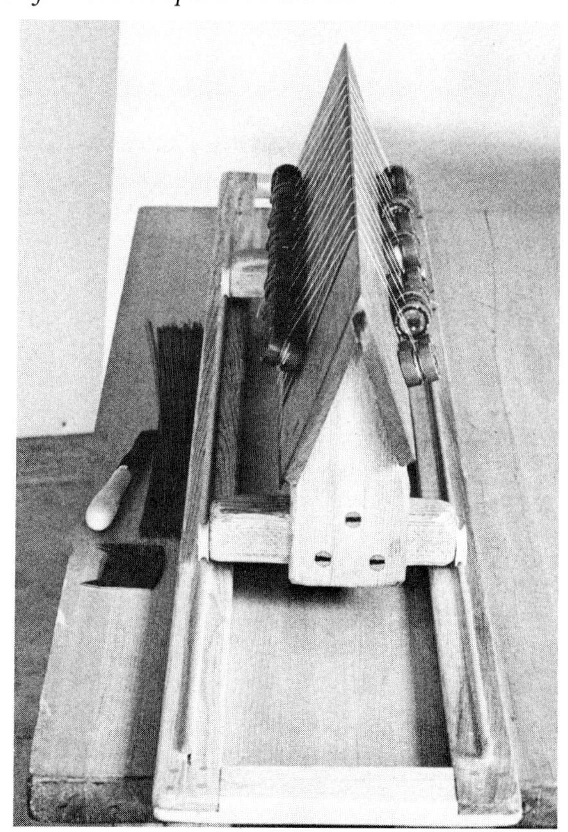

80. Su-*weaving stand (side view)*

81. Su-*weaving stand (front view)*

82. Su *weaving with tools made in the West*

83. Su *weaving in Japan*

84. Small Japanese mould (30 by 40 centimeters, or 12 by 16 inches) with su *in place*

85. Large Japanese mould (60 by 90 centimeters, or about 2 by 3 feet) with su *in place. Note: hands are gripping far edge.*

86. Traditional vat for use with small traditional mould (30 by 40 centimeters, or 12 by 16 inches)

87. Traditional vat (side view)

88. Traditional vat (disassembled on work table)

89. Equipment for simplified papermaking. Left to right: *press board and starting felt, spool holder, vat, mould on mould support sticks, and drain bucket. Note boards placed under plastic to form water dams.*

90. Equipment for traditional papermaking. Left to right: *drain bucket, rinse vat, press board and starting felt, couching guides, spool holder, vat, and drain bucket.*

91. Japanese cast-iron cauldron for cooking fiber

92. Japanese cast-iron cauldron (in use)

93. Drain basket (in use)

94. Japanese outdoor cement tank for washing fiber

95. Portable beating table and home-built beating sticks

96. Beating table covered with formica

97. Stamper (see Fig. 46 for construction plans)

98. Naginata *beater, with cover removed (see Fig. 47 for construction plans)*

99. Close-up of another naginata *beater*

100. Small Japanese hollander beater, roll cover removed

101. Large Japanese hollander beater (in use)

102. Lever press (see Fig. 49 for construction plans)

103. Small hydraulic press (home-built)

104. Japanese screw press

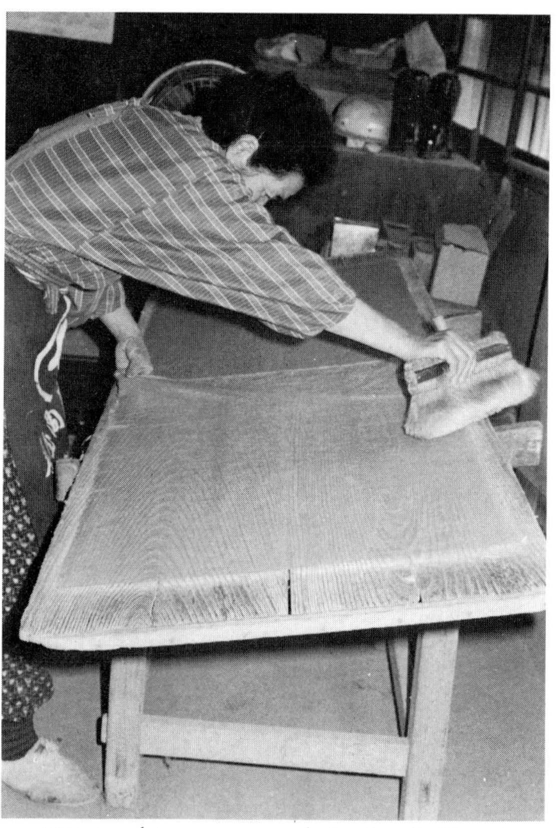

105. Brushing paper onto drying boards (Japan)

106. Japanese steam-heated dryer (with felts temporarily drying on top)

107. Drying yard in Japan

108. Heat-lamp dryer, cover removed (see Fig. 50 for construction plans)

109. Heat-lamp dryer, cover in place

110. Drying brushes. Top and bottom: *made from Western paintbrushes (see Fig. 52 for construction plans).* Center: *Japanese professional drying brush.*

111. Japanese drying brushes. Top: *made from palm fiber.* Bottom: *made from horsehair.*

112. Japanese mould suspension system

113. Work table with built-in drain holes (see Fig. 53 for construction plans)

114. Top to bottom: *kozo, mitsumata, and gampi*

115. Stripping kozo bark (Japan)

116. Scraping black outer bark from kozo

117. Close-up of scraping action

118. Kozo bark drying (Japan)

119. Removing foreign particles from kozo (Japan)

120. Bundles of dried scraped bark

121. Beating kozo fiber by hand (Japan)

122. A plot of home-grown tororo-aoi *in Michigan (plants on right allowed to grow tall for seed)*

123. Tororo-aoi *roots in bundles (Japan)*

124. Beating tororo-aoi *roots*

125. The viscous secretion of tororo-aoi *after soaking in water*

126. Wetting down the felt on the press board before couching

127. Mixing the vat solution with the mazè

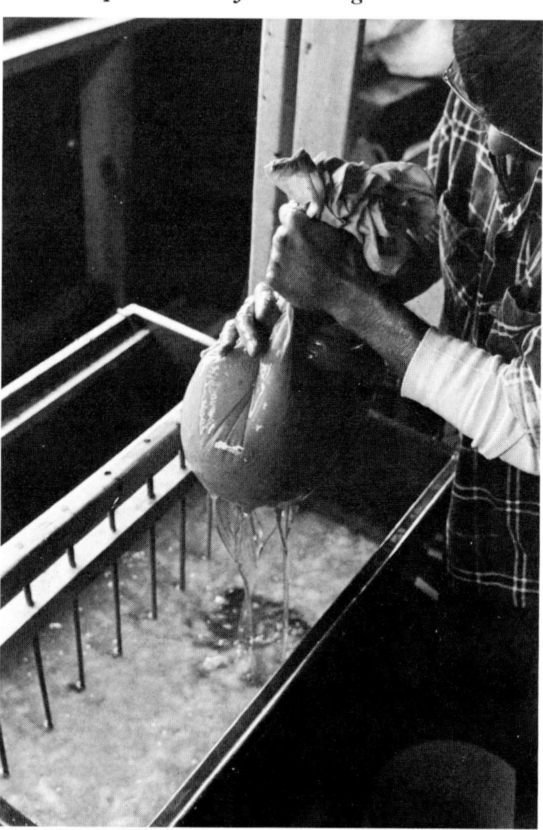

128. Adding the tororo-aoi *secretion to the vat*

129. Mixing the vat solution with a mixing stick

130. Equipment for the simplified method (in use)

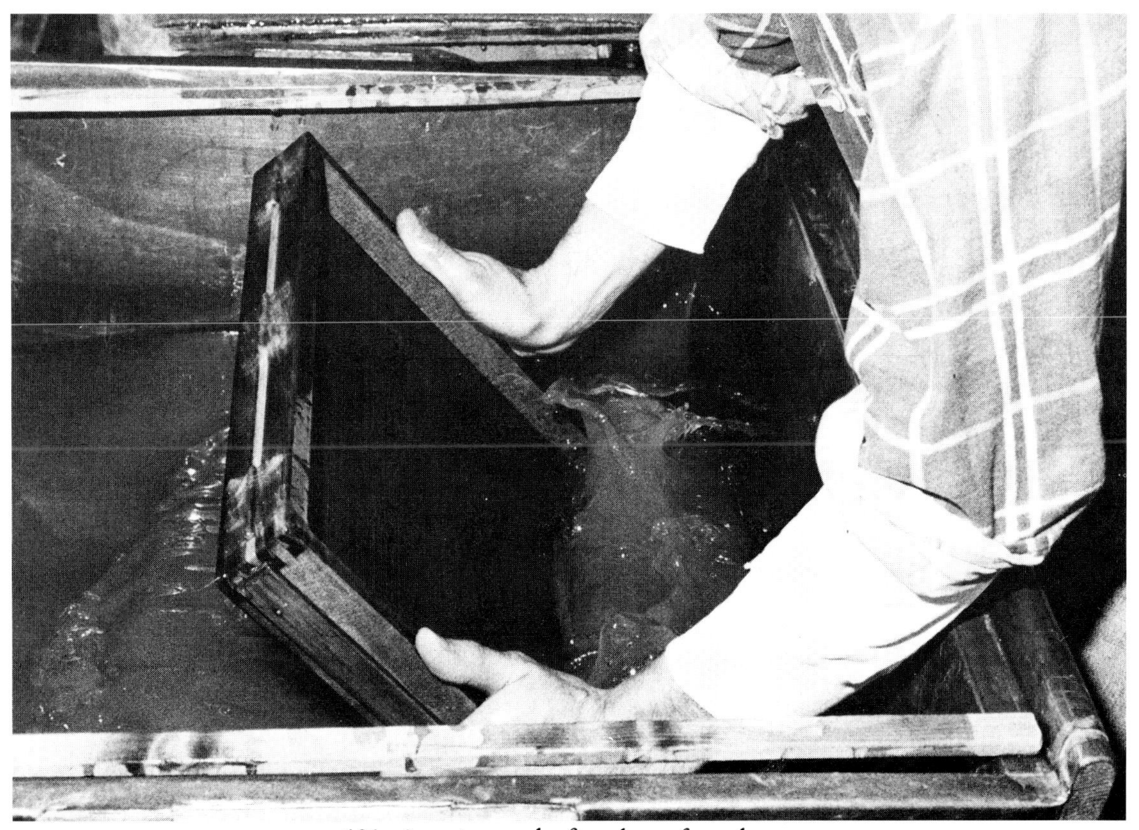

131. Scooping up the first charge from the vat

132. Tossing off excess solution from the first charge

133. Working the second charge from near to far edge of the mould

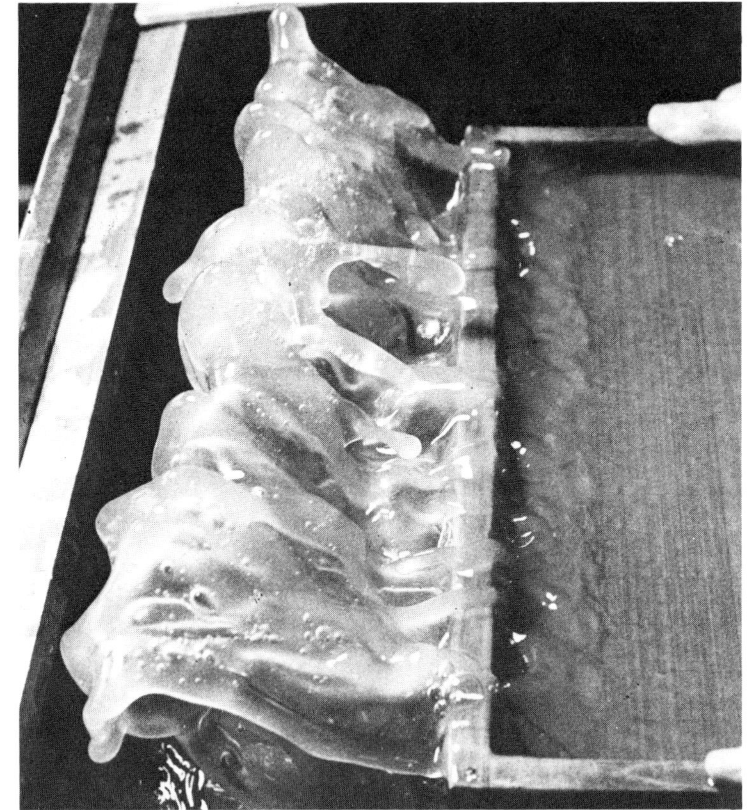

134. Tossing off excess solution from the second charge

135. Working the third charge from side to side

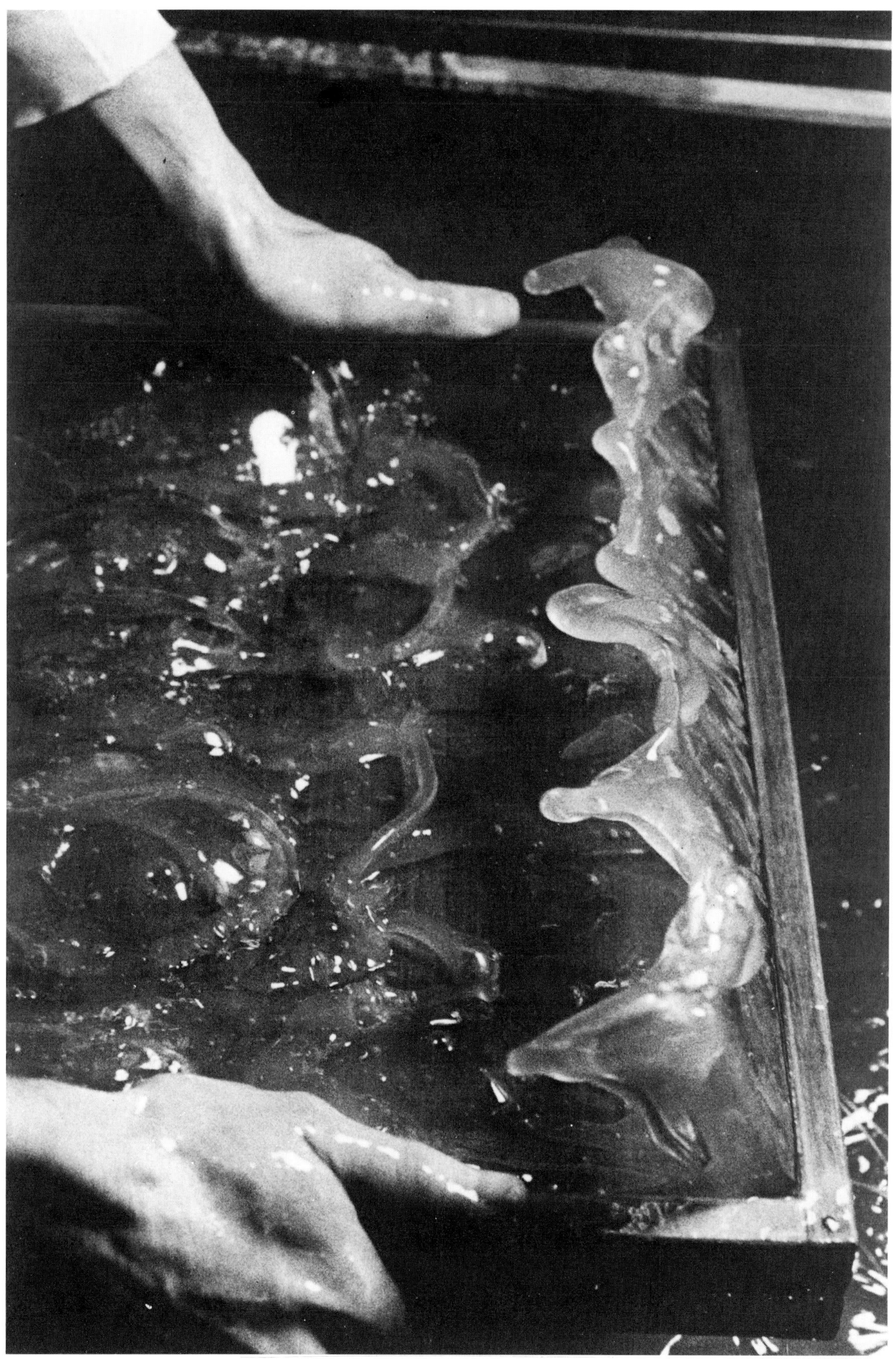

136. Advanced sheet-forming action

137. Starting to couch a sheet

138. Continuing to couch, maintaining a radical curl in the su *at the point of contact with the post*

139. Couching continued

140. Improper position of the su *during couching*

141. Depressing the near edge stick after folding it back over the su

142. Drawing the su *away from the post*

143. Continuing to draw the su *away*

144. Depressing the near edge stick of a mesh-covered su

145. Drawing a mesh-covered su *away from the post*

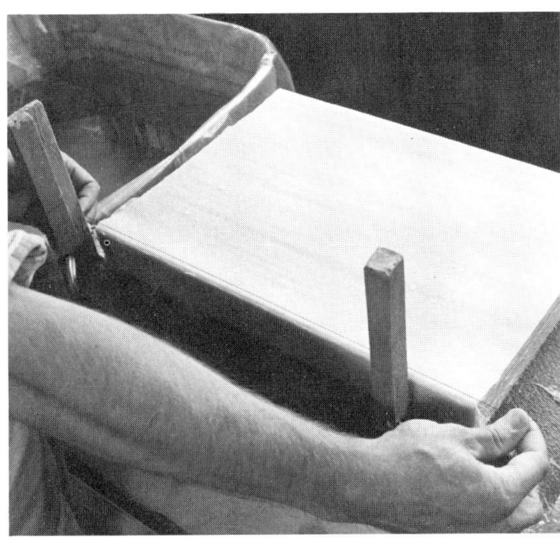

146. Laying thread on top of the couched sheet

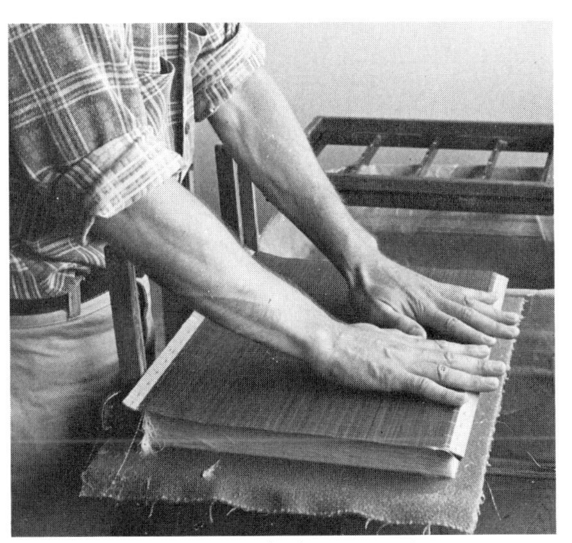

147. Depressing high areas in the post

148. Adding a press board to the finished post (top felt already in place)

149. Removing the first length of thread from the pack

150. Parting a sheet from the pack

151. Continuing to part a sheet from the pack

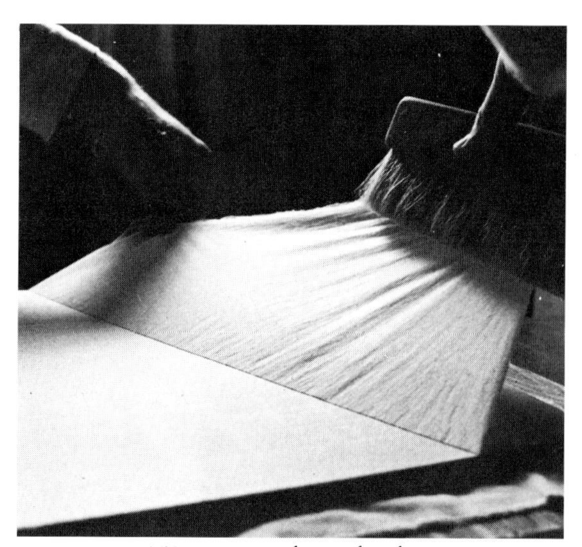

152. Using a drying brush to distribute strain during parting

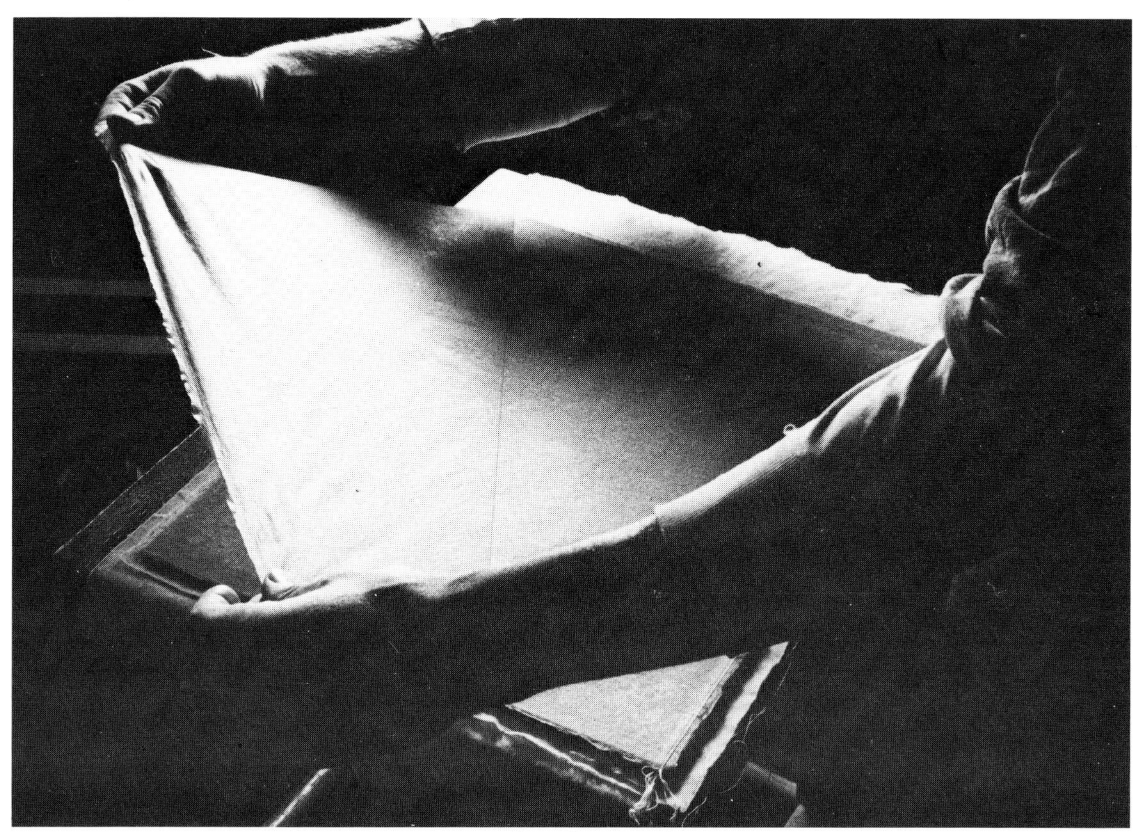

153. Proper angle and tension during parting

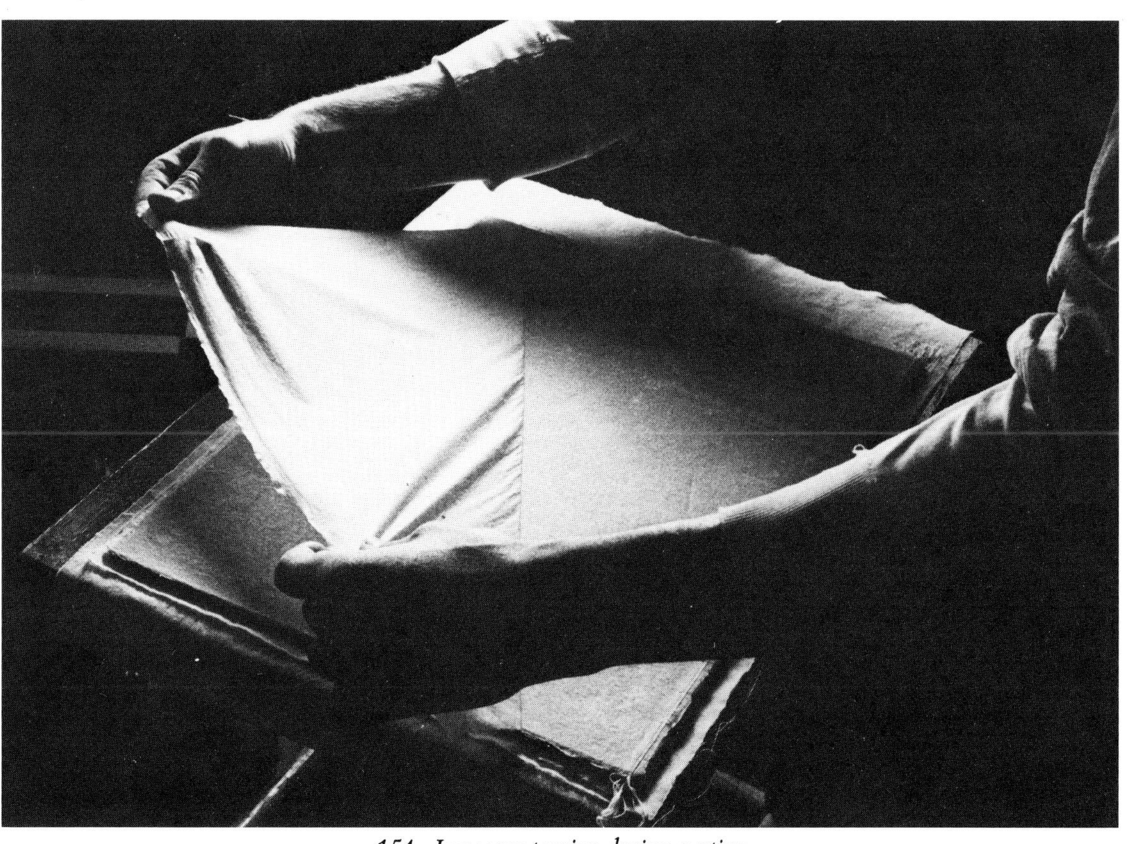

154. Improper tension during parting

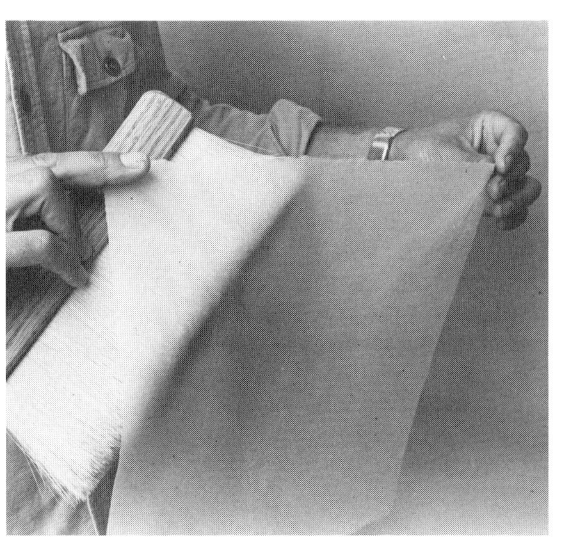

155

156

159

160

155–62. Applying paper to the drying surface. 155. Proper hand and finger positions for carrying a damp sheet to the drying surface. 156–57. Brushing the upper right corner of the sheet to the drying surface. 158. Brushing diagonally from upper right to lower left corner with one tip of the brush. 159–60. Brushing from the center to the upper left with full width of the brush. 161–62. Continuing to brush from the center out to adhere rest of sheet to the drying surface.

157

158

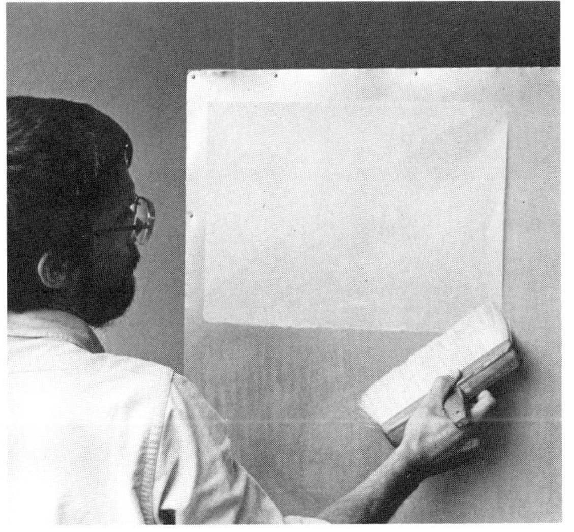

161

162

163. A kozo sheet, made from hand-beaten fiber, showing good formation quality

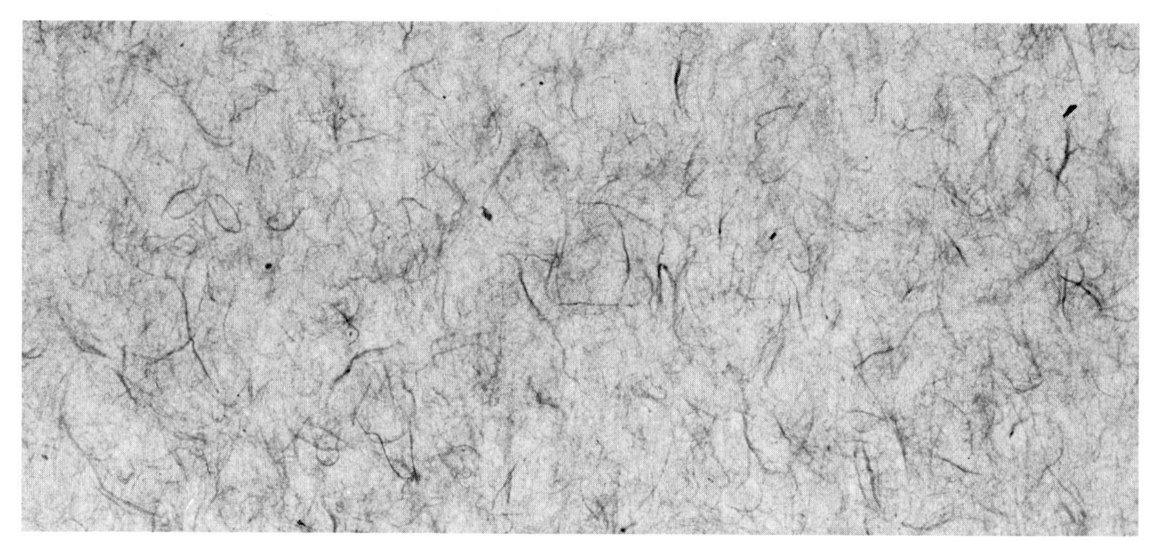

164. A kozo sheet showing poor fiber distribution

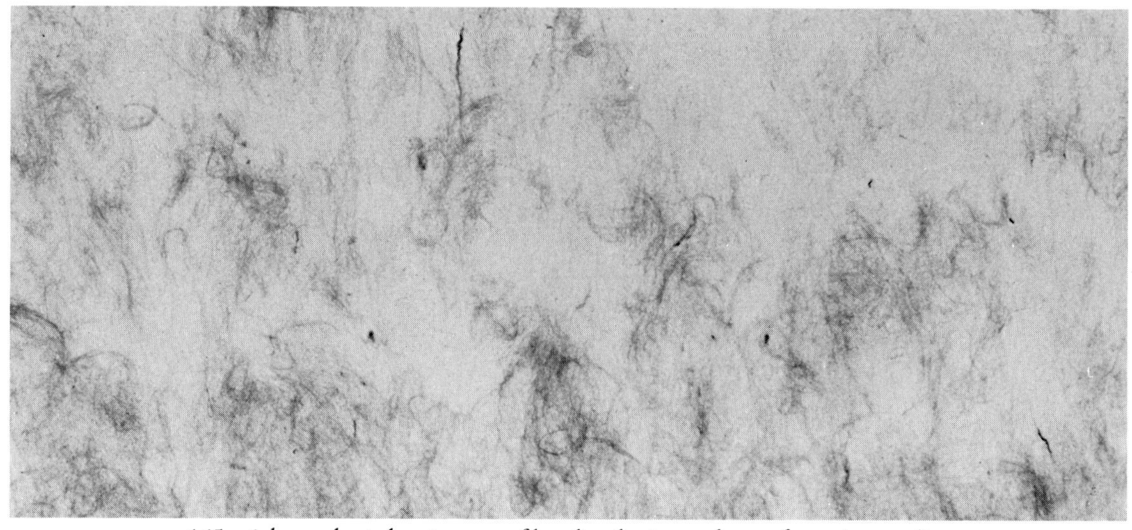

165. A kozo sheet showing poor fiber distribution and poor formation quality

rinse the *su*, and again leave it on top of the post. Rinse it again right before returning to sheet forming.

Add 1 liter (1 quart) of the beaten fiber mixture to the vat. Mix the fiber a few turns with the mixing stick (fifteen clockwise, fifteen counterclockwise), and then use the *mazè* again. Again, at least 125 strokes will be necessary because *tororo*, due to its viscous nature, makes dispersion more difficult at the beginning of mixing.

Stop once or twice during the 125 strokes to loosen any stray clumps of fiber from the corners of the vat with your hand. Add only a bit more *tororo*, perhaps 1 liter (1 quart). Or, you may elect not to add any additional *tororo*, particularly if you had problems with slow drainage before. Remember that you can always add more *tororo* later if necessary.

Once the vat is mixed, you can return to papermaking as before. Each time you run low on fiber (about every fifteen sheets) add more fiber and *tororo* as described above. If you encounter problems with the post sinking or collapsing in one area, delicately build up the area with a bit of damp beaten pulp or a strip of paper. The next sheet should couch correctly. If an area of the post begins to rise too high relative to the rest of the post (common at the near and far edges due to the sloshing action, which tends to produce a slightly thicker sheet at these locations), after a break of at least several minutes you may delicately press it down using the *su* placed on the post to distribute the pressure. Spread your fingers over a wide area on the back of the *su*, and push gently until you have reduced the pronounced high areas. Figure 147 shows the proper technique.

The fiber you have prepared (750 grams, or 1½ pounds, of dry bark) is sufficient for making at least 120 sheets of 30-by-40-centimeter (12-by-16-inch), fairly thin paper (20 grams per square meter, or 13½ pounds per 500-sheet ream, 25-by-38-inch sheets). The number of sheets you produce before stopping to press the paper depends on the thickness of paper you produce, the level of your skills, and the time available. A Japanese professional makes between 250 and 400 sheets in a regular 9-hour day. You should make *at least* 50 sheets, preferably 120, and experiment a bit with thicknesses and sheet-forming styles. (You may mark specific sheets or series of sheets for later identification by gently laying a damp tag along the edge. Use lightweight, white, machine-made or handmade paper marked with pencil.)

Any leftover beaten pulp, as well as pulp strained from the vat solution using the drain basket can be kept for later papermaking. (Remember to refrigerate it.) Only the freshest fiber, however, should be used for making traditional sheets.

Pressing (and Clean-up)

SIMPLIFIED

Using fresh water, clean any tools with fiber adhering, and set them aside to dry. Hang the *su* to dry from its sewn edge. If you would like to move the post prior to pressing, do so with care, keeping the press boards level at all times. Any drastic disturbance in the structure of the post from this point on can seriously complicate parting after pressing. A good location for pressing is on a cement floor equipped with a floor drain. If unavailable, a plastic tray or sheet plastic raised at the edges (with boards) on a kitchen floor, an outside sidewalk, or a driveway will also suffice. Use scrap blocks of wood to level the press board, if necessary.

Once you have moved the post to the pressing site, carefully rest a 16-liter (4-gallon) bucket containing 2 liters (2 quarts) of water on the top press board centered over the paper. This begins the pressing process. Leave the paper for 10 or 15 minutes, and then add another 2 liters (2 quarts) of water to the bucket. Continue this intermittent addition of weight until the bucket is filled—about 1 hour. (A labor-saving alternative here is to dangle a trickling hose into the bucket.)

From here on, pressing is a gradual 3-hour process consisting of continually adding more weight until the total weight on the post is at least 55 kilograms (120 pounds). This is most easily accomplished by adding water to a large plastic garbage can. The most trouble-free approach is to add the accumulated water from the 16-liter (4-gallon) bucket, and then adjust the flow from a trickling hose so it will gradually fill the remaining volume in a 3-hour period. Keep an eye on the whole set-up to make sure it does not overflow and spill water all over the pressing site. If you intend to work with the large plastic garbage can from beginning to end, you may eliminate use of the 16-liter (4-gallon) bucket initially. On the other hand, if you intend to shift the post to another press, the 16-liter (4-gallon) weight is recommended to solidify the post before the heavier pressing.

After 3 hours of pressing, with assistance, carefully lift (do not slide) the water weight off the top press board, and remove the top press board and damp top felt. You are almost certain to find the pressed pack still too wet for parting. Leave the pack where it is and cover it with a dry felt, replace the top press board, and invert the whole assembly. The bottom press board can now be removed and the bottom wet felt replaced with a dry one. If the pack is very wet (almost soggy), several dry newspapers can be stacked on top of the felt to help absorb the excess moisture. Replace the bottom press board and again flip the sandwiched pack so everything is in its original position. Replace the weight (filled garbage can). Let the pressure remain on the pack for at least 30 minutes. When you check after the second pressing, the pack should feel compacted and damp but not soggy. If such is the case, you are ready to part the sheets.

TRADITIONAL

When you are ready to stop making sheets, break the thread leading to the post and place the trailing end along the edge of the post so it will not get accidentally pulled during subsequent movement and pressing.

Let the post drain while you clean the mould and *su*. The *su* should be rinsed first in the rinse vat filled with clean, cool water. Keep cleaning the *su* until stray fibers have been cleared away. Note the discussion of *su* care in Chapter 5, Japanese Moulds.

Rinse the mould by shaking it under water in the rinse vat, and set it aside to dry. Any fiber left to dry on the mould or *su* (or any tool for that matter) will be much harder to remove later. Clean them both well while they are still wet. See Figure 28.

Remove any shims from under the press board so the post sits level. Carefully add the top felt and press board (see Fig. 148). Follow the 16-liter (4-gallon) bucket pressing instructions for the simplified method.

Unless you plan to be up and about for the next 4 hours, now (while the 16-liter, or 4-gallon, bucket is aboard) is a good time to stop for the day.

Final pressing and drying can be performed on the fourth and last day of papermaking. Finish cleaning up, but take care not to disturb the weighted post.

To resume pressing, remove the bucket from the top press board and very carefully move the sandwiched pack to the lever press. Position the press blocks, lever arm, and three empty buckets as shown in Figure 49. While adding water to the first bucket, watch for the post to "weep" (release a little water) for the first time. Stop as soon as it does, and introduce a slow trickle from a hose into the bucket so that it will fill in about an hour. Once the first bucket is full, move the hose to the second bucket. Repeat again for the third bucket.

Three hours later, after the third bucket has filled, remove the buckets, press arm, and blocks. Pull the pack from the press, and check for proper moisture content as discussed under the simplified method. In addition to touch, another way of evaluating moisture content in the pack is to try parting the first sheet. (See Figure 166.) Pull out the first thread and try parting the corner of the first sheet. If it seems wet and tears easily there is still too much water in the pack. On the other hand, if the first sheet comes off readily without problems you are probably ready to begin parting the sheets. If additional pressing with dry felts is required, use clean felts or old cotton sheets; avoid newspapers when making traditional papers.

Parting and Drying the Sheets

SIMPLIFIED

Very carefully draw the first length of thread from between the two top sheets. (Note the angles of proper thread removal indicated in Figure 166. Remember that the threads in the simplified-method pack run along the *short* near edge, not the long edge as in the traditional pack illustrated.) If the thread catches or binds, stop and very carefully draw the two sheets apart at the troublesome location. Once a snag is corrected, you should be able to continue pulling the thread again until the sheet is clearly raised along its entire near edge. Now carefully lift the lower righthand corner of this first sheet. Fold it back as you peel it away from the pack. See Figures 150, 151, and 153. Work

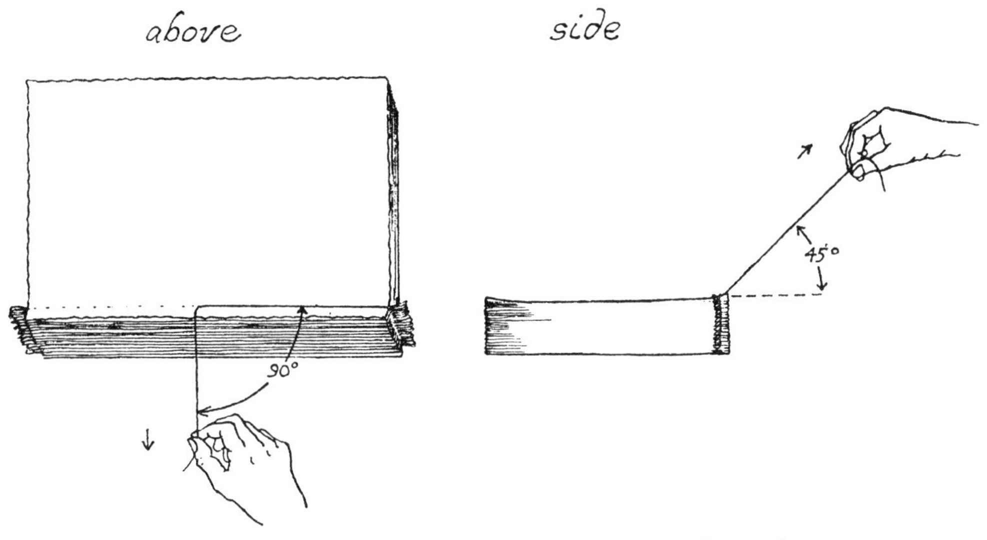

166. *Proper thread removal from pressed pack*

slowly and watch for picking between the first sheet and the sheet below. If luck is with you, all will go smoothly. If, on the other hand, the first sheet starts picking badly and starts to adhere to the second sheet, stop and try to correct the parting with your fingertips. If the paper refuses to cooperate, stop and try pulling the paper from the lower *left* corner. If worse comes to worst, you may lose one or two sheets getting the pack started. If the sheets are very wet and lack strength, you may have to subject them to more pressing with another set of dry felts.

(Any sheets lost in parting may be tossed into a bucket, mixed with a bit of water to loosen the fiber, and reused the next time papermaking is undertaken. If *none* of the paper parts agreeably, you have probably pressed the paper too quickly or made the paper too thin for a first attempt. Painful as it is, you will have to put the entire post into a bucket with water to be soaked overnight and then thoroughly mixed, in appropriate quantities, back into the vat to be made over again.)

Once the sheet is drawn from the pack, you can either set it aside on a sheet of dry newspaper to air-dry or brush it onto a smooth surface with the paintbrush to dry flat under tension. See the discussion of drying surfaces in Chapter 5, Boards and Drying Brushes. Brush the damp sheet on the surface as if you were applying wallpaper, and

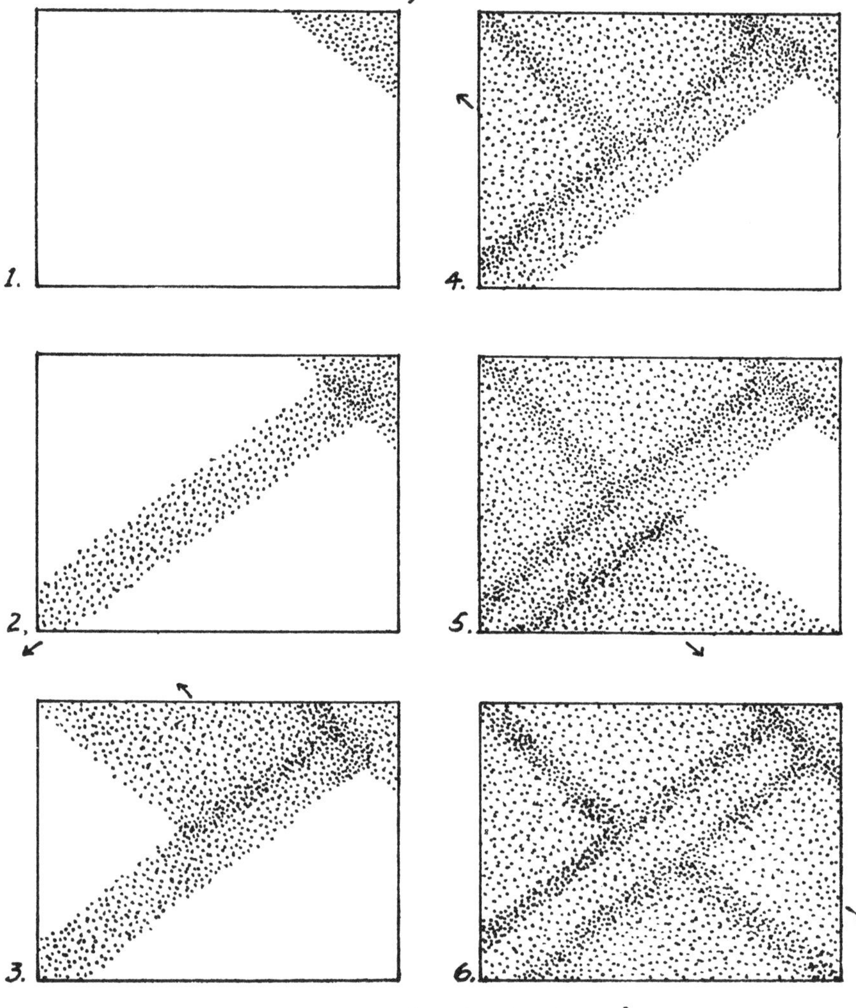

167. *Drying-brush stroke order*

experiment with techniques that allow you to smooth the paper on the surface without creases or folds. See Figure 167.

If the paper on the drying surface is exposed to sunlight, or warm air, drying will take only 5 or 10 minutes depending on sheet thickness. The paper should remain flat and adhering to the drying surface until it is completely dry. If you can slide your hand across the surface of the sheet without it dragging or without detecting *any* cool or damp areas, the sheet may be considered fully dry. Lift a corner off and peel the sheet away. Hallelujah! Your first sheet of *nagashi-zuki* paper! Sit down in a chair for a while if you are too excited to stand up. Congratulations!

Continue drying the remainder of the sheets in the same or varied fashions. If any of the paper pops or curls from the drying surface before it is entirely dry, chances are the paper needed a bit more moisture at the edges before application to the drying surface, was not brushed on hard enough, or was heated too fast or too unevenly during drying.

If a sheet pulls away from the drying surface prematurely, there is not much to be done about it. Do not try to push it back. Let the whole sheet dry and then peel it off. If you are set on saving the sheet, spray the whole sheet with a water sprayer or mister to a consistent after-pressing dampness, and try reapplying it to the drying surface or let it air-dry unrestrained.

TRADITIONAL

Locate and set up all the drying tools. Pull the thread at the angle indicated in Figure 149. Separate the top sheet from the pack and raise the corner (usually starting with the lower right) and lay it back as shown in Figures 150 and 151. Slowly pull the sheet away from the pack, being careful to distribute the strain over as wide an area as possible. (See Fig. 153.) If you are going to have a problem with sheets adhering to one another and delaminating, it will often occur along the edges of the sheet. Once the sheet is well started, it is a good idea to use the drying brush to distribute the strain of parting as evenly as possible. (See Fig. 152.) If you use only your fingers, spread them over a wide area and keep the tension uniform at the part line. Note proper and improper strain distribution in Figures 153 and 154, respectively.

Generally, the most successful parting occurs from the top of the pack, from the near to the far edge of the pack, with each successive sheet folded back as it is drawn from the pack. If you are experiencing continual problems, however, vary your approach. Turning the pack upside down and parting from the bottom can make a big difference. You can also try drawing the paper from the pack at different angles or from different directions. Improper parting can usually be traced to slow or inconsistent action at the vat, irregular couching, overly thin sheets, or too rapid pressing. As a last resort, if parting is failing miserably, dry the entire pack en masse by standing it on its edge in a location where both sides are exposed to plenty of fresh air. After it is completely dry (usually one to three days later), redampen it between wet felts, adding water to the top felt if necessary. (Redampening may take a full morning or afternoon.) When the pack is uniformly wet, press it again to the customary dampness, and try parting again.

When you separate the first sheet from the pack, carry it to the drying surface as pictured in Figure 155. Use the brush to push down the upper right corner of the sheet (Figs. 156, 157), and then immediately brush down the center diagonally using the brush tip only (Fig. 158). The remaining strokes are made with the full width of the brush, holding it almost perpendicular to the drying surface, in the order suggested in Figures 167 and 159–62. Remember also to brush *firmly*. You will be surprised at how much brushing the paper can take before the damp surface is disrupted. Brush especially hard at the edges of each sheet, as they are the areas most susceptible to peeling away from the drying surface prematurely.

As with sheet forming, brushing techniques vary greatly with the papermaker. You are free to develop your own routine or style. Practice makes for eventual ease. Any technique that smooths the damp sheet completely flat against the drying surface, without leaving wrinkles or folds, is acceptable.

If early in the course of brushing you fold a crease into a sheet, you may peel the sheet away from the dryer at the defect and try again to do it right, but only if you act quickly and concentrate on smoothing out the entire sheet as soon as possible. If you pause too long when a problem occurs the paper will lose some of its moisture content and, thus, its ability to stick tightly to the dryer.

The surface of the dryer should be kept warm enough to prevent you from holding your hand on its surface more than 15 seconds (approximately 75° C, or 170° F). Use the power switch occasionally, turning it on and off, to keep the dryer at the correct temperature. Generally, you will have fewer problems applying and drying paper if you keep the dryer somewhat on the cool side. Papers dried on a too-hot surface are much more prone to pull off prematurely. The disadvantage of the cooler temperatures, of course, is that they limit the amount of paper you can dry in a given amount of time.

Unless you were lucky enough to hit just the right moisture content during pressing, your first few sheets are likely to show a tendency to pull away from the drying surface before they are completely dry. This may be a result of not brushing hard enough during application of the sheet to the drying surface, but it is more likely a sign of insufficient moisture in the paper.

If this is the case, use the water sprayer or mister to moisten a 3-centimeter (1-inch) band around the edge of the pack. Let the water soak in a bit before parting the next sheet. Additional water at the edge should improve the adhesion of paper to drying surface (through capillary action) without detracting too much from sheet strength required at parting.[2]

Judge the sheet for final dryness by passing your hand over the sheet while it is still on the drying surface (see the simplified method). When you are convinced that the sheet is entirely dry, carefully peel away the two top corners with your fingernails and pull the sheet from the dryer surface straight towards you, without bending it downward. The latter action will leave an undesired curl in the sheet. Stack the dried sheets, and continue parting, brushing, and drying. Dry all your paper soon after pressing. If you must stop parting for more than an hour or two, keep the pack cool and wrapped in plastic. Note: The use of an electric dryer in this section is the only nontraditional aspect of the recommended procedures. Drying on boards in the sun is the more authentic alternative.

Keeping Notes

If you find yourself becoming serious about Japanese papermaking, start a well-organized notebook. The following are suggested headings for notebook dividers that follow the basic routine of the process:

Water
Fiber
Cooking and Washing
Beating
Sheet Forming
Pressing
Drying

Additives: Size
Retention aids
Formation aids
Loadings
Coloring agents (dyes and pigments)
Tools
Batch Record
Other: Suppliers
Bibliography

General comments or discoveries concerning the various topics should be recorded under the respective headings. Under "Batch Record" you should record each fiber cook, assigning a number to each and noting the details of all subsequent papermaking steps. When the paper is finished, attach a small sample for direct reference. Note any aberrant or interesting effects. Record any solutions to problems. Your notebook will soon constitute a perfect reference work for your own future papermaking.

Evaluating Quality

Evaluating quality in the finished paper is an important step. If you have adhered to the traditional techniques described (wood-ash cook, hand beating, fresh *tororo,* cold working conditions, good-quality water, the prescribed tools, and so on) you have very likely produced a paper that, properly stored, will last many hundreds of years.[3] Permanence, however, is only one consideration in judging quality in a paper.

The general appearance of the sheet and particularly the formation quality as viewed by transmitted light should be closely checked. A high-quality sheet is consistent in thickness throughout. (See Fig. 163.) Since a beginner's sheet-forming action lacks the relaxation and consistency of a professional's, beginners' finished sheets are likely to suffer somewhat in quality from a slight unevenness in thickness throughout each sheet and inconsistent thickness from one sheet to the next in a group of 120 or more sheets. Original fiber preparation should have been well enough executed that few, if any, strands, clumps, or specks of foreign matter are in evidence. Notice the poor formation and poor fiber distribution in the sheets in Figures 164 and 165.

To rate as "good quality" your paper should perform exceptionally in the application for which it was designed. If it was intended as a mending tissue, conservation specialists should approve of it in all respects. If it was made a bit thicker for calligraphy or thicker still for woodblock or other fine-art printing, the respective professionals should be called upon to critically evaluate the paper.

Finally, even if your friends are thrilled and amazed, do not become overly confident. If you are serious about making quality paper, do not compare your paper to machine-made paper or even to another contemporary handmade paper. Instead, seek out samples of similar papers from the best of the past, periodically look through them, smell and touch them—and more than likely they will show you there is still a great deal left to learn.

CHAPTER EIGHT

Variations

ONCE THE PRINCIPLES of Japanese papermaking are understood and the basic tools are at hand, specific papers or effects can be attempted following the guidelines presented in this chapter. While not a complete listing of all the possibilities, what follows is a good sampling of the potential of Japanese papermaking. Manipulative techniques for making art using *nagashi-zuki* are not described, but the artist who masters the techniques presented in the text is likely to succeed in implementing exciting and challenging ideas in his work no matter how nontraditional they may be. Many tools, techniques, and sensitivities remain largely unexplored in the field of standard Japanese papermaking as well as in the field of creative paper art. The papermaker, regardless of expertise or aesthetic persuasion, is encouraged to step beyond traditional bounds while watching for changes that may affect the permanence, durability, or character of the final product.

Papers for Specific Uses

Woodblock-Print Paper Under the general heading of *hosho* falls a variety of Japanese papers most commonly used for Japanese woodblock printing (typified by water-base ink and baren-printing). Most famous of all today is the very traditionally made Echizen *hosho*. Echizen *hosho* is made from a special short-fibered variety of kozo called *nasu* kozo. If the fiber is new it is usually boiled in an 11 percent soda ash cook for 4 hours. The washed fiber is then very carefully picked over by hand two or three times to make sure no foreign particles remain, beaten by hand, and treated lightly in a *naginata* beater to tease the fiber apart. The fiber is then thoroughly washed in a fine mesh net suspended at four points in pure water to lighten the color and soften the texture of the final paper. Before the medium-thick sheets (80 grams per square meter, or 54 pounds per ream, 25 by 38 inches) are formed, a small amount of white clay is added to the stock in the vat to further lighten the finished paper. Damp sheets are dried on boards either indoors in a specially heated compartment or outdoors. Usually, finished sheets are sized by a separate craftsperson, who brushes a gelatin alum mixture onto the dried paper. (See Sizing, below.)

Papers for Sumi-e Painting and Calligraphy Although some Japanese masters of these two arts prefer Chinese papers containing varying amounts of rice straw or bamboo fiber, very successful substitute papers can be made of pure kozo. Unsized, medium-weight sheets are in order. Mitsumata, gampi, and other short fibers tend to distort when wetted (by an ink-bearing brush), so they are generally not recommended for these applications.

Stationery Just about any *nagashi-zuki* paper can make beautiful stationery as long as you do not insist on writing with a metal-tipped fountain pen. All Japanese papers are traditionally long-fibered and unsized. As a result, they snag and bleed when written on with a fountain pen. (See Sizing, below.)

Book Papers *Nagashi-zuki* and the fibers commonly used in the process can yield exquisite, thin papers with exceptional drape characteristics. Unfortunately, these papers also tend to be very translucent, normally prohibiting their use as a single-thickness book paper. Printing on one side, using a medium-weight sheet, or adding a clay-opacifying agent may solve this problem. Traditionally the Japanese use a double, folded sheet as the single page in a book, thereby attaining the opacity required. The papermaker should experiment and alter the process in accordance with specific aesthetic goals. Even if not used as the main text paper, Japanese papers can serve as elegant title-page or chapter-head interleaves, or as unique protective interleaving tissue for prints or photographs.

Papers for Printmaking Although thick Japanese papers can yield successful and often sumptuous results, *collé* (application of a thin sheet to a thicker rag backing sheet) is potentially the best way to utilize these papers in fine-art printing, particularly intaglio, because of the expense of Japanese fiber and the preparation time involved. If a damp Japanese sheet is applied to a damp Western rag sheet during papermaking (before drying the sheets) and is immediately printed damp, superb detail can be attained. A dried sheet redampened for printing does not appear to have the malleability of the original never-dried sheet. The color and extremely plastic characteristics of the Japanese fibers make this approach to *collé* printing worthy of investigation by the printer/papermaker.

Archival Mending Tissue When making any paper that is intended for use in the conservation of irreplaceable artifacts, the strictest water-quality and fiber-preparation standards must be maintained. Thorough washing after cooking to remove undesirable residues is of the utmost importance. Very lightweight (13-grams-per-square-meter, or 9-pounds-per-ream, 25-by-38-inch sheets), uniform paper with even fiber distribution is often required for use as mending tissue. Maximum fiber length is maintained when hand beating is employed, although complete fiber distribution is hard to obtain. Better fiber distribution without substantial loss of strength is possible if hand beating is followed by light (1–3 minutes) *naginata* treatment. (Although a thin kozo tissue is appropriate to many conservation applications, the range of papers required by conservators varies considerably in thickness and fiber type. Consult conservators first if you intend to meet their specific needs.)

Other Papers For kites, use a medium-weight kozo paper. For collages, any archival paper will do (this is a good use for damaged sheets). Flexible book covers can be made from thick loft-dried papers of kozo, gampi, or a kozo-gampi mix.

Japanese Sheets from Western Equipment

Rather successful *nagashi-zuki* sheets can be made using European-style equipment, providing the following points are observed:

1. Stock make-up should simulate that for Japanese papermaking—i.e., very free, long fibers mixed with an appropriate formation aid.

2. Your deckle must be fitted with a slightly higher deckle wall (2–3 centimeters, or about 1 inch, higher) to contain the sloshing vat mixture during the gradual lamination of a sheet. If your mould is 55 by 75 centimeters (22 by 30 inches) or larger, you will have to rig a bungee or flexible bamboo suspension system to carry the weight of the mould while you work (see Chapter 5, Mould Suspension System).

3. Couching cannot be handled in the regular Japanese fashion, that is, one sheet on top of the next without felts. Instead, each successive sheet must be separated with a felt or other interleaving layer so the post does not become distorted and the sheets do not bond together when the pressure of the regular Western couch is exerted. Stiff-bodied silk mesh or nonwoven fabric may work well in place of felts. Try to work gently even though sheet separators are being used. Use clear, cool water poured over the back of the mould to obtain proper sheet release if the Western couch does not seem to work.

4. Press the post slowly, taking 20 to 30 minutes to reach the maximum, particularly if you have made thick sheets, to avoid distortion of the paper under pressure.

Western-style Sheets from Japanese Fibers

Very attractive Western sheets can be made from Japanese fibers employing more or less standard Western sheet-forming action and finishing steps. Generally, mitsumata and gampi yield better formation than kozo in the Western vat due to their shorter fiber lengths. During fiber preparation somewhat more beating of the Japanese fibers is permissible, and at the vat, higher fiber concentration and relatively little or no formation aid is necessary. The main objection to the use of Japanese fibers in making Western sheets is the expense and time required to prepare the large volume of necessary fiber.

Making Test Sheets

If you are interested in making paper from a certain fiber type but have only a small quantity of fiber available (30 grams, or 1 ounce, or more before cooking) you may elect to use the following test-sheet-making process commonly used in Japan. Proceed as follows:

1. Cook the fiber according to the normal gram/liter (ounce/quart) concentrations, with enough solution to cover the fiber, for the recommended amount of time. Beat the fiber by hand using a small implement appropriate to the amount of fiber you are working with—a 30-centimeter piece of 3-centimeter dowel (1-foot piece of 1-inch dowel), the smooth side of a meat tenderizer, etc.

2. Soak your *su*. Add a golfball-sized quantity of beaten fiber to 4 liters (4 quarts) of clear, cool water by tearing the fiber into dime-sized pieces. Mix well until the fiber is well dispersed. Mix 250 milliliters (8 fluid ounces) of prepared formation aid into the bucket.

3. Wet your mould in advance. Fit the wet *su* in the wet mould, and then, working over a draining floor or sink area, have a friend gently pour in a steady stream of enough stock to completely flood the mould surface. As he pours, be sure to keep the mould in continual action in the standard *nagashi-zuki* fashion. Work until most of the stock drains off, pouring the last back into the bucket. Do not attempt to add additional stock from the bucket beyond the initial pour. Doing so will disrupt the already formed sheet.

4. Couch onto a sheet of blotting paper, cotton linters, or a damp felt. If necessary, use a water wash on the back of the *su* to obtain proper sheet release. Make additional sheets if stock remains, using one of the separators described above between successive sheets. Cover the post, apply gradually increasing pressure for 30 minutes, switch separators for blotters or dry felts, and press again. Repeat if necessary until the paper is properly damp-dry for board or heated sheet-metal drying. Note: This procedure will provide no indication of a fiber's performance at parting when couched in a normal feltless *nagashi-zuki* post.

Watermarking

Successful watermarking of Japanese papers is difficult for two reasons. First, the exceptionally long fibers essential to Japanese papermaking do not conform well to watermark designs and yield marks without sharp edges or strong detail. Secondly, nothing that will interfere with the *su's* ability to curl radically during couching can be sewn to the *su*. Flexible pieces of plastic or string cut to form the appropriate design may be sewn to a normal *su*, but even if smooth couching is obtained, successive sheets may begin to yield a bubble-filled post because of the inconsistent areas within each successive sheet. Because of these problems, watermarking is rarely employed in Japanese sheets.

One technique that may be explored involves using silk-screening techniques (including photo silk-screening) to block out appropriate areas of a *sha*. Exceedingly short-fibered colored sheets are then made on the watermarked mesh and couched against a thicker backing sheet. The two sheets are then pressed and dried as a single unit. Experiment. Elicit the help of fellow papermakers or artisans in related fields.

Making Laminations

Laminations similar to the well-known Japanese "butterfly paper" are not hard to make when following the steps below. Materials for inclusion must be two-dimensional and not prone to bleeding or spoiling when wet. Test any suspect inclusions before use by wetting and pressing them between scraps of damp paper. Pressed flowers, grasses, and bits of string or cloth are all suitable materials for lamination.

1. Make up a fairly dilute kozo stock for producing thin paper. Form a medium-thin sheet and couch it. Add your objects for inclusion in the appropriate location. Make a second, very thin, cover sheet, and couch it on top of the first sheet and assembled objects. Rub the back of the *su* from the center out, and if necessary, use a water wash to obtain proper release of the *su*.

2. Use nonwoven silk-screen mesh or other separators if successive sheets in the same post are laminations.

3. Do not press too rapidly. Use one of the separating layers to carry the pressed and damp lamination to the drying surface. Brush through the mesh and then peel it away after the laminated piece is well adhered to the drying surface. Rebrush after the mesh is removed if areas of poor adhesion are apparent.

Using Pigments and Dyes

The following is a brief discussion of techniques required when adding natural dyes and pigments to paper pulp. For more information, consult dye and pigment suppliers, textile-dyeing manuals, and natural-vegetable-dyeing guides. (See also Koretsky, Hilton, and Clark, H. and K., in the Bibliography.)

When working with pigments or dyes, be sure to estimate the dry weight of the fiber you are about to treat in order to keep a record of coloring effectiveness.

Pigments Although pigments do not produce the more intense colors possible with dyes, and although they may weaken the paper slightly in higher concentrations, they are usually much more lightfast than dyes.

Pigments are best added to the fiber in the hollander or the *naginata* beater during the last minutes of treatment. Prepare the proper amount of pigment and retention aid for the entire batch by diluting each in at least 1 liter (1 quart) of water. Use a blender to thoroughly disperse the pigment. You should be able to decide on adequate amounts of both pigment and retention aid after consultation with suppliers and small-batch testing. After addition of the pigment, followed by the retention aid, let the colored fiber sit in the beater for several minutes before dumping it into the drain basket or box. If you are working with hand-beaten fiber, perform the final mixing in a plastic garbage bucket filled with clear water. In any case, after draining off the excess water you may proceed with papermaking as usual.

Dyes Natural vegetable dyes should be prepared as each species requires and in the same manner necessary for dyeing yarn or textiles. In Japan, the usual procedure for coloring papermaking fiber is to cook the plant material for about 1 hour and then strain out the spent vegetable matter. The fiber is cooked and washed normally, mixed with the prepared dye solution, cooked an additional half hour, drained, and finally washed in clear water. At this water-wash stage a mordant may be added to alter, intensify, or fix the color. Mordants commonly used in Japan with natural vegetable dyes include lye of wood ash, alum, caustic soda, cupric sulfate, and others. Consult natural-dye guides for more on mordants. Note that the use of some mordants, particularly those that leave an acidic residue, may affect the permanence of the finished paper. After a final wash the fiber is then beaten and made into paper as usual.

Notekeeping is especially important when you enter the field of paper coloring. Slight differences of technique can result in rather major color variations. Keep a close record of how you prepare the coloring agent and of the ratios of fiber (estimated dry weight) to quantity of coloring agent and other additives. Corresponding colored paper samples should be attached.

Mixing Fibers

Different fibers may usually be successfully mixed to obtain a combination of characteristics. If any mixture causes problems at couching or parting, increasing the concentration of kozo normally improves the situation. Using a mesh-covered *su* also increases your chances of working effectively with combinations of shorter fibers or fibers otherwise out of the ordinary and uncooperative on the regular *su*.

Sizing

Traditionally, Japanese papers were usually not sized. When required, a rabbit-skin glue and alum size was brushed on after the paper was made in the regular fashion. Gelatin surface sizes can give the paper a crisper feel and improve its strength, but residual acidity from the use of alum may affect the paper's permanence. The following recipe for a basic gelatin surface size is a composite of several similar recipes. More dilute versions may better suit the final application.

	Winter	*Summer*
Gelatin animal glue	13.5 grams (½ ounce)	37.5 grams (1⅓ ounces)
Crystalline alum	4.5 grams (⅙ ounce)	18.8 grams (⅔ ounce)

Water	670 milliliters (20 fluid ounces)	580 milliliters (17½ fluid ounces)
Preparation	Cook 2 hours at 60° C (140° F)	Cook 1 hour at 60° C (140° F)

In both seasons, soak the gelatin in cool water 2 to 3 hours before beginning the cook. Be careful not to get the size too hot during cooking. Note that the weather greatly affects the success of sizing. Proceeding with the whole operation during the winter is much easier according to one source. Once prepared, apply the size to the paper using a clean wide brush and careful even strokes in both the long and short direction of the paper.

For archival sizing with little alteration of surface texture or feel, synthetic internal size supplied by McDonald or Twinrocker (see Appendix 2) is recommended.

Air-Drying

Since most Japanese papers are dried flat and smooth on boards or dryers (resulting in slightly different textures on each side), you may wish to experiment with letting sheets air-dry. Because of the minimal beating most Japanese paper fiber has received, the damp paper will often air-dry without the violent cockling common to some Western papers when they are air-dried. Instead, the Japanese sheet will take on a textured clothlike feel that may be more desirable in certain applications than the standard, flat, smooth surface.

Calculating the Paper's Weight

Figuring the weight of your paper is a good way of comparing it to other papers. Use the following formula after determining the square-centimeter area and weight in grams of an average sheet:

$$\frac{\text{Average weight of a single sheet in grams} \times 10{,}000}{\text{Area of a single sheet in square centimeters}} = w$$

The quantity w is the weight of your sheet if it were a full square meter in size. This figure can be inserted into the common designation "w grams/m^2" and used to help document your paper. The quantity w may also be multiplied by .675 to arrive at the ream weight (weight of 500 sheets) if the paper were 25 by 38 inches in size. For reference, the weights of several types of paper are listed below. (Ream weights given are for sheets 25 by 38 inches in size.)

Very thin Japanese tissue	11 grams/m^2 (7½ pounds/ream)
Japanese *hosho* woodcut paper	80 grams/m^2 (54 pounds/ream)
Western-style book paper	85 grams/m^2 (57 pounds/ream)
Western heavy art paper	300 grams/m^2 (200 pounds/ream)

Afterword

IT WOULD SEEM, given all the tool drawings, the long and careful instructions, the cautions, and the appendices in this book, that making a truly beautiful sheet of paper is extremely difficult. It would seem that actually producing a paper that is a genuine pleasure to touch and see and smell must take a certain genius. In fact, it is deceptively simple.

Agreed, the young craftsperson must travel a very long road before acquiring an innate sense of the fiber and the way it changes in water as it gradually becomes a piece of paper. Part of this path must be shown by older teachers while much can only be traveled by the young artisan, working alone. But in the end, the act of making the successful sheet—a paper possessed of its own spirit—is a simple one.

Only three final ingredients are required—quality fiber and water, natural processes sympathetic to the character and integrity of the fiber, and the maker's careful avoidance of forceful manipulation of the other elements in the process. This last component is the most important, the most difficult, and the most crucial of the three. Without trusting the materials, the processes, and his own slowly acquired intuition, the craftsperson's finished paper will never have a spirit of its own. Genuinely successful sheets cannot be *created;* they already exist inherent in sound materials and sympathetic processes. The artisan's role is only to help the paper take form.

He is as the water in the cells of a tree—essential yet no more important than all the other elements in the final, moving event. Only when the papermaker realizes how truly minor his role is, will he become a natural element like all the others in the process. Only then will the paper become quite simply, and beautifully, itself.

APPENDIX ONE

Non-Japanese Fibers for Japanese Papermaking

by Winifred Lutz

A Japanese papermaker once told me that he could not understand why Americans who studied *nagashi-zuki* insisted on importing Japanese fibers once they had returned to their home studios. This made no economic sense to him. He suggested that in the United States plants must exist which would yield fibers comparable to kozo, mitsumata, and gampi and whose use would lend a distinctive quality to American *nagashi-zuki* papers so that a simple imitation of Japanese papers might be avoided. He urged me to look for such fibers myself. His words interested me very much, for I did not relish the difficulties of importing fiber. Also, the amount of land, the years, and the experience necessary make the alternative of growing one's own kozo impractical. Moreover, I like hunting. So I have followed Kubota Yasuichi's advice.

In the search for alternatives to Japanese fibers, there are two potential areas for investigation: plants, either indigenous or naturalized, which grow in this country, and processed plant fibers, such as those sold by craft-supply houses for weaving, ropemaking, and basketry.[1] Finding local plant sources for fibers appeals to me because this seems more in keeping with the basic gentle attitude of workmanship in *nagashi-zuki* since it involves paying attention to the attributes of one's materials and environment and working accordingly. Such an approach also has aesthetic advantages: the possibility always exists of finding a fiber with completely new attributes. At the very least, there is the certainty of finding a variety of textures and colors which, if not practical in a production sense, might be used for decorative manipulations or as additives to modify the appearance and behavior of the tried and true fibers. Finally, there is the pure excitement of the hunt.

If you want to look for alternative fibers, it is absolutely necessary to have had experience with at least one of the Japanese fibers, preferably kozo, so that you have a reference point. You should know how the Japanese fiber is harvested and should have handled the raw material before preparation, scraped the bark after soaking, and cooked, rinsed, removed black bark impurities from, and hand beaten the fiber, as well as formed sheets and dried them. Only then will you begin to have the necessary background to evaluate your new material. In addition to obtaining experience working with a Japanese fiber, there are four necessary steps to consider in the search for alternative fibers: (1) classifying the potential fiber according to the plant type and the location of the fiber in the plant; (2) selecting a strategy for locating good fiber-yielding plants; (3) conducting a preliminary evaluation of a fiber; and (4) testing a new fiber's potential for papermaking. Each of these topics is discussed more fully below.

Fiber Classification

Fiber may be obtained from different parts of a plant. There seems to be a direct correlation between what you may anticipate about the fiber's strength and its susceptibility to cooking, and the part of the plant it represents. Whether scientifically correct or not, my experience has revealed at least six practical categories:

1. Bast fiber. Kozo is an example of what is known as a bast fiber. This means that it is the skin of the branch or stalk of the plant. Botanically, this is the phloem, the structure which transmits liquids and food throughout the plant—the plumbing, if you will. Bast fibers of both woody (e.g., kozo) and herbaceous (e.g., flax) plants are useful.

2. Seed fiber. Cotton is the standard example. These are the hairs attached to the seeds of plants, which permit them to be propagated by the wind.

3. Petiole bast fiber. Abaca is one example. This is leaf-stalk bast fiber. Proportionately speaking, many plants do not have a large amount of leaf-stalk fiber, however abaca and other banana-related plants are predominantly petiole. On the same plant, petiole bast is usually a finer fiber than the bast from the main stem.

4. Leaf fiber. Sisal is an example that comes from the leaf of a plant of the agave family.

5. Grass fiber. Esparto and rice straw are two examples currently used in papermaking. According to J. N. Poyser, in his book *Experiments in Making Paper by Hand,* these fibers and those in the following category tend to be much higher in lignin (20 to 40 percent) than those previously mentioned and so, obviously, much lower in cellulose (compared to 80 to 95 percent cellulose in seed and bast fibers like cotton and ramie). In my experience, the fibers are also considerably shorter and more brittle.

6. Stem structural fiber. Bamboo, bagasse (sugar-cane stalk, a waste product of the sugar industry), and woods used in the machine papermaking industry are all examples. With the exception of the grasses, these fibers, when processed by hand, seem generally to be stiffer and shorter than all those preceding. They also require the most processing to free them of impurities and to ready them for papermaking.

However, refined industrial methods produce reasonably strong papers from these fibers.

Of the first five categories, bast and petiole bast fibers seem, in my experience, generally finer, longer, and stronger, with a higher yield per unit volume of harvested material (i.e., peeled bark versus picked stalks) than all other types (except cotton). A few other comments on these types seem in order here. Bast fibers themselves seem to differ for papermaking purposes by whether they derive from woody plants (trees) or herbaceous (soft-textured, green-stemmed) plants. Kozo bast is the white inner bark of the sapling of *Broussonetia kazinoki,* which is a tree. Flax bast is the fibrous outer layer of the stalk of *Linum usitatissimum,* which is an herbaceous annual. The former is cooked and hand-beaten easily, but the latter is difficult to cook to a tenderness suitable for hand beating and requires prolonged beating by hand or machine. The general rule seems to be that the bast of herbaceous annuals and perennials and of both woody and herbaceous vines is more resistant to cooking than the bast of trees. In fact, all the other fiber types are more difficult to cook to a tenderness suitable for beating than many types of tree bast. This observation is borne out by the Japanese papermaker Katsu Tadahiko,[2] who says that fibers traditionally used for textiles and the related crafts of rope making and basketry are generally resistant to standard *nagashi-zuki* preparation methods.

My own limited experience confirms that such fibers are indeed difficult to clean and soften by cooking and difficult to beat by hand. Often the substantially longer cooking and/or stronger alkalis necessary to allow these fibers to be hand beaten destroys their integrity because such treatment roughens the individual fibers and begins to dissolve the cellulose.[3] It seems better to prepare them by using fermenting techniques, which are discussed later. The outstanding exception to the general rule noted above is the bast of true hemp (*Cannabis sativa*), which was the first fiber used extensively by the Chinese for papermaking. It becomes beatable after an overnight soak in lye from wood ash.[4]

Locating Good Fiber-yielding Plants

A number of approaches are possible. The most obvious is to explore your local area and peel various trees and plants. Do *not* peel the trunks of large trees. Peel only branches or saplings of 1 to 2.5 centimeters (about ½–1 inch) in diameter for the best quality fiber. Before hunting, it is advisable to prepare yourself by reading field identification books on North American trees, shrubs, and weeds. I have found the Audubon and the Petersen field guides to be particularly helpful. *The Audubon Society Field Guide to North American Trees: Eastern Region* includes accounts of the historical uses of various trees. This type of information can provide useful clues to whether the bark is fibrous and strong.

In reading these books, pay particular attention to botanical orders and families.[5]

If one plant from a family is good for paper it often follows that the others are, too, and sometimes the whole order is good. For example, both mitsumata and gampi are of the family Thymelaeaceae. *Dirca palustris* (commonly called leatherwood or wikopi), a shrub indigenous to North America, is of the same family. When you look it up in a field guide, you find that its distinguishing characteristic is "bark tougher than the branch itself."[6] Elsewhere I have read that it was used for fish lines by the Indians. Such details are evidence in favor of the plant's potential for papermaking. Other families in the order, which is Myrtales, may also prove usable. An example of a whole order that so far in my testing is proving usable is Urticales. It includes Ulmaceae, the elms, and Moraceae, which includes both kozo and mulberry trees. I have tried both elm and mulberry barks, and they work well. This criterion may be used in reverse, as well, to eliminate species that are not likely to provide usable fiber. The order Salicales, whose one family is Salicaceae, includes both poplar and willow, both of which require prolonged processing and do not yield very good paper.

Books on fibers used in the textile and basketry crafts and on plant histories are also useful as is, of course, Dard Hunter's *Papermaking: The History and Technique of an Ancient Craft,* particularly the chapter on early papermaking materials and the chronology in the back, which lists many of the plant alternatives suggested by papermakers in the past. Since these fiber alternatives listed in Hunter's book were invariably for *tame-zuki,* they do not necessarily work well for *nagashi-zuki,* however. Also, most frequently they were only used as extenders, mixed with cotton or linen, rather than as an outright substitute. At any rate, these various sources will give you an idea of what may be worthy of attention in your area.

The best seasons for hunting are spring and summer, when plants are more easily identified and tree bark can be peeled without having to steam the branches. By the end of August, depending on your geographic location, many trees become difficult to peel on location, and many herbaceous plants begin to dry out.

Preliminary Evaluation

Specific qualities to look for vary with the location of the fiber in the plant and the type of plant, but there are some general qualities any fiber for *nagashi-zuki* should have:

1. High yield per volume of raw material. Does the bast or leaf seem mostly fiber, or is there a great deal of fleshy material?
2. Strength. How easily can you break the fiber unit of the plant with your hands? The tougher it is, the better.
3. Flexibility, fineness, length. It is highly desirable that the single fibers be long, fine, and flexible.
4. Light color. Is there a great deal of fleshy matter coloring the fibers (as in most

leaves), does the fiber darken when peeled and exposed to the air, or is the fiber white, yellow, or brown? Obviously, a very dark fiber would have limited value. Also, darkening on exposure to air or water may indicate a high tannin content, which is undesirable since tannin is acidic and darkens with age and exposure to light.

5. Availability. Is the plant either easily cultivated or naturally abundant?

6. Ease of harvesting. How difficult is it to pick, to separate from the rest of the plant, to clean, and to cook?[7]

7. Appropriate response to cooking. Does cooking soften the fiber so that it is more flexible and clothlike, or does it become more transparent and cellophane-like (i.e., nonabsorbent, hard, and smooth to the touch)? If the latter, you can eliminate the fiber immediately—it will not beat well. Neither less cooking nor a fermenting method will soften such fiber. The best you can expect from it is a very short-fibered, mealy paper.

In addition to the above, certain qualities take on added importance according to the type of plant and the part of the plant from which the fiber is derived. If you are picking tree, shrub, or woody vine bast, the following factors deserve special emphasis:

1. Ease of peeling. If it comes away from the full length of the branch easily and without breaking, that is a plus.

2. Thickness of inner bark. Obviously, a thin inner bark indicates low fiber yield unless it is very free of fleshy matter. Anything 1.5 millimeters (1/16 inch) or thinner is probably too thin.

3. Ease of separation of dark outer bark from white inner bark. Some black bark will simply flake or peel away easily from its inner bark, whereas others will require laborious scraping.

4. Apparent resin content. Some barks have a great deal of sap in them, which complicates processing. Siberian elm, for example, when soaked in water, yields a particularly viscous and tenacious slime that persists even in cooking.[8] The resin of pine is resistant to water.[9]

When peeling herbaceous plants, the most desirable characteristics are three that have already been mentioned but warrant repeating here:

1. Flexibility. The more flexible this bast is (like the feel of cotton or flax), the more likely it is to yield good paper. If it is springy or wiry, it probably will not process well.

2. Fiber luster. If the bast has a fine, smooth sheen like silk, this is a positive sign.

3. Ease of peeling. When peeling, if you have to crush the stalk to separate it from its skin, you will have a very time-consuming job cleaning the fiber later. Also, be on the watch for milky sap when peeling, for this could leave a rubbery residue in processing. Try picking the plant in early October if you encounter this problem, since the sap will usually have dissipated by that time.

With leaf and grass sources, pay attention to the amount of fleshy material and its effect on fiber color during cooking. In some cases (e.g., yucca), the green material dissolves in cooking and washes away without staining the fiber, but in others it stains the fiber green or yellow and will not wash away. The fastness of this color varies with the plant.

This brings up an important factor affecting the processing of not only leaf and grass fibers but the bast of herbaceous annuals and perennials as well: to discover whether cooking will render a fiber light or white after washing, you must cook the plant while it remains fresh and green. With every plant I have tested so far, if the green material is allowed to dry before cooking, it will not dissolve completely during cooking and the paper will be some shade of gray or brown or have flecks in it. This holds true even if the same plant yields a white or cream paper when cooked green (e.g., milkweed bast and yucca leaves).

My limited work with stem structural fiber has convinced me that it is not worth the effort necessary to harvest and process it by hand. The fiber is short, harsh, and either brittle or very soft and weak. For this reason, no further suggestions for processing stem structural materials are presented.

Testing for Use in Papermaking

Once you have harvested a fiber, there is the final question of what testing procedures to use and how to keep records. Shown on page 245 is a copy of a record sheet I designed for my own use. Testing methods used to evaluate a fiber will be discussed using this record sheet as an outline.

Material Find the botanical as well as the common name for the plant. If its fiber works well, you can check other genera and species in the same family and perhaps even other families in the same order. If you are unable to identify a promising plant, retain samples of its leaf, stem, bark, flower, and fruit so that you can consult an expert at an arboretum or at a college or university botany or forestry department. In any event, reserve a dried sample of the fiber as picked and note what part of the plant it came from. Collecting these specimens will give you visual and tactile references which, as they accumulate, will help you develop a feel for what marks a promising fiber. If your fiber is tree bast, make a note of the diameter range of the branches or saplings from which it was peeled since this bears directly on the maturity and, therefore, the strength and character of the fiber. Diameters of 1 to 2.5 centimeters (about ½–1 inch) are best. Smaller diameters complicate processing by prolonging scraping time, although diameters down to 7 millimeters (¼ inch) can be used. With larger diameters, the bark begins to get too tough, although this, too, varies with the tree. Obviously, you should never use dead branches.

Harvest Method Did you simply pick the leaves, or peel the branch or stalk? Were problems encountered? For example, milkweed bast is difficult to peel if you

Test Record

Material __________ Classification no. __________
Harvest method __________
Date picked __________ Start date __________ Finish date __________
Shop temperature and humidity __________
Weight of fiber __________ dry __________ green __________
Precook preparation __________
Cook __________ or fermentation __________
Alkali __________ weight __________ vol. water __________
  water: alkali ratio __________
Fermenting agent __________ vol. or weight __________
  vol. water __________ agent: water ratio __________
Fermenting or cooking time: __________ to __________ total __________
  cook pH: start __________ end __________
  ferment pH: after 1st day __________
    every 5 days __________
Standing time: __________ to __________ total __________
Washing __________

____
Beating method __________ time and routine __________
Forming method __________ formation aid __________
Pressing, area __________ wt. __________ time __________ drying __________
Additional notes: __________

PAPER RESULTS:
Weight of paper and left-over pulp (dry) __________
Single sheet weight __________ sheet dimensions (wet) __________
(dry) __________
Finished fiber as % of original fiber __________
Shrinkage in drying __________ %
Forming and parting characteristics __________

____
Paper strength __________
Paper absorbency __________ Appearance __________
Retest recommendations: __________

LIGHT-AGING TEST:
Exposure time: __________ to __________
Color change __________
Handling change __________

try to peel the stem immediately after cutting, but if you wait 30 minutes or so, it peels easily. And, another example: Recently I had the opportunity to peel some fresh flax and noticed that the bast is, in fact, as white as that of milkweed. This leads me to suspect that a very white paper, rather than the usual tan product, can be achieved by peeling the flax plant while it is still green rather than accepting the consequence of the traditional method of harvest wherein the bast is stripped when the stalk is dry.

Did you steam the plant stalks or the tree branches in order to peel them? This can make a difference either in the comparative ease with which the fiber may then be cooked or in whether or not it retains its desirable qualities throughout the papermaking process, or in both. Okra bast that has been removed by steaming cooks more easily than that which has not. On the other hand, gampi is never steamed in Japan. Instead, it is gathered in spring when the tree is easily peeled. Japanese papermakers say that steaming would damage the appearance of the fiber. Similarly, *Euonymus alatus* bark removed here in America by steaming is never as glossy as that peeled without steaming.

The bast from trees should be tested both in spring (or early summer), when it may be peeled easily without steaming, and in fall, when it must be steamed, to discover if time of harvest causes a difference in the fiber's behavior and appearance in papermaking.

The peeling of bast fiber, particularly herbaceous basts, may also be facilitated by soaking. This method is normally used only if the stalk has already dried, since at that point steaming or direct peeling seldom works. Simply submerge the plant stalks under stone weights in water. Soaking should be carefully monitored and the stalks removed from the water as soon as the bast can be slipped off the inner core. This is particularly crucial during warm weather (or in a warm studio) since otherwise the vegetable matter in the bast and stalk may begin to rot, with subsequent deterioration of the fiber itself. The times for soaking or steaming should be recorded.

Date Picked This is very important information, which may vary considerably from plant to plant. As previously mentioned, gampi is harvested in the early spring because then it can be peeled without steaming, which apparently is not good for the fiber. Milkweed bast, on the other hand, is best picked in September to early October, after the pods have formed, because if picked when flowering it exudes a milky sap that curdles in washing and cooking and leaves white rubbery flecks in the finished pulp; it also leaves a black residue on your hands. White mulberry should be harvested after it drops its leaves (early November) because the black bark is removed more easily at this time. Also, many plants do not develop their greatest fiber yield or strength until late in the season.

Start Date and Finish Date These should be recorded because: (1) the information indicates whether you stored the fiber for any length of time after you picked it, and (2) it provides a quick reference for how time-consuming the testing process was.

Shop Temperature and Humidity These affect a number of things and recording both will help avoid difficulties that might otherwise be encountered when trying to duplicate the first test's results. For example, the temperature of my workspace in winter is 13° C (55° F). Although I attempted in vain to ferment a fiber during winter, the same test in summer was successful. The winter temperature was simply too low for significant bacterial action to take place. Also, warm-weather papers (those made during high heat and humidity) are usually softer and thicker than cold-weather papers (assuming your workspace reflects outdoor temperature changes) because warmth promotes bacterial action and inhibits the effectiveness of natural formation aids. Finally, if you dry your paper on boards indoors, a warm dry shop will produce results different from those of a cool damp shop, simply because, in the former case, the paper will dry more rapidly.

Weight of Fiber With this information (the weight of the harvested fibrous material), you can determine the paper yield possible from a given quantity of untreated raw fiber. Specify whether it is green or dry weight. Only dry fiber weight will give you an accurate idea of the paper yield since the fiber in your paper will be dry when you weigh the final product for comparison. Thus, if the fiber must be cooked without drying, you might weigh a small sample green and then dry it and weigh it again to learn the relative water content of the green material. This will allow you to estimate the dry weight of the entire test batch. Any yield from dry harvested bark or other raw fiber to finished paper over 35 percent is good. Forty percent or over would be very good. Kozo white bark usually yields about 50 percent and sometimes more.

To conduct a fair test, you should start with at least 100 grams (3½ ounces), dry weight, of raw fiber. This depends in part on the sizes of the mould and vat you use. There must be enough material to permit you to form and press a *nagashi-zuki* post of at least 15 or 20 sheets. Otherwise you cannot test the properties of your fiber during parting of the sheets.

If you doubt the outcome of the fiber and do not wish to spend the time to form a full post, your first test could be accomplished with as little as 30 grams (1 ounce) of dry material, using the test-sheet procedure described on page 230. Several words of caution about this shortcut method are in order: Since the pressure used to remove excess water from the felts in this case will be greater than that used in feltless *nagashi-zuki* pressing, the paper can acquire a greater wet-web strength and become slightly denser and crisper when dry than if you had used normal *nagashi-zuki* procedures. Although handling the paper when you lift the moist sheet from the felt to brush it onto the drying board will give you a fair idea of the wet-web strength of the paper, nothing substitutes for observing the behavior of the sheet during parting from another sheet in a true *nagashi-zuki* post.

Precook Preparation If the fiber was tree bast, did you scrape the black bark away? Did you stop and use the green bark, or did you continue scraping to white bark? This makes a difference in the color of the final paper and is easy to forget. Also, remember that whether you dried your fiber or kept it moist for cooking also affects color and should be recorded. Finally, a long presoak of the fiber before cooking can favorably affect the speed and evenness of the cook and should be recorded. A presoak of at least one hour (before cooking) is recommended, and I prefer to leave it overnight. If circumstances allow, it is better to presoak in running rather than still water. Running water allows impurities released by soaking to be carried away and thereby inhibits bacterial action. Even with green material, presoaking is advisable in order to begin removal of impurities (the viscous material in Siberian elm bark, for example) and to render the fiber more susceptible to even cooking.

Cook The first way to try processing any fiber is to cook it in an alkali. Soda ash (Na_2CO_3, sodium carbonate) should be considered the standard cooking chemical. However, tough fibers, particularly herbaceous basts, may require the use of the more chemically active, or "stronger," caustic soda ($NaOH$, sodium hydroxide). (See "alkali" in the Glossary.) Both soda ash and caustic soda are used commonly in Japan, but they may not be ideal since they leave sodium attached to the fiber and this remains in solution with residual water molecules also on the fiber. If the pH of the paper is over 8.5, the fiber continues to "cook" over the years and deteriorates at a premature rate.[10] Conservators with whom I have discussed cooking have recommended lime ($Ca[OH]_2$, calcium hydroxide) as the best cooking alkali because it leaves calcium carbonate rather than sodium carbonate bonded to the cellulose in the finished paper. The calcium carbonate is desirable because it is insoluble and does not attack the fiber but acts as an alkaline reserve to counteract any future environmental acid contact. Conservators also suggest that fibers cooked with soda ash, caustic soda, or wood-ash lye (KOH) be mixed with a saturated solution of lime in water after cooking to facilitate rinsing out of the sodium or potassium during washing.[11] The more stable calcium in this final rinse will replace the more reactive sodium or potassium.[12]

An additional advantage of using lime is its tendency to lighten the color of fibers, without the destructive effects of standard chemical bleaches. It is, however, a less active alkali, and a higher concentration is required during cooking than with soda ash. Also, your supply should be checked for potency periodically since lime easily changes to calcium carbonate in humid conditions. To test your lime, make a slurry of lime plus water and add a small amount of vinegar. If the slurry bubbles, it is releasing CO_2 gas, indicating that carbonation has occurred; the lime has become insoluble in water and is no longer usable for cooking.

Cooking Concentrations and Volumes Since initial test samples are frequently small and require long cooks with the consequent evaporation that necessitates addition of more liquid, I have found it helpful to work with the alkaline solution concentration rather than alkali weight as a percentage of dry fiber weight when formulating cooks. I vary the volume of cooking liquid to the mass of the fiber (to cover and allow free movement of the fiber in the cooking bath), but I maintain a constant alkaline concentration by determining the alkali to be added as a ratio of grams per liter. For example, the volume of water necessary to cook a 50-gram (about 2-ounce) average fiber sample would be about 5 liters (5 quarts) whereas a 400-gram (14-ounce) sample could be done in about 12 to 16 liters (12–16 quarts) of water. If each sample were cooked in an alkali solution determined as a percentage of the weight of the fiber (15 percent is the average used by Japanese papermakers), it becomes clear that the 50-gram sample would be cooked in a much weaker concentration (7.5 grams/5 liters, or ¼ ounce/5 quarts) than the 400-gram sample (60 grams/12 liters, or 2 ounces/12 quarts). Using the alkaline solution concentration approach does increase the relative amount of alkali available in smaller cooks. It is an approach I have found quite successful. All discussion below follows this approach.

My standard testing concentration is 15 grams (½ ounce) soda ash to every liter (quart) of water. If I think a fiber is very delicate, I lower this to 7.5 grams (¼ ounce) per liter. I raise the concentration to 30 grams (1 ounce) per liter for tougher fibers before I shift to using caustic soda (of which I then use 20–30 grams to the liter, or ¾–1 ounce to the quart). For lime I use 30 grams to the liter. The pH of the cooking solution will be anything from pH 10 (soda ash) to pH 14 (caustic soda). Note: The typical Japanese "20 percent" soda ash cook translates to about 13 grams per liter. Thus, some of the cooking concentrations recommended here are quite strong by Japanese standards, but I have found them necessary when working with certain non-Japanese fibers. The long-term effects of these stronger cooks on the fibers are not presently known.

Total volume of water as well as alkali ratio and dry fiber weight should be recorded to develop a sense of the effect on cooking of a greater or smaller volume of fluid per volume of fiber.

A word about safety in handling strong alkalis: Never use aluminum containers. Aluminum reacts with all alkalis and gives off a dangerous gas when it comes in contact with caustic soda. Always wear rubber gloves and goggles or, preferably, a face shield when working with caustic soda to protect your eyes and face from possible splatter. Use a respirator or provide plenty of ventilation to protect yourself from the vapors emitted. When mixing any alkali with water, always add the alkali to the water. This is particularly important when working with caustic soda, which will splatter explosively if handled in the reverse manner. Further, when using caustic soda, add it gradually to a smaller volume of *cold* water, stirring constantly, and then add this solution to your cook pot of water before it boils. (Note that caustic soda will heat the water it is mixed with. Take care not to mix too much with too little water, particularly in a plastic container as the heat can melt the container.) Use only stainless steel, heat-resistant plastic, glass, or bamboo as stirring utensils and tongs when cooking fiber.[13] Fiber is always added after the alkali is well mixed with the water to insure even dispersal of the alkali with fiber in the cooking bath.

Cooking Time and pH Add the fiber when the cooking solution begins to boil and time from when the boiling starts again. Keep the solution at an active simmer, and stir at least every half hour to insure that the fiber cooks evenly and does not ride up in the pot and dry out. Cooking time can vary from 1 to 18 hours. Conservators advise slow cooking with a weaker alkali or alkaline concentration, since it does less damage to the cellulose in the fiber. Fast cooking at strong concentrations can make the cellulose begin to dissolve and thus weaken the paper.[14] Check the pH at the beginning and end of your cook, and record it. Anything over pH 11 begins to endanger the cellulose, and anything below 10, in my experience, is too weak. Check fiber at least every half hour while cooking by removing a piece, rinsing it, and then trying to tug it apart along the long axis of the fiber. When it parts with a gentle tug, it's done. Be careful not to overcook since this will result in weak, very soft or brittle paper regardless of the quality of the raw fiber. If you undercook, you simply will not be able to beat it by hand unless you beat for hours, and even that may not be enough.

If you want to depend on hollander beating or to make paper using only the *tame-zuki* technique, the cook could be stopped as soon as the fiber washes clean of fleshy material or, with tree bast, when the bark can be spread perpendicular to its length to reveal the fiber network. This is not necessarily an indication that the fiber is tender enough for hand beating. I do not advise the alternative of hollander treatment until a thorough test has been completed to discover if the material can be cooked to a state suitable for hand beating and made into good paper.

Standing Time It is safer to let the cooking solution cool before washing. In addition, the time the fiber stands in the hot solution can contribute to additional breakdown of the unwanted nonfibrous matter.

Fermentation If cooking does not soften the fiber enough to allow hand beating or if the cooking time proves unusually long (over 5 hours), you may try fermenting the fiber (also called retting) or, alternatively, allowing it to stand for a prolonged time in an alkali solution with a high pH (11–14).

The alkaline soak technique was used by the Chinese to prepare bamboo for papermaking. The bamboo was not cooked but was left to stand in water and then in a lime paste for months at a time and finally stamped to make the pulp.[15] I have allowed both milkweed and wisteria bast to stand in alkaline solutions (using either a wood-ash lye solution as described in Chapter 6 or 20–30 grams of caustic soda per liter of water, or about ¾–1 ounce per quart) over periods of 3 to 6 weeks as a successful substitute for prolonged cooking.

Fermentation can be achieved simply by leaving the fiber to stand in water in a warm place (over 20° C, or 68° F) until bacterial action on the fleshy plant material softens the fiber. Old European texts on papermaking sometimes recommend beer or urine as agents to accelerate bacterial action, and a few young Japanese papermakers have also mentioned using these agents. Milk added to the water will also accelerate fermentation. I normally use about 250 milliliters of milk per 5 liters (8 ounces per 5 quarts) of water. The total volume of liquid should be sufficient to cover completely whatever fiber is involved.

The time required to soften a fiber by fermentation varies according to fiber type and to ambient temperature during fermentation. The warmer the surroundings (i.e., 24°–35° C, or 75°–95° F), the faster the fermenting action will be. However, total time is seldom less than 2 weeks and more usually 3 to 5 weeks. Sometimes it requires months.

The fiber should be stirred in its fermentation bath once a day, and the bath should be kept covered with cheesecloth, or a plastic screen, and a lid to cut out light but not all air. If the bath is not covered with some sort of screen, flies may deposit their eggs in the liquid and you will find maggots in your fiber.

Fermentation requires careful monitoring if you are to avoid total disintegration of the fiber. Test the fiber every day after the first week of fermentation until it pulls apart with a gentle tug on its long axis. Record daily the pH in your fermentation bath. I have found that the pH tends to correlate with fiber readiness although this is not an absolute indicator. The pH in a milk fermentation progresses from 4.5 after the first 24 hours to 7, at which point the fiber is usually ready.

Generally, you may expect a softer paper from fermentation than from cooking or a cold alkaline soak. Fermentation also tends to yield a grayer fiber than does cooking if the original fiber is white, and a paler result if the original fiber is dark or tan. Fermented fibers also generally yield pulps with greater freeness than do cooked fibers. For example, a milk-fermented Belgian flax, if beaten by hand, will yield a soft, grayish white paper. The same fiber beaten in a hollander after light cooking in lime and water will produce a crisp tan paper. (Soaking flax for a month or more in lime, however, yields a very white paper). The fermented flax paper is soft; the hollander-beaten cooked flax paper is crisper and harder. Another example, okra bast, is a cool greenish white if fermented but turns a light yellow-tan if cooked either in soda ash or lime. Unlike the flax, however, the fermented okra paper eventually darkens on exposure to light. This may be due to residual lignin (which is very reactive to light) in the paper.

After a fiber has been fermented it should be washed thoroughly and perhaps boiled to insure that no residual bacteria or mold spores remain to cause deterioration later. If it is also rinsed in a saturated calcium solution (1.5 grams $Ca[OH]_2$ to 1 liter of water, or about ½ teaspoon to 1 quart), the retained calcium carbonate will act as an alkaline reserve against acidity in the environment. Rinse lightly once more before beating.

Fermentation may prove to be the treatment that allows use of fibers otherwise unsuitable to the *nagashi-zuki* process. I have been testing fermented flax, milkweed, okra, dogbane, and basswood with promising results.

Washing How did you wash it and for how long? Begin by draining the fiber in a stainless-steel sieve to remove the cooking broth. Washing may proceed by placing the fiber in a bucket of clear water, vigorously agitating and then draining it, and then repeating the process, using fresh water each time, until the fiber drains clear.

Other rinsing methods include placing the drained fiber into a large plastic bucket (don't use galvanized or aluminum containers) with a plastic screen tied over the top, and running water into this continuously for 4 to 12 hours.[16] The screen prevents fiber loss. A more effective version of this is to cut a hole in the bottom of the bucket so that a hose connection can be inserted with rubber washers used for sealing. As before, the bucket should have a screen tied across the top. A bottom feed of this type causes better circulation of fiber and water. Still, although it is the most tedious, the first, vigorous method mentioned above seems to provide the most thorough washing. It is a must if you are processing leaf fiber or herbaceous bast because so much fleshy matter must be separated from the fibers.

A rough test to determine the thoroughness of your washing is to disperse a sample of your fiber in 100 millimeters (about ½ cup) of distilled water (pH around 7) and measure the pH of the mixture. It should be below pH 11 if cooked in lime and below pH 8.5 if cooked in wood-ash lye, soda ash, or caustic soda. (By the way, you should periodically check the pH of your regular water supply since you cannot rely on its remaining constant. If it is below 7 (neutral) you should add calcium hydroxide or magnesium bicarbonate to bring it up to a neutral or slightly alkaline level. Also, although expensive, you may wish to consider a mixed-bed ion-exchange system if your water is high in iron or copper content. However, since this alternative renders the water chemically active, you must still add an alkaline reserve to your water. Washing beyond what is necessary to obtain a low enough pH may be done to lighten the fiber since, particularly in the case of leaves and petioles, a great deal of vegetable matter may be dissolved during cooking.

Washing may be repeated after beating. The Korean papermakers do this as a matter of course, as does the Japanese papermaker, Iwano Ichibei. He says that the additional washing removes hemicelluloses released by the beating process. I have found that certain fibers, such as wisteria, appear pale when washed after cooking but then release a dark material when beaten. If this is left in the fiber, the final paper will be dark and crisp. If it is rinsed out, the paper will be lighter but also softer. In any event, this second washing should be done using an extremely fine sieve or a muslin sack to avoid losing the finer fibers.

Beating Method Did you beat it by hand, by stamper, or by hollander?[17] Try it first by hand. With some fibers, due to a tendency to splatter even if well drained, you will need either the equivalent of a mortar in which to beat your material or you will want to make a wooden frame to place on your beating surface as a splatter guard. Otherwise, you will lose a substantial quantity of fiber during beating. To alleviate the splatter problem, I use a long-handled wooden mallet with a notched face rather than a stick for beating. I use a round basin as deep as the length of the mallet head from face to handle intersection. It is cast of white portland cement and white silica sand.[18]

Some fibers are so tough that hand beating is impossible and hollander beating will prove essential. This should be done with care to preserve fiber length. Do not try to speed up the beat by lowering the roll or raising the bed so that the fiber is cut. It is important to try the hollander if hand beating or mechanical stamping is not successful, since you may find that your new fiber, while it does not process well for *nagashi-zuki,* will, in fact, make a very good *tame-zuki* paper. Basswood bark is one case in point. Also, some fibers knot excessively during stamping and may be de-knotted by being run through a hollander. If this is done for more than 30 minutes and/or if stamping was prolonged (i.e., exceeds 2 hours), washing the fiber carefully after beating insures higher freeness.

Beating Time and Routine This is important data if you are ever to duplicate the results. With a hollander, record all beating times and tackle adjustments. If a stamper is used, record any water added during beating. This is also important when recording hand beating. Note whether the fiber was squeezed quite dry before beginning beating or left relatively wet. Some fibers swell or compact drastically during hand beating and stamping and require several additions of water to permit the fibers to shift and separate.

Forming Method Remember that if the finished fiber does not work for *nagashi-zuki,* you might want to try it for *tame-zuki.* Also, sometimes the sample may have been too small for a regular *nagashi-zuki* post and so may have required the test-sheet procedure previously mentioned, or couching directly onto the drying board.[19] Record the technique you used.

Formation Aid Note whether a synthetic substitute for *tororo-aoi,* natural *tororo, noriutsugi,* or some other formation aid was used. Note details of the behavior and effects of the formation aid and if more or less was required than is normally used with a traditional fiber. In your search for fibers you will probably find plants that seem usable as formation aids. One I discovered was Siberian elm (*Ulmus pumila L.*) inner bark. Okra (*Hibiscus esculentus*) root is a very acceptable substitute for *tororo-aoi.*

Pressing Was it a standard slow press, wherein the post was left overnight and then weight was slowly added? How much weight was added? What was the size (surface area) of the paper pressed? Obviously, the larger the paper area pressed, the greater is the weight required to attain a standard kilograms per square centimeter (pounds per square inch) pressure on the paper.[20] If the paper was rapidly and heavily pressed in a hydraulic press, with the use of interleaving silkscreen mesh, felts, or other separators, record this and the amount of final pressure.

Drying Was the paper dried on boards, plastic, glass, or hot metal? Was it dried in the sun, or in the shade? Was it loft-dried? Each makes a difference in the final surface and handling qualities of the paper. Generally, the faster it is dried, the crisper it will be (and the more likely it will prematurely pull off the drying boards).[21] Sun drying usually results in a subtle lightening of the paper. It is probably best to have a standard drying method. It can be useful to loft-dry a few sheets each time for comparison with your board-dried sheets to get an idea of sheet shrinkage and character differences.

Additional Notes This space is for recording anything unusual that you may have noticed during preparation. Also, use it to remind yourself whether you added water or more alkali solution during a long cook or perhaps changed the cook solution completely to compensate for evaporation. Include a notation if you feel you underbeat or overbeat the fiber and if you refrigerated or froze the fiber between cooking and beating. (Freezing a fiber sometimes has the effect of lightening its color. The defrosting process breaks down the fiber so that it is more susceptible to cooking.) Reminders of ways to retest, and so on, are best recorded here.

Paper Results The headings in this section of the test record sheet are self-explanatory. I do not have laboratory testing equipment so my notes on paper strength are very general and involve observing the ease with which a paper tears, its wet-web and wet strengths, and its ability to stand repeated folding without coming apart. I run a rough absorbency test by drawing on the paper with a fully loaded brush of sumi ink, to see if the ink spreads or not and if the paper cockles in the brushed areas. The paper appearance category is used to record type of surface (e.g., shiny, matte, dense, or porous), color, and crispness or softness. I also keep a notebook of samples, correlated by number to the test data, which usually includes both thick and thin versions of the paper.

Light-aging This heading is included in response to a suggestion by Betty Fiske, who works in the paper conservation department at the Metropolitan Museum of Art in New York. A light test is important because it will reveal whether the new paper discolors or becomes brittle on exposure to sunlight. To conduct this test, cut two samples of at least 6 by 6 centimeters (2½ by 2½ inches) from the same sheet. Tape one in a window where it will be exposed regularly to sunlight, and store the other in a drawer in an acid-free glassine envelope. Check for color and handling differences at monthly intervals. It is probably not necessary to extend the test beyond

3 months. (Note that this procedure is a simplified, inexpensive version of more accurate reproducible measurements normally made in the industry with standardized testing equipment and methods.)

Fiber Charts

This section consists of data, in chart form, on some of the fibers I have tested to date. The charts are condensations of data collected on record sheets as described above.

The most promising fibers I have tested so far for *nagashi-zuki* are white mulberry, slippery elm, yucca, dogbane, and milkweed. Milk-fermented flax also produces good results. It is included in the charts even though I have never actually harvested flax. I have only used line flax as sold for spinning and weaving purposes.

The charts on tested fibers included here are divided into four groups: (1) highly successful fibers, (2) moderately successful fibers that might be better for *tame-zuki* or that might simply require different preparation techniques to qualify for *nagashi-zuki,* (3) fibers that do not yield strong papers but have decorative or other unusual characteristics, and (4) totally unpromising fibers (one of these is included to familiarize the reader with the characteristics judged as "undesirable"). Not all of the fibers I have tested are included here.

When reading the charts, note that washing is not mentioned unless it is done after beating. It should be assumed that the fiber is always washed after cooking until it has the same pH as the water source or until it rinses clear, or both, depending on what is most relevant to the fiber type.

Beating is described as "by hand," "by stamper," or "by hollander." Stamping time can be assumed to be about the same as that which would be required for hand beating, give or take 15 minutes. Except where the roll was never brought near the bed, hollander beating adjustments are not described because my hollander is a very old, noncalibrated Valley model, and all my adjustments would be meaningless to anyone with a different machine. Beating was judged complete in all cases when a small amount of fiber shaken in a jar of clear water dispersed evenly.

"Standard slow press" means the post was left overnight to drain (8 hours minimum) and then pressed very slowly by adding weights over an 8-hour period to a maximum of 300 grams per square centimeter (4 pounds per square inch) calculated according to the surface area of the paper being pressed, not the press bed. Initially, every hour just enough weight was added to make the drips of water from the post recommence; then, after the post lost half its thickness, weight was added every half hour. "Hydraulic press, fast" refers to use of a 20-ton hydraulic press that exerts a full bed pressure of 3.2 kilograms per square centimeter (44 pounds per square inch). Hydraulic pressing was always performed with wool blankets faced with muslin for 5 minutes or less. Fast hydraulic pressing allows formation of test sheets in quantities too small for a post while still obtaining some indication of potential parting behavior.

My description of qualities such as strength, absorbency, and appearance is admittedly vague. I am not a paper chemist nor do I have access to a laboratory and the equipment required for TAPPI standard testing. Thus, my comments are made from the point of view of an artist familiar with many papers, including those made from kozo, gampi, and mitsumata. My criticism of new fibers is made relative to my knowledge of Japanese fibers.

"Yield" refers to the total amount of dry fiber left after processing and sheet forming relative to the total amount of dry fiber weighed after removal from the plant. Where the reference is only to the total amount of paper produced, there is a note to that effect. This has not been done in any standardized fashion and is only included where it was measured to give an idea of the practicality of the fiber source.

The reader interested in other alternative plant fibers should be sure to refer to Lillian Bell's recent compilation noted in the bibliography. Finally, immediately following, I have included a list of failures and moderately successful fibers both for comparison purposes and to save the reader time in testing. For the same reason, fibers that I have not yet tested but believe to be particularly promising are also listed below.

Failures and Moderately Successful Fibers The following material is a condensation of information gleaned from my tests on fibers that are not represented in the charts below.

Tree and woody vine bast tests included shining sumac, silver maple, scotch pine, American basswood, tulip poplar, Carolina poplar, Russian olive, shagbark hickory, and bittersweet. Of these, only the basswood and the bittersweet yielded good paper and only by *tame-zuki* methods. Basswood inner bark is very thick and fibrous, although quite coarse. Unfortunately, it dyes itself brown, and the bark contains a gelatinous resin that complicates processing. Also, the black bark is not easily separated from the inner bark. I have since tried fermenting this bark in water for several months. Although this seems to solve the problems of the resin and the black bark, I am not sure of the durability of the resulting fiber. Bittersweet, when steamed, peels easily, and the black bark separates easily from the white. The fiber is very fine and strong but does not respond to *nagashi-zuki* methods. However, when bittersweet is processed in a hollander beater, a pulp of low freeness results, which produces a crisp, high-shrinkage, grayish beige paper that resembles sheets made from unbleached linen. It may be that bittersweet would respond to milk fermentation as does flax, and thereby become useful for *nagashi-zuki.*

The other barks mentioned above either yielded a mealy, short-fibered paper, became wiry or cellophane-like during cooking, or required extensive processing (e.g., pine) not justified by the quality of the resulting paper.

Among the herbaceous basts, I have tried several types of goldenrod, hollyhock, and true hemp. Goldenrod fibers are strong but become like wiry cellophane when cooked, a sure sign that they will beat poorly and yield short-fibered, brittle paper.

Hollyhock is not as fibrous nor is its fiber as fine and supple as okra, its near relative. True hemp processes easily and makes excellent paper but is not readily and legally obtainable. This is regrettable since recent research in China indicates that it was the first fiber used to make paper.

Leaf fibers usually appear more promising than they actually prove to be. Although most iris leaves are quite fibrous, they still do not compete favorably with yucca in terms of fiber yield, amenability to *nagashi-zuki* methods, color, or abundance for harvest. Lily-of-the-valley leaves, picked dry, give a brown, crisp, slightly shiny paper if cooked with lye and then beaten and formed *tame-zuki* style, but the fiber yield is very low. Phragmites, a common and abundant reed, has leaves which would seem to have very strong fiber but cook to yield only small quantities of short fibers of a rather bilious green color.

As I have mentioned before, stem structural fibers are normally not worth the trouble of processing due to the absence of distinctive characteristics of strength or appearance in the finished sheets. I have tried bagasse (the waste from sugar-cane processing) and chicory. Both papers had to be made *tame-zuki* style and resembled brown wrapping paper.

Of course, the above condensation of negative results is only negative if the goal is a supple, translucent sheet of book-quality paper. For artists needing bulk pulp for massing into a slab or onto a sculpture armature, such fibers might serve very well, particularly if their visual characteristics answer the needs of the user.

Plants with Potential An overwhelming number of plant sources are yet to be tried. Some, I am sure, will yield better results than any listed in my charts. I offer a few promising plants here as a guide for the fiber hunter.

WOODY BAST

1. Leatherwood (*Dirca palustris*) and mezereon (*Daphne mezereum*), both of the same family as gampi, are reputed to have very-long-fibered, tough bark. According to the Petersen *Field Guide to Trees and Shrubs,* the Indians used the inner bark of *Dirca palustris* for bowstrings and fish lines.
2. Eastern burning bush (*Euonymus atropurpureus* Jacq.) and spindle tree (*Euonymus europaeus*) are of the same family as winged euonymus (*Euonymus alatus*), which I have tested, and perhaps they are stronger and longer-fibered. I base this on the fact that they are of the same family as the bittersweet vine (*Celastrus scandens* L.), which does yield good fiber. Dard Hunter mentions the spindle tree as having been tried by Leorier Delisle, director of the Langlee Paper Mill, in 1786.[22]
3. Cork elm, also called winged elm (*Ulmus alata* Michx.), might yield good fiber since elms tend to be good fiber sources. In the *Audubon Society Field Guide to North American Trees: Eastern Region,* the inner bark of cork elm is described as having been used in the eighteenth and nineteenth centuries to make rope to fasten cotton-bale covers.

4. Red mulberry (*Morus rubra* L.) and Osage orange (*Maclura pomifera* [Raf.] Schneid) are close relatives of white mulberry. Red mulberry inner bark, according to the *Audubon Society Field Guide to North American Trees: Eastern Region,* was used by the Choctaw Indians to weave cloaks. The same guide describes the Osage orange as having root bark that yields a yellow dye.

HERBACEOUS BAST

1. Kudzu (*Pueraria thinbergiana*) grows "flagrantly" in the U.S. South. It is used for textile fiber in Japan, the plant's native habitat. According to Shimura Asao's sample book, *U.S. Papermakers '78,* Bob Tauber, now director of the Logan Elm Press at Ohio University, cooks the kudzu vine with lye and beats it with a hollander for *tame-zuki* paper. Tauber uses the whole vine, and his paper is relatively soft and yellow white with a matte surface. Paper made from only the bast might be entirely different.

2. Velvet leaf, also known as butterprint (*Abutilon theophrasti* Medic.) grows throughout the United States except in a large area along the northern boundary. It has been described as a convenient "emergency thong material,"[23] which would seem to indicate that its bast may be serviceable for paper as well.

GRASSES, STEM-STRUCTURAL FIBERS Two other plants are mentioned in Dard Hunter's "Chronology of paper and allied subjects." They may be good fiber sources.

1. Life-everlasting plant, also called cudweed (*Gifola germanica* [L.]), was apparently successfully used for paper in New England in 1862.[24] It's a member of Compositae, the thistle family.

2. Tule (*Scirpus lacustris* and *Scirpus tatora*), which is said to grow abundantly in California, was judged in 1850, by "experienced manufacturers," to have great potential for papermaking.[25] This plant is a type of rush.[26]

I. HIGHLY SUCCESSFUL FIBERS

White mulberry (*Morus alba* L.)	
Fiber type	bast, tree
When and how to harvest	November, after the leaves fall from the tree—at this time the black bark is easiest to remove. Cut branches or saplings. Steam to peel.
Precook preparation	Soak bark until black bark slips off—about 4 days. Leave as green bark and dry to weigh, or scrape to

white bark and dry. Presoak at least 24 hrs before cooking, or the bark may be cooked immediately without drying.

Cook method 13 g soda ash to 1 l water (½ oz to 1 qt) for 2–3 hrs depending on branch diameter. Let stand overnight after cooking.

Fermentation method

Beating method By hand, 30 min. Be careful not to beat too long. A very sticky, low-freeness pulp can otherwise result, causing severe parting and board-drying problems, although this can be remedied by washing the pulp after beating.

Forming method *Nagashi-zuki*

Press method Standard slow press

Drying Board

Forming and parting qualities Excellent

Strength Tear, wet, and fold strengths comparable to kozo papers

Absorbency Moderate

Appearance Pale greenish white, slight luster, soft but tending to slight crispness, tight but not dense surface.

Yield 36.6% for branches very small in diameter—i.e., 3–5 mm (¼″–3⁄16″)

Comments Paper will be whiter and warmer in tone if bark is scraped white. Thicker branches will give higher yield. A good source because it grows everywhere, like a weed. Paper quality varies with the growing environment of the tree. I have obtained different results from bark of trees found in the same large geographic area but different growing sites. Particular care must be taken not to overcook or overbeat this bark. Also, avoid using branches over 2.5 cm (1″) in diameter—the bark begins to get woody and the paper is not as good. The Osage orange tree (*Maclura pomifera* [Raf.] Schneid) is a close relative of the white mulberry and should be tried for papermaking, as its root bark purportedly yields a yellow dye and might successfully be added to the branch or sapling bark to make yellow paper.

American elm (*Ulmus americana* L.), **slippery elm** (*Ulmus rubra* Muhl.)	
Fiber type	bast, tree
When and how to harvest	May through mid-November. Cut 1–2.5 cm (3/8″–1″) branches. If picked after August 1, steam to peel.
Precook preparation	Scrape black bark and then green bark immediately after picking. If first dried, green bark can be removed after soaking bark for 1 hr. Presoak overnight before cooking. Slippery elm requires several soakings to remove the slippery gel it exudes. If dry, it requires 5 days of soaking.
Cook method	15 g soda ash to 1 l water (1/2 oz to 1 qt) for 3 hrs. If bark not steamed, cook takes longer. For slippery elm destined for hollander beating: 12.5 g soda ash to 1 l water (1/2 oz to 1 qt) for 1 1/2 hrs. Let stand 24 hrs before washing.
Fermentation method	
Beating method	By stamper, 1 hr 24 min. For slippery elm: by hollander, 1 hr 20 min. Wash slippery elm fiber briefly after beating.
Forming method	*Nagashi-zuki.* Have tested with both Siberian-elm formation aid and synthetic *tororo-aoi.*

Press method	Standard slow press
Drying	Board in shade
Forming and parting qualities	Good. Wet-web strength at parting not as great as mulberry, but this could be due to my lack of experience in beating this fiber.
Strength	Good, much like a mitsumata paper
Absorbency	Like kozo
Appearance	For American elm: medium pink-brown color, slightly crisp, tight, smooth surface. For slippery elm: if stamped, yellow-pink tan color, soft surface; if hollander beaten, light dusty-rose color, slight luster, resembles mitsumata.
Yield	45%
Comments	This fiber dyes itself. Remove green bark unless you want a very dark paper. The color is not light-fast; it lightens on exposure to sunlight. Be careful to stamp this fiber sufficiently; otherwise, the coarseness of the long fibers causes parting problems. I remedied this by beating the slippery elm in the hollander and washing it after beating and before forming. Slippery elm bark has a pleasant fragrance that, unfortunately, does not persist in the paper. Some health-food stores carry slippery elm white bark as a sore-throat remedy. Slippery elm is not as rare nor as disease-decimated as American elm.

Milkweed (*Asclepias siriaca*)

Fiber type	bast, herbaceous (perennial)
When and how to harvest	Best if picked after pods have fully formed but before they dry and open—late August through September. Cut stalks; remove leaves by cutting. Peel no sooner than 30 min and no later than 3 hrs after cutting.

Otherwise, steam to peel. Wipe any black residue from stems before peeling, for it will contaminate the eventual pulp. This black residue is produced by aphids drinking the sap of the milkweed, which turns black on exposure to air.

Precook preparation

Do not allow peeled bast to dry. Immerse immediately in water. Soak overnight before cooking. If dark areas are present, scrape or cut away because they will cause discoloration in final paper. Additional precook preparation (optional): presoak 1 to 4 weeks in 40–50 g (about 1½–2 oz) caustic soda to 1 l (1 qt) of water until green material begins to separate from white bast. Rinse thoroughly.

Cook method

Caustic soda soak described above; then cook 2–3 hrs in solution of 50 g lime to 1 l water (about 2 oz to 1 qt). OR without caustic soda soak, cook 1½–2 hrs in solution of 50 g caustic soda to 1 l water, and let stand 12 hrs. Rinse and then soak in solution of 20 g lime to 1 l water (¾ oz to 1 qt) for 1–12 hrs.

Fermentation method

Soak in water to cover at an ambient temperature of 21° C (70° F) or higher for 2–6 weeks or until fiber tests for hand beating. May be accelerated by soaking in a solution concentration of 60 ml milk to 1 l water (2 oz to 1 qt). Stir once a day.

Beating method

If cooked: by stamper, 6–7 hrs, with water added as the fiber compacts and with thorough rinsing and soaking (overnight) for every 2 hrs of beating. May also be hollander beaten to make *tame-zuki* paper similar to fine flax paper. If fresh fiber is fermented: by stamper, 6 hrs. De-knot this pulp in a hollander for 25 min. Wash pulp before forming. If dried fiber is fermented: by hand or stamper, 30 min to 1½ hrs.

Forming method

Nagashi-zuki, with natural or synthetic formation aid (soak fiber in vat overnight before adding formation aid and starting to form). OR *tame-zuki,* with synthetic formation aid.

Press method	For *nagashi-zuki,* standard slow press. OR hydraulic press, fast, with felts.
Drying	Board, in shade first then in sun. OR loft- or press-dried.
Forming and parting qualities	Excellent for both *nagashi-zuki* and *tame-zuki.* Must be stamped (as described above) or fermented and stamped for *nagashi-zuki.* Otherwise, pulp is not free enough and parting problems occur.
Strength	Excellent wet-web and wet strengths. Moderate tear and fold strengths in *nagashi-zuki* paper. Excellent tear and fold strengths in *tame-zuki* paper.
Absorbency	*Nagashi-zuki:* moderately absorbent. *Tame-zuki:* non-absorbent; behaves like a strongly sized sheet.
Appearance	Varies according to whether fiber was treated while green, whether cooked or fermented, whether beaten and formed in *nagashi-zuki* or *tame-zuki* style. If fresh fiber, cooked, *nagashi-zuki* stamping and forming: white, soft, slight sheen to paper. If dry fiber, fermented, *nagashi-zuki* stamping and forming: tan with dark flecks, soft, dull surface. If fresh fiber, fermented, *nagashi-zuki* stamping and forming: greenish white, moderately dense surface, slightly crisp. If fresh fiber, cooked, *tame-zuki* beating and forming: white, crisp, dense surface.
Yield	44% of harvested bast fiber if cooked green
Comments	A "cold" cook of this fiber may be done by soaking it in the caustic soda concentration for precook preparation described above until all green matter rinses away. This will take 2–8 weeks (or longer if the environment is cooler than 18° C, or 65° F). Once this cold cook or one of the hot cooks mentioned above has been done, the fiber may be dried, after thorough rinsing, and stored as one would store flax or sisal rope. This is a very strong, very white, and fine fiber.

It is easy to harvest and naturally abundant. The seed fiber of milkweed is not as strong as the bast but may be used to make paper. Untreated milkweed "silk" may be added to any pulp for decorative effects or the fiber may be beaten in a hollander. This yields an ivory-colored, short-fibered, crisp paper with a soft sheen. To harvest seed fiber, it is best to pick the pods when large and mature but still green and closed. It is easier to remove the seeds from the bundle of "silk" at this point and easier to handle the fiber without having it fly in every direction. This paper shrinks 35% from its fresh-formed area if prepared and formed *tame-zuki*-style and loft-dried.

	Yucca (*Yucca filamentosa*)
Fiber type	leaf
When and how to harvest	This is an evergreen, and any season seems fine for harvesting. Only mature leaves should be cut. If white paper is desired, cut only green leaves. Dead, dried leaves around base of plant may be cut and used separately for brown paper.
Precook preparation	If green: just wash. If dried: wash and presoak 12 hrs. Cut points off all leaves to avoid dark flecks in the final pulp.
Cook method	23–27 g caustic soda (NaOH) to 1 l water (about ¾–1 oz to 1 qt) depending on leaf toughness. Cook 2–4 hrs depending on leaf toughness.
Fermentation method	
Beating method	By hand, 30 min to 1½ hrs depending on cook and quality of paper desired. By hollander, 2½ hours if crisper paper desired.
Forming method	*Nagashi-zuki*, with synthetic or natural *tororo-aoi*

Press method	Standard slow press
Drying	Board
Forming and parting qualities	Very good
Strength	Moderate tear, wet, and fold strengths. Varies with cooking and beating strategy and whether leaf is dry or green.
Absorbency	If green leaf: moderately to very absorbent. If dry leaf: moderately to slightly absorbent.
Appearance	If green leaf: a cool cream color, no flecks, smooth semi-matte surface, soft. If dry leaf: light warm brown, with gold flecks, smooth, semi-matte surface, harder than green-leaf paper.
Yield	There is a high volume of fiber in the leaf, but I have never performed a weight test with this.
Comments	Very easy to harvest. Yucca grows everywhere in the U.S. if you just look for it. The U.S. government used it to make paper sacks in World War II. Combined with one-third muslin or ramie, it makes a very beautiful and strong paper that is crisper than pure yucca paper.

Flax (*Linum usitatissimum*)

Fiber type	bast, herbaceous (annual)
When and how to harvest	Entries below refer to line flax, unbleached, such as may be purchased at a good weaving supply store.
Precook preparation	Cut into pieces 7.5–15 cm (3″–6″) long. Wash by agitating in water and draining several times. Soak overnight (up to 24 hrs) in clean water.
Cook method	Boil in plain water 2 hrs, or in solution of 20 g lime

to 1 l water (about 3/4 oz to 1 qt) 2 hrs. This is a prefermentation preparation.

Fermentation method — Cover wet fiber with a solution of 250 ml milk to 5 l water (8 oz to 5 qt). Keep at ambient temperature of 24°–35° C (75°–95° F), stirring once daily, till fiber tests for hand beating. After washing, soak in solution of 7.8 g lime to 2 l water (1/4 oz to 2 qt) overnight (up to 24 hrs). Rinse well.

Beating method — By stamper, 2 1/2 hrs followed by hollander for 30–45 min. Rinse fiber twice (draining each time) before adding to vat.

Forming method — *Nagashi-zuki,* synthetic formation aid

Press method — Standard slow

Drying — Board and loft

Forming and parting qualities — Excellent

Strength — Very good wet-web strength. Good tear and fold strengths if not made too thin.

Absorbency — Like a kozo paper

Appearance — Cool, slightly grayish off-white. Surface like a medium-weight, slightly coarse kozo paper. Color varies with the type of flax.

Yield

Comments — Fermentation and beating strategies still need refining. Keep a gauze or screen cover over the fermentation bucket to keep flies from depositing their eggs. Keep away from light. More extensive washing before and after beating could yield a whiter paper. This paper shrinks 18.26% from board- to loft-dried dimensions. Loft-dried sheet is stronger and has more distinctive character than the board-dried sheet. Looks a bit like old European handmade paper.

II. Moderately Successful Fibers

	Okra (*Hibiscus esculentus*)
Fiber type	bast, herbaceous (annual)
When and how to harvest	Late September to early October, after pods have formed. Cut off leaves and roots. Steam to peel. Bast of both stalk and petiole may be used.
Precook preparation	Scrape away outer bark. If not to be cooked immediately, remove outer bark by putting to soak in water till mold forms and green material washes away easily (1 month) or in milk water (1:10 by volume), which takes only 2 weeks. This white bark may be dried and stored after washing or cooked or fermented immediately.
Cook method	15 g soda ash to 1 l water (½ oz to 1 qt) for 2 hrs or 15 g lime to 1 l water (½ oz to 1 qt) for 9 hrs.
Fermentation method	A milk-water fermentation instead of cooking may be used to further soften the fiber for beating as well as for initial cleaning away of green material. Takes about 2 weeks for cleaning and 1 month for softening.
Beating method	By stamper, 1 hr.
Forming method	*Nagashi-zuki*, with synthetic *tororo-aoi*
Press method	Standard slow press and hydraulic press
Drying	Board
Forming and parting qualities	Good forming properties. Some, but not insurmountable, problems with parting due to what seems to be the coarse or rough nature of the individual okra fibers.
Strength	Moderate wet-web strength. Hydraulic-pressed sheets had better wet-web strength and were crisper after drying. Moderate tear and fold strengths.

Absorbency	Moderate to low
Appearance	Pale yellowish cream color, slight crispness, coarse fibers clearly evident.
Yield	
Comments	Cooking turns the cool white glossy fiber dull and yellow. Fermentation does not alter the color, but the sheets will yellow later on exposure to light. It could be that fermentation is the better way to prepare this fiber. Hollander beating should be tried as well. The roots yield a formation aid comparable to *tororo-aoi*. The petiole bast is finer than the main stalk bast and yields crisper, paler paper with some sheen.

Dogbane, Indian hemp (*Apocynum cannabinum*)

Fiber type	bast, herbaceous (perennial)
When and how to harvest	Mid-July through September. September preferable to avoid milky sap, but plant is not easily peeled on location in September.
Precook preparation	Peel stems on location if harvesting while it is flowering; otherwise, steam to peel. To avoid coloring pale fiber, pick while flowering, peel without steaming, and scrape away outer "bark." Otherwise, this outer bark acts as a dye during steaming and/or cooking.
Cook method	20 g Na_2CO_3 to 1 l water (about ¾ oz to 1 qt) for 11 hrs 45 min. OR, for a paler fiber, 20 g NaOH to 1 l water for 2 hrs.
Fermentation method	In plain water for 3 months. Rinse and soak in lime solution, pH 11, overnight. Rinse and cook as above for soda ash.
Beating method	Proved impossible to beat by hand or stamper if

cooked, so beat by hollander. If fermented and then cooked: by stamper, 2 hrs to crush outer bark, which is then removed by washing. Then beat by hollander 2 hrs. Wash fiber before forming.

Forming method

If cooked: *tame-zuki*. If fermented and then cooked: *nagashi-zuki*.

Press method

If cooked: hydraulic, fast. If fermented: standard slow.

Drying

If cooked: board, loft, and press drying. If fermented and cooked: board drying.

Forming and parting qualities

If cooked: excellent *tame-zuki* qualities; low freeness not good for *nagashi-zuki*. If fermented and then cooked: picked at *su*, and caused some parting problems. Both problems could be remedied by more washing after beating.

Strength

If cooked: excellent wet-web and wet strengths, excellent fold and good tear strengths. If fermented and then cooked: good wet-web and wet strengths.

Absorbency

If cooked: nonabsorbent. If fermented and cooked: very absorbent.

Appearance

If cooked: warm light tan with longer cream white and golden tan fibers; crisp, dense surface; translucent, like a good flax paper. If fermented and cooked: medium mauve brown; dense, even surface; crisp; translucent when thin.

Yield

Unknown

Comments

Steaming dyes the fiber pinkish brown, a color that derives from the outer bark and also stains the stem core a strong sienna color, which has good lightfastness. If cooking is done without removing the outer bark, the fiber will become tan during cooking (the soda ash acts as a mordant). Loft-dried, hollander-beaten sheets shrink 33% in drying. I fermented some fiber to try to maintain a light color; however, when light-colored fermented fiber (from which all black bark was removed) was added to lime water it turned pink. Care must be taken not to overferment this fiber. I have yet to conduct a successful fermentation but feel sure of eventual success due to the fiber's similarity in behavior to flax.

Japanese wisteria (*Wisteria floribunda* [Willd.] D.C.)	
Fiber type	bast, woody vine
When and how to harvest	May through December. Doesn't ever seem to require steaming. Used vines 13 mm (½") in diameter. It is possible that bast from smaller-diameter vines picked in spring would be easier to cook, but I haven't tried this. Be careful not to peel too much—i.e., to start removing woody stock instead of phloem.
Precook preparation	May be scraped immediately or, if dried, soaked to soften (1–12 hrs) and then scraped. Remove both black and green bark unless you don't mind a dark paper.
Cook method	15 g soda ash to 1 l water (½ oz to 1 qt) plus 15 g caustic soda to 1 l water (1 oz to 1 qt) for 3 hrs. (A 10–18-hr soda ash cook alone might be enough.) Let stand 18 hrs.
Fermentation method	Soak in lye of wood ash to cover for 65 days or until tender. Change lye every 30 days.
Beating method	For cooked: by stamper, 1 hr 45 min.
Forming method	For cooked fiber: *nagashi-zuki,* with synthetic *tororo-aoi.* Note: I rinsed this fiber after stamping because it exuded a purple-brown liquid on stamping. Should be tested again without rinse.
Press method	For cooked fiber: standard slow press
Drying	Board in shade

Forming and parting qualities	Good formation qualities, fair parting due to only fair wet-web strength. This needs more testing.
Strength	Fair fold, tear, and wet-web strengths
Absorbency	For cooked fiber: very absorbent. Takes sumi in an interesting way—stroke edges become feathery according to dispersal along longer fibers.
Appearance	For cooked fiber: pale tan with pinkish tone, no sheen, slightly crisp.
Yield	For cooked fiber: 18%, but this is calculated from black-bark weight, not white-bark weight. Since barks I've weighed to compare black to white usually show up to 50% weight loss in scraping, the yield from white bark is probably much higher.
Comments	This is a good fiber that bears more testing. Close examination of white bark shows it possesses a purplish resin in the interstices of the fibers. This comes out in stamping. Needs test done leaving this in rather than washing it out.

Winged euonymus (*Euonymus alatus*)	
Fiber type	bast, shrub
When and how to harvest	June to mid-November. Peels easily. Steam to peel after August 1 (in New England).
Precook preparation	Black bark flakes away easily; green bark may be scraped away immediately or after soaking 1 hr.
Cook method	7 g soda ash to 1 l water (¼ oz to 1 qt), 20 min to 1 hr. Let stand to cool only.
Fermentation method	
Beating method	By hand, 12–15 min, if cooked. By hollander, 1–3 hrs, if not cooked.

Forming method	If cooked: *nagashi-zuki* onto muslin blankets over wool blankets (due to shortness of fiber); synthetic *tororo-aoi*. If uncooked and hollander beaten: *tame-zuki.*
Press method	Hydraulic press, fast
Drying	Board in shade
Forming and parting qualities	Picks at *su*. If used by itself, better for *tame-zuki*. The woven metal screen and Western couching eliminate the problem of picking.
Strength	Weak due to fiber shortness
Absorbency	Low absorbency. Acts as if it has been sized. If uncooked and hollander-beaten: nonabsorbent.
Appearance	If cooked: cream white with a hint of green; slight sheen with otherwise porous-looking surface. Has a lot of sheen if cooked with a 15 g/1 l (½ oz/1 qt) concentration. A crisp paper. If uncooked: white with slight pinkish cast; very crisp.
Yield	40%–67% depending on whether cooked or not. This is figured on finished paper weight only (i.e., no dried pulp residue weight taken).
Comments	Imparts a distinct sheen to any fiber with which it is mixed. This would seem to be its best use for *nagashi-zuki*. For *tame-zuki*, if the very white bast is hollander beaten without cooking, it makes an excellent dense, white paper with moderate shrinkage and no absorbency.

III. Distinctive Fibers

Siberian elm (*Ulmus pumila* L.)	
Fiber type	bast, tree

When and how to harvest	June through mid-November. Bark still peels easily by end of October without steaming. Black bark falls away easily during peeling.
Precook preparation	Peel away black bark that doesn't fall away with harvesting. Leave green bark. Reserve innermost white bark for formation aid; do *not* use it for paper. Presoak 5 days, drain through a muslin bag to remove formation aid. Put in solution of 30 g lye to 1 l water (½ oz to 1 qt) to cover. Soak again for 5 days. Rinse.
Cook method	20 g caustic soda to 1 l water (¾ oz to 1 qt) for 3 hrs. Let stand overnight.
Fermentation method	
Beating method	By stamper, very wet, 4 hrs 15 min. Wash after 10 min of stamping and soak in solution of 38 g lime to 4 l water (1¼ oz to 1 qt). Rinse and complete stamping. Probably should be tried with hollander.
Forming method	*Nagashi-zuki;* have tested both with its own formation aid and with synthetic *tororo-aoi*. Some delamination problems with its own formation aid, but these may have been due to other factors.
Press method	Standard slow press
Drying	Board in shade
Forming and parting qualities	Good. Fiber is long and permits formation of mending-tissue-thin sheets, which will part, but wet-web strength not as good as kozo or gampi.
Strength	Fair due to extreme softness
Absorbency	Very absorbent
Appearance	Light tan, smooth soft surface. This is very much a consequence of the strong cooking solution. A shorter,

	milder cook and hollander beating would probably yield very different qualities.
Yield	10%–15% figured by finished paper weight only
Comments	Might give better yield and be easier to cook if picked in fall and steamed. Although nice color, low yield makes difficult processing not worth it. Gives a strong formation aid, which should be tested more. The formation aid exuded by the bark is darker and purplish in the fall but amber-colored in the early summer. Kim Yon Yong, a papermaker in Korea, informs me that Siberian elm bark is used as a formation aid there when *tororo-aoi* is not available or when paper is being made which need not be pure white. Formation aid is made by soaking the innermost white bark in water to cover (although the complete bark may be soaked, it will always yield a darker formation aid). The viscous product is strained through a moist muslin bag before using. It does not lose its effectiveness in warm weather as rapidly as does *tororo-aoi,* but it is also not as clear in color. Bark may be resoaked to produce more formation aid. The bark may be dried for storage; up to a year and a half after harvesting it will yield formation aid when soaked.

	Dwarf Cavendish banana (*Musa cavendishii*)
Fiber type	petiole
When and how to harvest	(Plant was obtained from an experimental greenhouse.) Cut plant after fruit ripens. Cut off leaves. Disassemble stalk layers (the petiole). Separate each layer into outside long fibers and inside fleshy material, and hang to dry or cook immediately. Each side is cooked separately because the fiber yield is different as is the paper produced.
Precook preparation	If dried: presoak 12 hrs. I have not cooked this yet from the dried bast, only from fresh. Fresh does not

need presoak. From here, "A" is inner part of petiole, including majority of fleshy structure of petiole, and "B" is outer part of petiole, mostly long, fine fibers and very little fleshy material.

Cook method

A. 10 g caustic soda to 1.6 l water (3/8 oz to 1.6 qt). Let stand 9 hrs.
B. 10 g caustic soda to 1 l water (3/8 oz to 1 qt). Let stand 1–2 weeks.

Fermentation method

Beating method

A. By hollander, 3 hrs. B. By hollander, 1 hr 20 min. Both probably hand-beatable with the right cooking or fermenting strategy.

Forming method

A and B. *Nagashi-zuki,* synthetic *tororo-aoi.* Couched onto cotton blankets over wool blankets.

Press method

A and B. Hydraulic press, fast.

Drying

A. Board, loft-dried in shade. B. Board in shade.

Forming and parting qualities

A. Due to large amount of sediment still left from fleshy material, despite washing, this fiber picks at *su* and back of *su* must be flooded with water to make couching possible. No wet-web strength. Therefore, not really good for *nagashi-zuki.*
B. Good forming qualities, good wet-web strength, will probably part well.

Strength

A. Poor tear strength, moderate wet strength due to non-absorbency rather than fiber length, moderate fold strength.
B. Good fold and wet strengths, moderate tear strength.

Absorbency

A. Nonabsorbent, behaves as if strongly sized.
B. Low absorbency, behaves as if moderately sized.

Appearance

A. A dark cool brown, moderate luster, very crisp and translucent where thin, very smooth.

	B. Light creamy pink-brown, tight, slightly lustrous surface, moderately crisp, opaque.
Yield	A and B. Unknown (due to starting with undried material).
Comments	A. Despite forming difficulties, this is a beautiful paper. The sediment settles in the laid lines and is apparent when paper is held to light. Also makes a handsome paper mixed with B since the light fibers float separately from the dark ones. Dark color. Has good lightfastness. B. Comparable to abaca (*Musa textilis*), but the fibers are much finer. Both A and B deserve a great deal more testing.

	Siberian iris (*Iris sibirica*)
Fiber type	bast, herbaceous (perennial)
When and how to harvest	Cut stalks after blooms die. Peel immediately.
Precook preparation	Presoak in water, 10 hrs.
Cook method	
Fermentation method	Soak 1 month in solution of 50 g lime to 1 l water (½ oz to 1 qt) to cover
Beating method	By hand, 20 min.
Forming method	*Nagashi-zuki,* synthetic *tororo-aoi.* Should have beaten sample longer—disparity between fine particles and very long fibers caused formation problems.
Press method	Formed on blankets and hydraulic pressed, fast
Drying	Loft-dried on blankets due to sheet fragility

Forming and parting qualities	Poor but might have improved if fiber were beaten an hour. Perhaps would be good *tame-zuki* paper if beaten in hollander.
Strength	Poor tear and fold strengths
Absorbency	Nonabsorbent, as if pre-sized
Appearance	Pale greenish yellow, lustrous, crisp, translucent. Coarse shiny long fibers in a translucent, very-short-fibered matrix.
Yield	Low
Comments	Very impractical due to low yield and laborious harvesting. However, the unusual appearance of the paper does seem to recommend it for art uses.

IV. Unsuccessful Fibers

Black willow (*Salix nigra* Marsh.)	
Fiber type	bast, tree
When and how to harvest	June through mid-November. Peels easily. Steam to peel after August 1.
Precook preparation	Scrape to white bark. Presoak overnight before cook.
Cook method	Have tried both standard soda ash solution and 30 g caustic soda to 1 l water (3/4 oz to 1 qt). Both 2–6 hrs.
Fermentation method	
Beating method	By hand, 40 min. Have not tried hollander beating.
Forming method	*Nagashi-zuki,* synthetic *tororo-aoi.* Couched onto muslin blankets over wool blankets due to coarseness of fiber.

Press method	Hydraulic press, fast
Drying	Board in shade
Forming and parting qualities	Fair. Disperses evenly but fiber is coarse (ribbonlike). Did not try standard *nagashi-zuki* post because in all cases fiber obviously formed too rough a sheet to allow for parting.
Strength	Poor in every category
Absorbency	Moderate
Appearance	Medium brown, matte, porous, coarse-fibered surface. If bleached, cream yellow.
Yield	
Comments	The same results were obtained with weeping willow (*Salix babylonica* L.) and pussy willow (*Salix discolor* Muhl.). Does not make a good *nagashi-zuki* paper. Have not tried beating with hollander and *tame-zuki* forming. This fiber does combine well with other fibers as a decorative element. *Salix nigra*, particularly if used as black bark, yields a pleasing red-brown dye that colors whatever it is added to. Dye is not lightfast.

APPENDIX TWO

Supplier List

Fibers

ITEM	SUPPLIER
Kozo, mitsumata, gampi, and abaca. Abaca, sisal, and flax pulps. Cotton rag half-stuff, bleached and unbleached cotton rag, cotton linters, ramie, flax tow, and Belgian line flax. Any quantity.	Lee S. McDonald Fine Hand Papermaking Equipment 523 Medford Street Charlestown, MA 02129 U.S.A.
Kozo and mitsumata. Bleached and unbleached abaca, sisal, and Indian hemp pulps. Any quantity.	Carriage House Handmade Papers 8 Evans Road Brookline, MA 02146 U.S.A.
Kozo, mitsumata, and gampi. Usually small or medium quantities.	Shimura Asao Cannabis Press 431 Fukuhara, Kasama-shi Ibaraki-ken 309–15 Japan
Abaca, sisal, and other pulps, dry or fully prepared (concentrated and wet).	Twinrocker Handmade Paper Brookston, IN 47923 U.S.A.

Tools, Equipment, and Other Supplies

ITEM	SUPPLIER
Simple *nagashi-zuki* moulds and imported Korean *su*. Placemats, *sha* material, splint stock, and threads for making *su*. Mesh material for drain baskets, beating sticks, sheet plastic, wheat starch, synthetic formation aids,	Lee S. McDonald Fine Hand Papermaking Equipment 523 Medford Street Charlestown, MA 02129 U.S.A.

pH test strips, pigments, retention aids, and loading agents. Western moulds, felts, non-woven fabric, gelatin, and alum. Stampers and other custom equipment.	
Japanese moulds and *su,* drying brushes, and other special requests from Japan.	Shimura Asao Cannabis Press 431 Fukuhara, Kasama-shi Ibaraki-ken 309–15 Japan Richard Flavin Jion Zenji 218 Kibe, Ogawamachi Hiki-gun, Saitama-ken 355–03 Japan
Orvis fly-tying bobbins	Orvis Manchester, VT 05254 U.S.A.
Tororo-aoi seeds. (Order: "*Abelmoschus manihot,* Golden Bowl No. 0992.")	George S. Park Bros. Greenwood, SC 29647 U.S.A.
Custom presses, beaters, and other specialized hand papermaking equipment.	Twinrocker Equipment Corporation Brookston, IN 47923 U.S.A.
Western moulds	Edwin Amies Hayle Mill Maidstone, Kent ME15 6XQ U.K. Cooper-Taylor Moulds 18414 Lynton Road Cleveland, OH 44122 U.S.A. Lee S. McDonald Fine Hand Papermaking Equipment 523 Medford Street Charlestown, MA 02129 U.S.A.
Beaters, used	James F. Gormely 7072 Spier Falls Road Gansevoort, NY 12831 U.S.A.
Beaters, new	Voith, Inc. P.O. Box 2337 Appleton, WI 54911 U.S.A.

	Twinrocker Equipment Corporation Brookston, IN 47923 U.S.A.
Internal size, retention aids, pigments, gelatin, books, and other supplies	Twinrocker Handmade Paper Brookston, IN 47923 U.S.A.
Internal size and retention aids	Carriage House Handmade Papers 8 Evans Road Brookline, MA 02146 U.S.A.
Live-plant importing permit applications (U.S.A.)	United States Department of Agriculture Federal Building Hyattsville, MD 20782 U.S.A.
Laboratory flat diaphragm screens	Voith, Inc. P.O. Box 2337 Appleton, WI 54911 U.S.A.

APPENDIX THREE

Metric Conversion Chart

Throughout this book the metric system is used for all measurements. Though new to many, once used in practice the metric system will soon become familiar; you will grow to appreciate its simplicity and international appeal. Do not be disheartened by the initial confusion encountered in the transitions between the two systems. In the end, learning the metric approach is very much worth the effort.

Approximate Conversions to Metric Measures

When You Know	Multiply by	To Find
	LENGTH	
inches (in)	2.5	centimeters (cm)
feet (ft)	30	centimeters (cm)
yards (yd)	0.9	meters (m)
miles (mi)	1.6	kilometers (km)
	AREA	
square inches (in^2)	6.5	square centimeters (cm^2)
square feet (ft^2)	0.09	square meters (m^2)
square yards (yd^2)	0.8	square meters (m^2)
	MASS (weight)	
ounces (oz)	28	grams (g)
pounds (lb)	0.45	kilograms (kg)
pounds (lb)	454	grams (g)
	VOLUME	
fluid ounces (fl oz)	30	milliliters (ml)
quarts (qt)	0.95	liters (l)
gallons (gal)	3.8	liters (l)

When You Know	Multiply by	To Find
	TEMPERATURE (exact)	
degrees Fahrenheit (° F)	(5/9 after subtracting 32)	degrees Celsius (° C)

Approximate Conversions from Metric Measures

When You Know	Multiply by	To Find
	LENGTH	
millimeters (mm)	0.04	inches (in)
centimeters (cm)	0.4	inches (in)
meters (m)	3.3	feet (ft)
kilometers (km)	0.6	miles (mi)
	AREA	
square centimeters (cm^2)	0.16	square inches (in^2)
square meters (m^2)	1.2	square yards (yd^2)
square meters (m^2)	10.9	square feet (ft^2)
	MASS (weight)	
grams (g)	0.035	ounces (oz)
kilograms (kg)	2.2	pounds (lb)
	VOLUME	
milliliters (ml)	0.03	fluid ounces (fl oz)
liters (l)	2.1	pints (pt)
liters (l)	1.06	quarts (qt)
liters (l)	0.26	gallons (gal)
	TEMPERATURE (exact)	
degrees Celsius (° C)	9/5 (then add 32)	degrees Fahrenheit (° F)

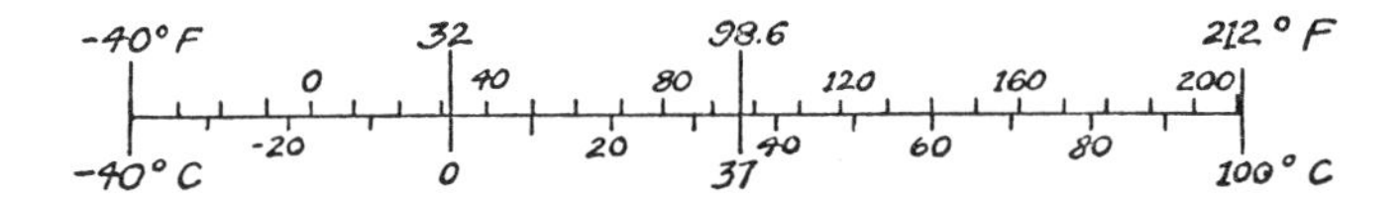

Temperature Scale

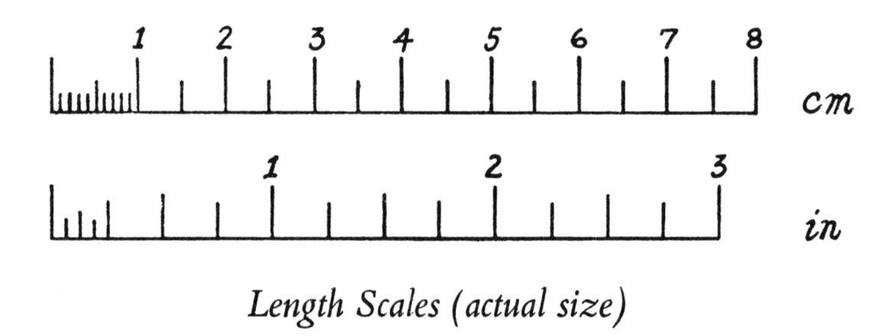

Length Scales (actual size)

Notes

CHAPTER ONE

1. *Shifu* was often made with a warp of cotton or other textile fiber, but sometimes both the warp and weft were of twisted paper threads. Today a few craftspeople continue to make *shifu* on a part-time basis, but the quality is rarely like that of the *shifu* produced in the past.

2. Robert C. Mikesh, *Japan's World War II Balloon Bomb Attacks on North America,* Smithsonian Annals of Flight, no. 9 (Washington, D.C.: Smithsonian Institution Press, 1973): 13.

3. Seishi Machida, Sadanori Nishikori, and Tadashi Ueno, "Studies on the Mucilaginous Solution Concerning Japanese Hand-made Paper (Part III). On the Change of Papermaking Properties of *Tororo-aoi* Mucilage in Preservation," *Bulletin of the Paper Pulp Technical Society* 17, no. 149 (1963): 501–4.

4. In the past most *washi* was not sized. When it was, animal glue with some alum was used as a surface size and applied with a brush to the dry sheet. Very early (pre-1400) sutra papers seem to show a surface size that was glazed or pounded into the paper after application of the size. Rice paste may have been added to the vat before sheet forming of some early Japanese papers to act as a size or to change the paper's texture.

5. A household was usually a family operation with one or two vats, but occasionally it was a large-scale operation with five to twenty or more vats.

6. At this writing, well-made *washi* containing no wood pulp costs from a dollar a sheet in Japan or America up to four or five dollars a sheet (at 200 yen to the dollar). Paper produced by a famous craftsperson may cost fifteen or more dollars a sheet. The price of labor and economics in general have changed so radically in Japan since the end of World War II that *washi* is no longer the inexpensive commodity it once was.

CHAPTER TWO

1. Papermakers in some areas of Japan make a point of not removing this green layer, claiming it makes the finished

paper impervious to insects, more pleasing in color, and crisper. The crispness is probably due to a prevalence of glue-like, water-loving hemicelluloses between the green and white layers. The resistance to insects is thought to be the result of essential oils present in the green layer.

2. The black bark of mitsumata and gampi is removed in much the same way as that of kozo, but since both mitsumata and gampi trees branch eventually into little twigs, they have to be meticulously cleaned down each tiny twig. A kozo tree, on the other hand, tends to take the shape of one long shaft and can be knifed clean in only a few passes. The stripped black and green bark, particularly of kozo, was once used to make crude paper, but it is often discarded today.

CHAPTER THREE

1. B. Hickman, "Japanese Handmade Papers: Materials and Techniques," *Japanese Society of London,* Bulletin 81 (April 1977): 13.

2. Traditionalists in the countryside do not necessarily think in terms of kilograms and liters. I asked one craftsperson, "If you cook forty kilograms of fiber in this cauldron, how many liters of water do you add?" "Water? Oh, up to about here," he said, indicating a stained line below the rim of the cauldron. "Yes," I said, "but how many liters would that be?" "Liters? I really couldn't tell you. My dad always used to fill it up to here, so I do too." His work was consistent and his finished paper of superior quality, and that was, admittedly, the most important thing. Still, I wondered how many liters he had in his pot.

3. Most similar tedious work is performed by women. In fact, up to seventy percent of actual production-level papermaking work, including forming sheets, is done by women in Japan. Men are usually found cooking, beating, and purchasing fiber, packing paper, and dealing with customers. In some areas they are also found at the vat, but more often than not, they are busy overseeing the operation.

4. For more on flat diaphragm screens, see Chapter 5, note 2, and Chapter 6, note 1.

5. Tubs for most Japanese beaters are made of steel-reinforced cement. The rolls and bedplates are usually built by machine shops. Although some are well-made, most are not designed for beating rag.

CHAPTER FOUR

1. The time required to form a sheet, whether using Western or Japanese techniques, varies considerably depending on the fiber type, degree of beating, temperature of the stock in the vat, and thickness and quality of the sheets being formed. The figures given here are rough averages.

2. This is only a basic description of the *tame-zuki* process. Professional production techniques are much more involved, requiring more people and yielding a greater output per day. For more on the *tame-zuki* process, see Dard

Hunter, *Papermaking: The History and Technique of an Ancient Craft* (New York: Alfred A. Knopf, 1947), 428–52, or J. B. Green, *Papermaking by Hand in 1967* (Maidstone, Kent: Hayle Mill, 1967).

3. While only bast fiber was used traditionally, today less-expensive wood pulp is increasingly being added to Japanese handmade paper. By the same token, many contemporary Western papers are being made from the traditional cotton or linen rag mixed with cotton linters (the short fibers that adhere to the cotton seed). In both cases, the finished paper lacks the distinctive character and often the durability of sheets made entirely of traditional fiber.

4. Suspension systems and large moulds (40 by 60 centimeters and larger) first appeared around 1860. Prior to the late 1800s most moulds were small, entirely hand-held tools, measuring 35 by 60 centimeters and smaller.

5. Occasionally the inner bark of the Japanese *noriutsugi* tree (*Hydrangea paniculata* Sieb. or *Hydrangea floribunda* Regel) is used to produce *neri.* Its secretion differs from that of *tororo* in its stronger resistance to breaking down when subjected to a rise in temperature or continued stirring. It costs more than *tororo,* and papermakers who use it claim it is a superior formation aid. Nevertheless, its use is rare. For more on *noriutsugi,* see Seishi Machida and Mitsumasa Inano, "Chemical Studies on Polyuronides. VI. On the Mucilage of *Nori-utsugi* Plant, *Hydrangea Paniculata,* Sieb.," *Bulletin of the Chemical Society of Japan* 28, no. 9 (1955): 629–32. During the history of the craft, before the cultivation of *tororo-aoi,* secretions from other wild plants in addition to *noriutsugi* have been used as formation aids. See Dard Hunter, *Papermaking Pilgrimage to Japan, Korea and China* (New York: Pynson Printers, 1936), 21–25.

6. Several professors in the agriculture or forestry departments of major Japanese universities have done considerable research on *tororo* in attempts to define its composition, its effect upon fiber, and its contribution to the hand papermaking process. Experiments performed in 1954 by Seishi Machida and Norito Uchino showed the essential element of the secretion to be a polyuronide composed of rhamnose and galacturonic acid. Subsequent research by Machida and others has clarified several questions about *tororo* and its elusive nature.

At least two properties seem readily accepted. First, *tororo* attaches easily to fibers bearing hemicelluloses. This rapid association is explained by the strongly hydrophilic (water-loving) nature of both *tororo* and hemicelluloses; the similar chemical groups borne by their polymers; and the hydrogen bonding that occurs between *tororo,* hemicelluloses, and water. Secondly, once attached, *tororo* produces a splendid deflocculating effect, which John W. Swanson has described as a function of its stringiness. ("It is found that the effectiveness of these latter materials [deacetylated karaya gum and certain extracts such as those obtained from tororo, *Hibiscus manihot*] depends on a peculiar rheological characteristic possessed by their dispersions in water. This characteristic is referred to as stringiness, ropiness or, more elegantly, pituitousness. The latter term is defined as, full of, resembling, or due to mucous. The greater the degree of pituitousness possessed by an aqueous dispersion of gum or mucilage in water, the greater will be the deflocculation quality of this dispersion on very long fibered pulps." John W. Swanson, "The Science of Chemical Additives in Papermaking," *TAPPI* 44, no. 1 [January 1961]: 151A.) The mechanism of deflocculation may be explained more specifically, however, in terms of electrical charge. *Tororo,* like certain components of hemicelluloses, is known to be negative in charge. Once attached to a cellulose fiber, *tororo* gives the fiber a concentration of negative charges, which repel other like-charged fibers, thereby dispersing fiber and inhibiting flocculation. This "force field" may also be physically globular in shape. Though it is not well understood, *tororo's* very high molecular weight and the configuration and alignment of its molecules on the fiber surfaces are considered to be connected with its favorable deflocculating characteristics.

Beyond attachment and deflocculation, however, a description of *tororo* and its effect at the vat becomes more difficult. In attempts to evaluate *tororo's* character, Seishi Machida and Sadanori Nichikori conducted extensive tests on *tororo* and various synthetic substitutes, comparing filterability, viscosity, sedimentation rate, and deflocculation of fiber. Although none of the variables considered independently was found to relate directly to good papermaking properties, as a result of their research Machida and Nichikori were able to suggest that *tororo* (or any good substitute) provides good deflocculation with minimal loss of freeness in minimum concentrations. The research did not, however, clarify *tororo's* specific effect and contribution during papermaking. Concise evaluation during testing was difficult because *tororo* secretions easily change character with continued shear action, changes in temperature, and the passage of time. Also, hand papermaking, a non-mechanized process, does not lend itself readily to mathematical quantification.

Due to the lack of concrete information or extensive research, the following hypotheses regarding *tororo* and its effects are based on available research, interviews with several experts, and my personal experience at the papermaking vat.

Tororo is a formation aid used to control the otherwise rapid drainage of a dilute stock made of very free bast stuff and water. In addition to deflocculating, it also functions to prevent sedimentation of fiber and appears to "lubricate" fiber. (This latter term is used loosely to refer to the certain slipperiness of *tororo* and fiber mixed with it. A hydrated shell of attached water and *tororo* molecules, which encapsulates fibers and fibrils and produces a kind of protective colloid effect, may account for this slipperiness.) At the vat the slippery quality of the stock allows the smooth lamination of a sheet in the mould.

It may also be suggested that, for a given amount of freeness of an ideal stock (fiber, water, and formation aid), *tororo* lubricates and deflocculates fiber-bearing hemicelluloses exceptionally well. Its hydrodynamic properties during the formation of a sheet also seem exceptional compared to those of synthetic alternatives. In another view, a synthetic substitute having deflocculating, lubricative, and hydrodynamic properties identical to those of *tororo* would probably yield a stock with less freeness and therefore less efficient papermaking than that possible with genuine *tororo*.

In summation, the interrelationship between *tororo's* pituitousness and viscosity, its effect on the stock's lubricity, freeness, and rate of sedimentation, and its contribution to deflocculation and hydrodynamics during hand papermaking is an extremely complex one. Although I make further suppositions below, as of this writing it has not been possible to describe in any concrete scientific form exactly how *tororo* performs at the vat.

It may be suggested that the deflocculating effects of *tororo* are counteracted during papermaking as fiber and stringy *tororo* are strung or laid out flat and straight by the *nagashi-zuki* action while hydraulic forces push and rub the fiber together. The combined hydraulics at play are the pressure of the stock in the mould above the fiber mat, the shear forces resulting from sheet-forming action, and the drainage from below the fiber mat enhanced by the string-forming nature of *tororo*.

As mentioned in the text, and contrary to previously published information, *tororo* is not added to the stock solution in the vat primarily as an adhesive or size. True, it does act as an adhesive in that its ready interaction with cellulose, hemicelluloses, and water contributes to bonding. And in a strict sense it may be considered an internal size because it does contribute to a tightly formed sheet that shows slightly more controlled absorption of water or ink than a sheet made without *tororo* (i.e., a *tame-zuki* sheet). These effects, however, are negligible compared to *tororo's* role as a formation aid, and thus the terms "adhesive" and "size" are not appropriate when applied to *tororo*. Normally formed *nagashi-zuki* sheets do not exhibit an obviously "sized" resistance to water.

Since there is no immediate physical indication of *tororo's* presence in finished paper, there is some question about *tororo's* very existence after drying. During papermaking (and after breaks of an hour or more), *tororo* must be periodically replenished in the vat. *Tororo* breaks down and loses its effectiveness rapidly in acidic stock solutions (usually those containing rosin-alum internal sizing), in the presence of chloride (usually from bleaching), with the passage of time, with continued agitation, and, particularly, in warm weather. Damp, pressed sheets show no sign of stickiness whatsoever. Many authorities in Japan suggest it disappears altogether at drying. Although this seems highly unlikely, the most up-to-date infrared spectrum analysis shows only traces of *tororo* on the surfaces of fiber from dried paper. *Tororo's* quantity and effect in finished paper are considered negligible.

7. Due to a lack of grazing land for livestock in Japan, human waste, rather than animal manure, has played a major role in the history of Japanese agriculture.

8. There are, however, modern powdered synthetic substitutes for *tororo*, which are occasionally used. See Chapter 6, Synthetic Formation Aids.

9. The amount of *tororo* required in the vat stock is directly related to the fiber type, thickness, and quality of the paper being made. Mitsumata and gampi fibers are shorter and narrower than kozo fibers. Because of this and their larger amounts of hemicelluloses and fines (loose fiber particles), they are less free and thus require less *tororo*. Kozo—particularly, bleached or well-washed kozo, which bears fewer hemicelluloses—is freer, and requires more *tororo* for good formation. Thinner papers require more *tororo* to slow the drainage of a low consistency (dry-fiber-to-water ratio) stock and to provide working time. Thick papers require less *tororo* to permit continued drainage because as the sheet thickens on the mould, it blocks the passage of more liquid from above. High-quality paper may require more *tororo* to yield a clean finished sheet, while low-grade paper takes less. In the latter case, less *tororo* means faster overall drainage and less time per sheet but more lumps and coarser fiber in the final sheets. Surprisingly good paper can be made from "dirty" stock by adding a great deal of *tororo* to help keep the undesirable clumps and strands in suspension; however, drainage time will increase considerably, and efficiency will decrease.

Fiber preparation, the most important of all steps, has great influence on the quantity of *tororo* required. A superior fiber, free of coarse strands or lumps, can be made into fine sheets more quickly with less *tororo*. Cruder fiber requires more *tororo* and time to produce clean paper.

10. The magic of strength in any paper is related to hydrogen bonding between cellulose molecules of neighboring fibers or fibrils of those fibers. The interlocking of fibers as they lie together in a mat is only a secondary reason for strength. Hydrogen bonding occurs when two fibers or fibrils are forced so close together that electrons from free hydroxyl groups of cellulose molecules from both are involved in a certain electrostatic resonance. (Similar bridging bonds may occur between cellulose and water or *tororo*.) The mechanism that brings fibers into intimate molecular contact during drying is referred to as the Campbell effect. Stemming from surface tension forces of water existing between fibers or fibrils in damp paper, the Campbell effect shows linearly increasing compacting forces which are believed to approach 110 kilograms per square centimeter (1500 pounds per square inch) as the sheet nears dryness. The more intimate the contact between fibers at all points during the process, the greater the compacting forces, the more prevalent and larger the bonds, and the stronger the paper will be in the end. Beating is normally used to make fibers more plastic and inclined to intimate contact, but in the *nagashi-zuki* process, sheet-forming action, *tororo,* hemicelluloses, and easily collapsed thin cell walls all contribute to intimate contact between exceptionally long unbeaten fibers and thereby to sheets with surprising strength even when still damp during parting.

In addition to the compact nature of the long-fibered sheet, smooth *nagashi-zuki* sheet surfaces and the freeness of the stuff are important to eventual parting. *Nagashi-zuki* action leaves an even surface on each sheet that is not prone to grabbing at the sheet below in the pack. The high freeness of bast stuff allows it to part with water readily during pressing, thus contributing to wet-web strength during parting.

Tororo does not help keep sheets divided at couching and during pressing. In fact, during the making of some papers, an effort is made to let each sheet drain water and *tororo* an extra moment or two before it is couched to reduce its presence and to lessen problems at parting. *Tororo's* only contribution to eventual separation of sheets occurs during sheet forming, where it helps produce a compact, cohesive sheet, and during pressing, when it aids in bonding between fibers. Both effects help yield a strong paper able to withstand handling during parting.

11. After damp Japanese paper is brushed onto a board (or metal surface), it sticks without falling for several reasons. First and foremost, water surface-tension forces act between the fiber in the sheet and the drying surface. As the paper dries, these forces draw the sheet more and more tightly toward the board. If stress factors within the sheet do not exceed forces pulling the sheet to the board, the sheet will adhere. Hemicelluloses, the "plasticizers" of cellulose, contribute by making bast fiber more willing to lie in intimate contact with the board surface during brushing and drying. Another major reason Japanese paper sticks is its relatively low shrinkage rate. Any paper made of lightly beaten free stuff shrinks very little at drying. Low shrinkage means less strain as the sheet dries and less chance it will break away from its drying surface. The exceedingly smooth surface of the *nagashi-zuki* sheet is also a factor in its ready attachment to the drying surface.

Board drying of *nagashi-zuki* papers is possible partially because the characteristic thinness of the papers allows ready passage of moisture from within the sheet. Thicker papers are much more inclined to cause trouble. The surface area is the same, but more internal stress factors are at work and the moisture has a harder time leaving the sheet evenly.

Proper moisture content is critical to successful drying: if too dry, the sheet will not stick; if too wet, it will be very difficult to handle at brushing. Problem papers are often remoistened along the edges after pressing to improve edge contact. If a paper fails to respond to watering, thin rice or wheat paste may be applied to the drying surface or to the paper edges, but this is bothersome and is not done unless absolutely necessary. In some shops thicker papers are rubbed from behind with a smooth-surfaced Japanese camellia leaf (*Camellia japonica* L.) to force more intimate contact between fibers and the drying surface.

CHAPTER FIVE

1. The fermented persimmon juice mentioned here is produced from a special inedible species of persimmon (*Diospyros lotus* L., *Diospyros japonica* Sieb. et Zucc., or *Diospyros kaki* Thunb.).

The fermented juice's active agent seems to be tannin or possibly lactic acid. It is used in other applications where water-resistance is desired: *su* threads, paper book-covers, and laminated paper for stencil dyeing, to mention only a few.

2. If you are working with mitsumata, gampi, or Manila hemp, you may mechanically remove foreign particles with a flat diaphragm screen. Flat screens are rarely one-hundred-percent effective, and since they also constitute an additional washing step, flat-screened fiber often yields paper less crisp and lustrous than its hand-cleaned counterpart. Flat screens are, however, considerably quicker and may be of interest to the serious papermaker. The ideal piece of equipment for the home workshop is a laboratory flat screen with a slotted plate area of at least 30 centimeters (12 inches) square. Optimum slot size for mitsumata, gampi, or abaca is approximately .15 to .2 millimeters (.006 to .008 inches). The professional *nagashizuki* papermaker will need something a bit larger, perhaps two full-sized screen plates giving a working surface of about 60 by 120 centimeters (2 by 4 feet). New equipment is available from suppliers listed in Appendix 2. Used equipment, although harder to come by, is a good deal cheaper. See also Chapter 6, note 1.

CHAPTER SIX

1. The manufacturer's instructions concerning the operation of a flat screen should be followed, but the general procedure is as follows: Introduce a continuous flow of fresh, cool water into the reservoir above the plates. When water begins to pass out the discharge vent, turn the motor on and adjust the water flow so there is always about 2.5 centimeters (1 inch) of water on top of the plates. Run the machine until the exiting water is clean and free of any stray fiber that may have been adhering to the inside of the machine.

If the discharge water continues to contain suspect material, it is a good sign that the last operator did not thoroughly flush the machine at the end of his work session. (Note: If you have acquired a used machine, you may want to disassemble and thoroughly clean it of any remaining stray fiber and/or chemicals.) Make it a habit to thoroughly flush the flat screen, before and after use, to avoid unwanted specks in finished paper.

When the water runs clear, begin introducing beaten fiber into the reservoir a handful at a time. Very quickly you will learn how fast the machine can handle the fiber. If you are processing very dirty fiber, you may want to stop and squeegee the strained foreign matter from the surface of the plates at intervals. During operation, a wooden stick with a T-shaped end may be helpful in keeping the plate slots clear of debris.

Exiting water and clean fiber should be directed into the drain basket. Continue working until all the fiber has been cleaned. Squeegee any waste from the plate surfaces, and flush the machine by operating it until the water runs clear.

2. If the reader has access to a Canadian Standard Freeness Tester, or the similar Shopper-Riegler Tester, he may want to

consider its use in assigning special values to the gradually changing freeness as beating proceeds. Such tests are not terribly important when working with kozo or any hand-beaten fiber, but as soon as the hollander or *naginata* comes into play, a freeness tester can be very helpful in keeping the stuff from falling below an acceptable freeness level. For explicit instructions on use of the C.S.F. Tester, see Technical Association of the Pulp and Paper Industry, *Freeness of Pulp T227* (Atlanta, Georgia: Technical Association of the Pulp and Paper Industry, 1958).

For those interested in utilizing the freeness testers, the Japanese consider a minimal allowable freeness to be approximately 425 milliliters Canadian Standard Freeness (30° Shopper-Riegler). Kozo will generally come out much "faster" (around 650 milliliters, or 17° S R rating), particularly when beaten by hand. Mitsumata, gampi, and abaca, however, will approach the minimum very rapidly during machine beating. Hence, use of a tester is advisable in a production or research facility.

CHAPTER SEVEN

1. While the production of reliable, quality paper for unspecified uses is the goal here, the instructions given, if properly executed, should yield paper functional for letter writing, sumi-e, Chinese calligraphy, Oriental-style woodblock printing (when made thicker), and possibly some conservation applications.

The term "permanent" is used here not in the absolute but in the relative sense. Papers produced according to these traditional methods, if properly stored and handled, will easily last for centuries although they, and all papers, will naturally lose some of their durability over time.

2. Some papers—especially thick sheets—may cause special drying problems. If additional water does not keep the paper on the dryer, try using a soft rubber brayer on the back of the sheet after it is brushed on the dryer. If the sheet still pulls away before it is fully dry, as a last resort, a bit of weak wheat paste applied at the edges of the sheet may be necessary. Mix a small amount of wheat starch into a thick slurry with cold water. Then, while whipping the mixture, add boiling water gradually until the starch swells and forms a thick mass. More boiling water should then be added to thin the paste to a very dilute consistency. Apply just a bit to the very edges of each successive sheet with a soft brush. Brush the sheets onto the drying surface as usual. After they are completely dry, remove them with a pallet knife or a similar thin knife made from bamboo.

3. Remember that the ideal iron content is below 300 parts per million; and the ideal copper content, below 30 parts per million. The pH should be neutral or slightly alkaline and may be determined using TAPPI Method RC-29, as follows: "Place one gram of air-dried paper (cut in approximately ¼-inch [6-millimeter] squares) in a beaker, add 20 mL of distilled water (pH 6.5 to 7.0) and macerate with a stirring rod until the paper is uniformly wet. Then add 50 mL more of distilled

water, stir well, cover with a watch glass, and allow to stand for not less than 1 hour. At the end of that time stir once more and determine the pH of the unfiltered mixture at room temperature in the usual manner, either colorimetrically or electrometrically [i.e., use color indicator strips or solutions, or a pH meter]." The method recommended here is TAPPI Routine Control Method RC-29, pH of Paper (Cold Extract). More accurate results may be obtained using TAPPI suggested method T 509 su-68, Hydrogen Ion Concentration (pH) of Paper Extracts, Cold Extraction Method. Both are published by the Technical Association of the Pulp and Paper Industry, Inc., One Dunwoody Park, Atlanta, GA 30338.

APPENDIX ONE

1. Several examples are abaca (*Musa textilis*), flax (*Linum usitatissimum*), ramie (*Boehmeria nivea*), sisal (*Agave sisalana*), and jute (*Corchorus capsularis*). Of these alternatives, only abaca seems to combine the qualities of long fine fiber, comparative ease of cooking, and susceptibility to hand beating, and the good dispersion and parting properties so necessary in *nagashi-zuki*. By contrast, ramie (the name of the degummed fiber of "China grass," the bast removed from a non-stinging variety of nettle native to China) is a high-quality, very white fiber, and lower in lignin than sisal, abaca, or jute. This fiber is unusually heat-resistant and exceptionally long and broad. It does not require cooking to be made into paper by Western methods since the degumming done to prepare it for textile use has removed impurities. Ramie may be beaten with a hollander, but cooking—even for extended periods in caustic soda—will not render it soft enough to beat by hand. If beaten in a hollander it develops very low freeness, which means that it drains too slowly when mixed with *tororo-aoi* and that the sheets of paper will tend to stick to each other in the post after pressing. Sometimes this stickiness and loss of freeness can be remedied by washing the fiber extensively after beating and before adding it to the vat.

Flax presents problems similar to ramie. I have been working with strategies for fermenting flax to render it hand-beatable and these have yielded encouraging results. (It could be that ramie will ferment well also.) Sisal, too, seems better suited to *tame-zuki* production. If the fiber (as processed for textile use) is cooked, it yields a very soft paper, low in fold and tear strengths, but beaten in the hollander without cooking, it gives a crisp, dense, strong paper. Due to the negative information I have read about the high level of lignin impurities in jute and its short fiber, I have so far avoided experimenting with it for *nagashi-zuki*.

2. Formerly an apprentice of the renowned gampi papermaker Eishiro Abe, Katsu is presently specializing in the processing of *basho* (abaca, or *Musa textilis*) for paper. My information on Katsu is based on a conversation with Louise Allison Cort, a longtime resident of Japan and author of *Shigaraki: Potters' Valley* (Tokyo: Kodansha International, Ltd., 1980)—who knows him and had

visited him in the summer of 1979 to discuss his work. Katsu is working with abaca because he discovered that papermakers in Okinawa (where he now lives and works) long ago used the waste from the weavers' abaca preparation for paper. The unusually high amount of lime in the natural water supply helped to whiten and soften the fiber during its washing in the streams.

3. Boiling a fiber in an alkaline solution with a pH of over 11 will start to dissolve the cellulose of the fiber, according to paper research scientists.

4. Asao Shimura, *Early Chinese Papermaking* (Tokyo: Bunseido Press, 1980). See also Pan Chih-hsing, "China," in *Handmade Papers of the World* (Tokyo: Takeo Company, Ltd., 1979), 29–41.

5. There are two types of plant classification: the oldest (which does not imply kinship) groups plants for convenience of identification, as in poisonous and nonpoisonous or woody and herbaceous. The second and more modern system is based on genetic, structural, functional, biochemical, and developmental relationships. It is still being elaborated, and several variations by different authors exist. The main groups in this classification system proceed from the Plant Kingdom (as opposed to the Animal Kingdom), to subkingdoms, to divisions, to subdivisions, to classes, to orders, to families, to genera, to species, to races (as the smallest subgroup so far). All the main groups can have subgroups (a class and a subclass, a race and a subrace). All papermaking fiber plants come from the division Spermatophyta, the plants which bear seeds. Thus, using kozo as an example:

KINGDOM	Plant
DIVISION	Spermatophyta
SUBDIVISION	Angiosperm
CLASS	Dicotyledoneae
ORDER	Urticales
FAMILY	Moraceae
GENUS	*Broussonetia*
SPECIES	*kazinoki*

Usually, the plant, when listed by scientific name, is listed by genus and species with initials sometimes following to indicate the source author. For more information on plant classification see Harold C. Bold, *The Plant Kingdom* (Englewood Cliffs, New Jersey: Prentice-Hall, 1977, 4th edition) and Nathaniel Lord Britton and Hon. Addison Brown, *An Illustrated Flora of the Northern United States and Canada,* 3 vols. (1913; reprint, New York: Dover Publications, 1970).

6. G. W. D. Symonds, *The Shrub Identification Book* (New York: William Morrow and Co., 1963).

7. A German friend told me that in his country a type of nettle is used for papermaking. Historically, a linen-type cloth and cordage were manufactured from the stinging nettle. It is also eaten in soups. However, gloves are necessary in harvesting and handling until the fiber has been either cooked or dried. The unpleasant handling conditions would have to be tallied against the desirability of the fiber once tested.

8. I have tried using this slippery gel from Siberian elm inner bark as a formation aid and it works well; however, the gel has a very light, clear

amber color in the summer, and bark picked in the fall yields a gel that is dark and purplish. I do not know if using such a formation aid would cause eventual darkening of the paper. The Siberian elm formation aid is remarkably resistant to heat. I recently learned from a Korean papermaker that it has been used traditionally as a low-grade formation aid in Korea when whiteness of the paper is not important.

9. Due to the water-resistant nature of the pitch, I would normally advise against using bark from trees of the pine family. However, Jim Fortune of Plymouth, New Hampshire, has sent me samples of paper he has made from spruce bark harvested in the spring and cooked with soda ash. Paper made from the pure bark seems crisp and nonabsorbent, very short-fibered, and with little tear or fold strength, although it apparently has good wet strength. Fortune normally uses the bark as an additive to give a different character to cotton fiber papers. The fiber yields a brown to tan paper.

10. This information is derived from discussions with conservators and paper research scientists.

11. (Source is same as note 10.) A saturated solution of lime is obtained by mixing an excess amount in water, allowing it to settle overnight, and siphoning off the resulting solution.

12. It is believed that some early Western papers may have been made using water from streams that had dolomite (Georgia limestone) beds. Since dolomite is composed of both calcium and magnesium, it is believed that this helped to buffer the paper. At this point, research indicates, but has not proven, that magnesium may inhibit the oxidation of iron and copper, which can cause foxing or premature degradation of the finished paper. This leads me to believe that there might be some advantage in using dolomite for the suggested cook rinse-out rather than lime. Dolomite can be obtained by that name from ceramic chemical supply houses since it is also a ceramic glaze ingredient.

13. Wood utensils tend to deteriorate more rapidly on exposure to alkali solutions in my experience, so I do not recommend them. They splinter more easily, creating the possibility of wood fragments in your fiber, and the fiber strands may snag on the deteriorating tool.

14. This is confirmed by all Japanese papermakers with whom I have spoken. They all stress gentle processing and avoidance of caustic soda.

15. Dard Hunter, *Papermaking: The History and Technique of an Ancient Craft* (New York: Alfred A. Knopf, 1947; New York: Dover Publications, 1978), 215–16.

16. This method was suggested by Yasuichi Kubota, maker of *sekishu-hanshi* paper in Shimane Prefecture, Japan, when we were discussing methods for washing fiber in the absence of a river or stream.

17. A ball mill may also be used. This is a beating method employed by Lillian Bell, a papermaker using natural fibers in Oregon.

18. A plywood box with a hardwood floor (e.g., a bread board) can also be used. However, it is not as convenient

as a round container for mallet beating (unless your mallet is square-faced). Also, abrasion of the fiber does not seem to occur as well as it does against the more porous and rougher cement. The fiber being beaten slips on the wood and ends up sticking to the mallet.

19. In *su-buse* forming, the paper is couched directly onto the drying board. Tilt the boards horizontally for drying if they are plastic- or glass-surfaced or of treated wood to avoid residual water from one sheet running into and disrupting another sheet or perhaps causing a whole sheet to slide off the board. As the sheets become damp-dry, a brush should be used to work out air bubbles. *Su-buse,* or directly board-couched, sheets invariably are the softest type of sheet possible from a given fiber since they are never pressed.

20. I have been pressing paper at from .15 to .3 kilograms per square centimeter (2–4 pounds per square inch) at the surface of the paper. Weights are added gradually over an 8 to 9 hour period.

21. This is based on interviews with Japanese papermakers and subsequent personal experience. It came up as an issue for me in trying to board-dry thin sheets of gampi paper. They constantly peeled off the board during drying. I was advised by Yasuichi Kubota of Shimane Prefecture and by Tetsuo Naruko, a maker of gampi paper from the village of Kiryu in Shiga Prefecture, Japan, that drying of gampi paper should be started in the shade and then completed in the sun to equalize the shrinkage stresses that result from the edge drying before the center. Naruko claims that speed of drying affects the hardness relationship of the surface to the core of a sheet of paper and, therefore, its flexibility and fold strength. He does not think that high-shrinkage paper like gampi should ever be dried on hot metal surfaces for that reason. Both Naruko and Kubota said that drying in the shade alone produced a softer, limper sheet than sun drying. Since drying in the shade, given Japan's humid climate, generally means slow drying, I interpreted this to mean that slow drying produces softer paper. In practice, this has proved to be the case.

22. Hunter, op. cit., 327.

23. Harlan G. Metcalf, "The Outdoor Cordage Workshop: Cordage from Raw Material to Finished Product," in *Whittlin', Whistles, and Thingamajigs* (Harrisburg, Pennsylvania: Stackpole Books, 1974), 43–45.

24. Hunter, op. cit., 565.

25. Ibid., 557.

26. Nathaniel Lord Britton and Hon. Addison Brown, *An Illustrated Flora of the Northern United States and Canada,* 3 vols. (New York: Dover Publications, 1970). Additional information on both tule and cudweed can be found in this book.

Glossary

abaca: The more widely accepted name for Manila hemp (*Musa textilis*), a leaf fiber usually raised in the Philippines.

alkali: A material that shows a very high pH when mixed in water. Alkalis differ from one another in their readiness to combine chemically with other materials. To the non-chemist this translates as meaning that some alkalis are "stronger" than others. More active alkalis can be hazardous to work with and can degrade cellulose if their concentrations are not carefully controlled. Lye (sodium hydroxide, $NaOH$), soda ash (sodium carbonate, Na_2CO_3), and lime (calcium hydroxide, $Ca[OH]_2$) are all alkalis.

alkaline reserve: A paper additive such as calcium carbonate that serves to counteract the deleterious effects of acidic inks, sulfur dioxide in the air, and any other acidic components in the environment that may contact the finished sheet of paper. Also commonly called "buffer," a less appropriate term since a true chemical buffer will offset either an excess alkaline or an excess acidic condition.

alum: Although often used as a mordant in dyeing, alum is most commonly used to precipitate rosin and other sizing agents or chemicals onto fiber. Alum is the prime source of acidity in many papers and, unless neutralized, contributes to a lack of permanence. Papermakers' alum is aluminum sulphate ($Al_2[SO_4]_3\,14H_2O$, $Al_2[SO_4]_3\,18H_2O$, or a mixture of these hydrates).

archival: Originally meaning "of or pertaining to archives," the term is now loosely used (as is the term "permanent") to refer to a material that can be used without deleterious effects in the conservation or care of important artifacts, or in the production of new items designed to have very good aging properties.

backfall: A part of a beater tub that, because of its high sloping profile, causes the stuff just passed under the roll to begin its downhill return trip to the roll.

bast fiber: The phloem or inner bark fibers of woody plants (dicotyledons), which occur in an outer ring of vascular tissue. Bast fibers serve to conduct liquids down from the leaves in the plant, while the inner woody portion of the plant offers support and carries liquids up from the roots. The term also refers to fibers found in cortex and pericycle rings of herbaceous plants. Thus, in addition to kozo, mitsumata, and gampi, flax, hemp, and jute are also considered bast fibers.

beater: Usually refers to the hollander beater, a common piece of fiber preparation equipment used in modern hand papermaking shops around the world, which was developed in Holland at the end of the seventeenth century. In use the beater cuts and plasticizes fibers by working them in water between the rotating bars of the roll and the stationary bars of the bedplate.

beating: Any treatment of fibers to plasticize (soften) them, engorge them with water, collapse cell walls, raise fibrils, and cut, split, or otherwise prepare them for hydrogen bonding, which occurs during papermaking and drying. Beating affects the finished character of any paper by improving formation and smoothness, increasing tensile and fold strengths (to a degree) and hardness, while lowering opacity, absorbency, and tear strength. Japanese beating and the treating of some wood pulps is a very light, gentle process, while beating cotton rag and other very strong fiber can be an aggressive, prolonged process.

black bark: All three layers (white, green, and black) of the bark stripped from trees for Japanese papermaking. The term also occasionally refers to only the outermost black layer of the bark.

bonding: Refers to hydrogen bonding, a type of electrostatic resonance that occurs between hydroxyl groups of cellulose molecules of neighboring fibers within a sheet of paper during processing and drying. Hydrogen bonding accounts for most of the strength in any paper. In addition to interfiber bonding, hydrogen bonding may also occur between hydroxyl groups attached to molecules of water, hemicelluloses, adhesives, and *tororo-aoi*.

bonding agent: Any substance added to papermaking stuff to improve the strength of bonds already occurring or to create new bonds during papermaking and drying, thereby increasing the strength of the finished paper.

brightness: The degree to which a paper reflects light compared to that of a white reference surface, normally of magnesium oxide.

cellulose: Chemically, a high-molecular-weight polymer of glucose. In papermaking, cellulose fibers, except for cotton, are not pure but actually consist of cellulose plus varying amounts of other materials such as hemicelluloses and, especially in woody plants, lignin.

chain lines: Wires or silk threads used to weave together the laid lines of a mould surface. The term comes from the chainlike stitch used to hold the laid wires, splints, or sticks in place.

charge: to pick up, with the mould, sufficient stock from the vat to flood the surface of the mould, as in "to charge a mould"; or to load the beater with fiber and water, as in "to charge a beater." Or, a scoop of enough stock to flood the mould surface, as in "to manipulate the charge in the mould."

collé: The process of applying a thin sheet of paper to a thicker, usually rag, backing sheet at the moment of impression during fine-art printing. Also called *papier collé*.

consistency: The amount of fiber in a given volume of water, usually expressed in percent, used to describe the fiber concentration in stock. One-percent consistency is one gram of dry fiber in ninety-nine milliliters or ninety-nine grams of water.

cotton linters: The short fiber left on the cotton seed after the long staple fiber has been ginned away for the textile industry. Because of very thick cell walls and resistance to fibrillating, linters do not respond well to beating and are not generally used where strength is an important factor. Not to be confused with cotton rag fiber.

cotton rag: Any material made originally from the long staple fiber of the cotton seed. Cotton rag may be "old rag," such as discarded bed sheeting, but today usually means "new rag," such as shirt and underwear cuttings from clothing factories. Natural cotton fiber from the plant varies in length from twelve to thirty millimeters, but beaten rag fiber is generally between one and four millimeters, depending on the type of paper being made.

couch: To remove a newly made sheet from the mould and transfer or stack it elsewhere so the mould can be used again at the vat. From the French *coucher,* "to lay down."

deckle: The open wooden frame that fits on top of the mould, contains the stock, and defines the edge of the sheet during hand papermaking.

deflocculate: To disperse and prevent the entanglement or clumping of fibers in the stock and thereby provide more even and consistent sheet formation.

fast: Fast-draining, said of stuff or stock. *See also* freeness.

felt: A rectangle of interleaving fabric used in Western (*tame-zuki*) papermaking to keep sheets separate in the post. Rather than a true nonwoven felt, today most are cut from woven woolen yardage.

fibrillate: To raise fibrils on the surface of cellulose fiber to provide greater flexibility and surface area for forming fiber-to-fiber bonds. Although fibrillation is important, some people consider plasticization to be of equal or greater importance in producing strength in a finished paper.

fibrils: Microscopic strands raised from the outer cell walls of cellulose and other fibers during beating. Their diameter depends on the degree of mechanical treatment the fiber receives.

filterability: The rate of drainage of a mixture of water and fiber through a given mesh size or through the fiber mat that forms on the mesh.

fines: Very short fibers, loose fibrils, or other fiber fragments produced during the beating process, or ray and parenchyma cells that occur naturally. The presence of fines usually increases the strength and density of the final sheet while decreasing freeness during papermaking. (In some cases, however, fines may *decrease* strength in paper.)

flat screen: Commonly used term for flat diaphragm screen, a device for removing the majority of foreign particles or knots from a fiber mixture in water after beating. Use of a flat screen in Japanese papermaking greatly decreases or eliminates the need for hand removal of foreign particles prior to beating.

flocculate: To clump together. Fibers that have a tendency to flocculate in water usually yield paper with poor formation quality.

formation aid: Substance added to a papermaking stock to improve formation quality, usually by its deflocculating effect.

formation quality: The degree of even distribution of fibers within a sheet, judged by observing the degree of cloudiness of a sheet when held up to light. Formation quality influences not only appearance but all other properties of the sheet as well.

foxing: Reddish brown spots or stains in paper attributed to the presence of iron, copper, combinations of the two, or biological organisms.

freeness: The rate at which a papermaking stock or stuff gives up water while draining through a mat of fibers being formed on a standardized mesh size. Very free (or "fast") stuff drains rapidly and has a "high freeness." Slow-draining (or "slow") stuff has a "low freeness."

galacturonic acid: A chemical building unit which, repeated many times, forms the molecules of such natural materials as *tororo-aoi*. Galacturonic acid is an oxidized form of the simple sugar galactose, which is related to glucose, the building unit of cellulose.

gampi: The rarest of the three trees bearing bast fiber used for papermaking in Japan. As with kozo, several varieties are used, but *Diplomorpha sikokiana* Nakai is usually considered to yield the best fiber. Gampi, like mitsumata and Nepalese papermaking fiber, is a member of the family Thymelaeaceae. Gampi fibers vary in length between 2 and 4.5 millimeters, averaging 3.4 millimeters. Their diameter averages .018 millimeters. Pentosan hemicelluloses account for twenty-two percent of the white bark; and lignin, for approximately three percent.

green bark: The middle of the three layers of bark removed from the wood of kozo, mitsumata, and gampi trees. Refers also, in this book, to the green and white bark combined, as opposed to "black bark" (all three layers) and "white bark" (white bark alone).

hemicelluloses: Any of a number of cell-wall polysaccharides. Hemicelluloses form a noncrystalline sort of matrix that: (1) imbibes water and contributes to fiber swelling leading to internal lubrication and a readier response to beating, (2) due to its adhesive nature, tends to harden as fiber and fibrils shrink during drying, resulting in a stronger, crisper, less opaque, and less absorbent dry finished sheet, and (3) because of its mucilaginous qualities, contributes to fiber dispersion during papermaking.

hemp: *See* Manila hemp.

hydrated shell: A thin, closely associated layer of liquid on certain fibers, a result of attached water and/or formation-aid molecules.

hydrodynamic: Of or relating to the behavior of liquids in motion.

hydrogen bonding: *See* bonding.

hydroxyl group: A chemical group (O–H) present on cellulose, hemicellulose, water, and *tororo-aoi* molecules that serves as the center for hydrogen bonding.

kan: A Japanese term meaning sixth sense or the ability to judge intuitively.

knot: A twisted or tangled mass of fiber, usually larger than a pinhead but smaller than a pencil eraser, sometimes found in a batch of beaten fiber. In quantity, knots can seriously detract from the quality of an otherwise uniform high-quality sheet.

konnyaku: The Japanese vegetable *Amorphophalus konjac* K. Koch, used for food or to make a type of glue.

kozo: A mulberry tree from which the most common Japanese papermaking fiber is produced. Although there are several varieties used, *Broussonetia kazinoki* Sieb. is considered to yield the best fiber. Another variety, *Broussonetia papyrifera* Vent., commonly designated "paper mulberry," is occasionally found in North America from New York to Missouri and south. Kozo is of the family Moraceae and is closely related to the white and red mulberry trees common in areas of North America and to *kuwa, Morus alba* L., the leaves of which are fed to silkworms in Japan. Kozo fibers vary in length between three and twenty-five millimeters, averaging twelve millimeters. Their diameter averages .025 millimeters. The pentosan hemicellulose content of kozo white bark averages nine percent; and lignin, about four percent.

laid: Refers to the laid and chain style mould surface as opposed to the "wove" mould surface covered with woven mesh. The laid lines—i.e., wires, splints, or sticks—can leave parallel watermarked lines in the finished sheet.

lignin: The non-carbohydrate portion of most plant cell walls, which serves to bond fibers together and give structural strength to the plant. Large quantities of lignin in paper contribute to premature discoloration of the sheet and interfere with hydrogen bonding of fibers during papermaking leading to weakness in the paper.

loading: Materials (also called "fillers") added to the fiber, usually at the end of beating, to change the opacity, printing quality, weight, or feel of the finished sheet. Common loading agents are kaolin clay, titanium dioxide, and calcium carbonate.

loft drying: Formerly, the drying of Western-style sheets in specially ventilated lofts. Now the term refers to any unrestrained, natural air-drying procedure.

Manila hemp: An older name for abaca, or *Musa textilis,* a plant related to the banana that bears leaf fiber used in papermaking. Manila hemp is not to be confused with the only true hemp—*Cannabis sativa,* or marijuana.

mazè: A comblike mixing device used in the Japanese papermaking vat. Pronounced "mah-zeh."

midfeather: A longitudinal partition in the tub of the beater, which serves to control the flow of water and fiber in the tub during beating.

mitsumata: A tree, the inner bark of which yields a fiber traditionally used in Japanese papermaking. Usually cited as *Edgeworthia papyrifera* Sieb. et Zucc. or *Edgeworthia chrysantha* Lindley. Mitsumata, like gampi and bast fiber used for papermaking in Nepal, is a member of the family Thymelaeaceae. Mitsumata fibers vary in length between 1 and 5 millimeters, averaging 3.3 millimeters, and have an average diameter of .020 millimeters. Pentosan hemicellulose content averages sixteen percent of the mitsumata white bark; and lignin, about two percent.

mordant: A substance used to cause increased fixation of a dye to a fiber.

mould: The main hand-papermaking tool in any country, the mould is a flat screen manipulated to filter an even layer of fibers from a dilute fiber and water mixture in the vat. (Note: This is the British spelling of "mold" but has come to refer specifically, throughout the West, to the hand papermaking tool.)

nagashi-zuki: A laminating form of papermaking used in Japan that is characterized by: the use of several charges from the vat and energetic action during sheet forming, very long bast fibers, the addition of a viscous formation aid to the stock, the use of a removable flexible mould surface, couching without using felts, and very light pressing. (For more on the differences between *nagashi-zuki* and Western papermaking, or *tame-zuki,* see Chapter 4.) Along with *tame-zuki, nagashi-zuki* is one of the world's two highly evolved, contemporary production methods for making sheets of paper by hand in large numbers.

naginata beater: A unique beater designed for the preparation of bast fiber. The *naginata* beater is identical to a hollander except for its lack of a bedplate and backfall and its incorporation of curved knives, which replace the standard beater roll. See Figures 15, 16, 47, 98, and 99.

National Living Treasure: A person who has been designated a "holder of an intangible property of cultural importance" by the Japanese government. Along with the title, the recipient is awarded a stipend, which enables him to continue in his field and train others to carry on the traditional art or craft.

neri: General term for any viscous formation aid added to the *nagashi-zuki* vat. Thus, an artificial substitute for *tororo-aoi* is termed *kagaku-neri,* meaning "chemical *neri.*" Related to the verb *nebaru,* or "to become sticky or viscous."

noriutsugi: The inner bark of a wild

shrub, a species of Saxifragaceae, which yields a formation aid occasionally used in place of *tororo-aoi*. Usually cited as *Hydrangea paniculta* Sieb. or *Hydrangea floribunda* Regel.

pack: In Western (*tame-zuki*) papermaking, after the post has been pressed the felts are removed and the paper is restacked without felts and pressed again lightly. This feltless pile of paper is called a "pack." In Japanese (*nagashi-zuki*) papermaking, "pack" is used to refer to the block of damp paper after pressing.

parting: In Western papermaking, the removal of freshly pressed sheets from the post or pack. In Japanese papermaking, the peeling away of successive sheets from the freshly pressed, feltless pack of paper.

permanent: A term that ideally would always appear in quotes since all papers made of cellulose fiber degrade naturally and are never truly permanent. The term refers more accurately to a paper or material "of a high degree of permanence." See Barrow, Clapp, and W. J. Barrow Research Laboratory in the Bibliography.

pituitousness: The string-forming character, or "ropiness," of a viscous liquid.

plasticize: By beating, to soften cellulose fiber, collapse its walls, and imbibe it with water. Although the term "hydrate" is commonly used for the same process, it is not appropriate since it implies a chemical change that does not actually take place.

polysaccharide: a polymer chain made up of simple repeating units formed by splitting water from simple sugars such as glucose, galactose, and xylose.

polyuronide: A polymer made from sugar units that bear attached acid groups due to oxidation. Galacturonic acid is a polyuronide.

post: In *tame-zuki* papermaking, the wet stack of newly made sheets of paper interleaved with felts before pressing. In *nagashi-zuki* papermaking, the feltless stack of newly made sheets prior to pressing.

raw fiber: Fully harvested and dried black, white, or green bark before preparation for papermaking.

rhamnose: A pentose sugar building unit of hemicellulose molecules.

rice paper: A common misnomer applied to *washi*, Japanese handmade paper, or *nagashi-zuki* papers. Rice rarely plays a part in the manufacture of Japanese papers. Occasionally rice-straw fiber is used with other fibers, and sometimes rice paste was used as an adhesive or size in earlier papers. Rice alone, however, will not make paper. According to Dard Hunter, true rice paper is made from a plant that grows in Taiwan (*Tetrapanax papyriferum*). Thin white sheets are cut spirally from the inner pith of the plant, like veneer from a log. This "rice paper" is, in fact, not paper at all, since it is not made from cellulose fiber that has been beaten, suspended in water, reformed into an even mat, and dried.

sha: Treated silk or synthetic mesh attached to a regular *su* to eliminate the mark of the laid and chain lines in the finished paper and give the finished sheet a wove surface.

shear action: Any action that causes disruption of a liquid or solid in a uniformly planar direction, as in sliding the cards in a deck.

sizing agent: Any material added to paper that increases the paper's resistance to penetration by liquids. A material mixed with the stuff or stock prior to papermaking is called an "internal size." The most common internal size in machine papermaking consists of a rosin emulsion precipitated with alum. Cellulose-reactive internal sizes (such as Hercon 40) are used in making permanent papers since alkaline conditions and the freedom from acidity are requisite. A size applied after the sheet is formed and dried is called an "external" or "surface" size. Surface sizes (such as starch or gelatine) not only alter resistance to liquids but also affect surface smoothness, erasability, strength, gloss, stiffness, and printability.

slow: Having low freeness. *See also* freeness.

stock: The dilute, fully prepared mixture of water, fibers, formation aids, sizing agents, and any other additives present in the vat during papermaking. (In the continuous-process machine industry, "stock" refers to the fiber and fiber-water mixture at all stages of papermaking, thus encompassing the term "stuff.")

stuff: Used in this text to refer to concentrated, beaten fiber before it is mixed with other ingredients into stock for papermaking.

su: The flexible removable mould surface used in *nagashi-zuki.* Usually made of bamboo splints woven together with silk threads.

tackle: beater roll, bedplate, and adjustment apparatus.

tame-zuki: Japanese term for the Western style of hand papermaking that employs one charge from the vat, a gentle shake during sheet forming, felts between each sheet at couching, and heavy initial pressing. Although the term is sometimes used to refer to early Chinese papermaking as well as pre-*nagashi-zuki* Japanese papermaking, in this book it applies only to the contemporary Western production method. *Tame-zuki* is sometimes used in Japan for making thicker papers. See also *nagashi-zuki.*

TAPPI: Abbreviation for Technical Association of Pulp and Paper Industry, an organization of professionals from the machine papermaking and allied industries. TAPPI standard testing procedures are used internationally in paper research.

tororo: Abbreviated term for the plant *tororo-aoi,* secretions from the root of which yield the most common formation aid used in contemporary Japanese hand papermaking. Usually cited as *Abelmoschus manihot* Medikus or *Hibiscus manihot* L., a species of the family Malvaceae. *Tororo* is an annual herb believed to be of Chinese origin.

traditionalist: A term used in this book to refer to any papermaker who values the old techniques and places the quality and character of his paper above profit considerations. Also refers to those artisans who refuse to use wood pulp and strong chemicals, and rarely use machinery during production of their papers.

washi: From the Japanese *wa,* meaning Japan, and *shi,* meaning paper, *washi* is used today to refer to Japanese handmade paper of any type, traditionally made or not, and in some cases even to certain varieties of machine-made papers.

washing: Used in this text to refer to the process of rinsing fiber after cooking, bleaching, or dyeing.

Western hand papermaking: The European method of making paper by hand, usually employing linen or cotton rag as a raw material. Called *tame-zuki* in Japanese.

wet strength: The strength of finished paper after it is saturated with water.

wet-web strength: The strength of paper while still damp after pressing (and before drying).

white bark: The innermost layer of the bark used in making Japanese papers. The white bark bears the majority of the fiber rendered from "black bark" and is used exclusively when making very-light-colored, high-quality papers.

wood pulp: Refers to a wide variety of chemically processed softwood and hardwood fibers normally used by the machine papermaking industry. Fiber length varies considerably depending on the source and the degree of treatment of the pulp. Unbeaten softwood fibers usually have an average length of 3 to 5 millimeters and an average width of about .040 millimeters. Hemicellulose content ranges from several percent to twenty percent; and lignin content, from zero to twenty-seven percent, depending on pulping yield and bleaching. Hardwoods by comparison average 1 to 2 millimeters in length and .035 millimeters in width, and have similar hemicellulose and lignin contents.

wove: A mould surface of woven wire cloth (in *tame-zuki*) or woven silk cloth (in *nagashi-zuki*) used in making papers where a very consistent sheet, free of a laid and chain-line watermark, is required.

Bibliography

Arrow Art Works, Inc. *Handmade Papers by Eishiro Abe.* Tokyo: Arrow Art Works, Inc., 1976.

Arrow Art Works, Inc. *Handmade Papers by Yasuichi Kubota: Sekishu-hanshi.* Tokyo: Arrow Art Works, Inc., 1978.

Barrow, W. J. *The Manufacture and Testing of Durable Book Papers.* Edited by Randolph W. Church. Richmond, Virginia: The Virginia State Library, 1960.

Bell, Lillian A. *Plant Fibers for Papermaking.* McMinnville, Oregon: Liliaceae Press, 1981.

Bold, Harold C. *The Plant Kingdom.* 4th ed. Englewood Cliffs, New Jersey: Prentice-Hall Inc., 1977.

Brockman, Frank C. *Trees of North America.* New York: Golden Press, 1968.

Britton, Nathaniel Lord, and Hon. Addison Brown. *An Illustrated Flora of the Northern United States and Canada.* 3d ed. New York: Dover Publications, 1970.

Clapp, Verner W. "The Story of Permanent Durable Bookpaper, 1115–1970." *Scholarly Publishing* 2 (January, April, July 1971): 107–24, 229–45, 353–67.

Clark, Howard, and Kathryn Clark. "Final Descriptive Report, N.E.A. Art Services-Grant No. R50–41–215. Standards for Light Fastness in Handmade Artists' Papers." Brookston, Indiana: Twinrocker Handmade Paper, 1977.

Clark, James d'A. *Pulp Technology and Treatment for Paper.* San Francisco: Miller Freeman Publications, Inc., 1978.

Goto, Seikichiro. *Japanese Handmade Paper.* Vol. 1, *Northeastern Japan,* Vol. 2, *Northwestern Japan.* Tokyo: Bijutsu Shuppansha, 1958.

Green, J. B. *Papermaking by Hand in 1967.* Maidstone, Kent: Hayle Mill, 1967.

Hickman, B. "Japanese Handmade Papers: Materials and Techniques." *Japanese Society of London,* Bulletin 81 (April 1977): 9–16.

Hilton, Crockett. *Dyeing Cellulosic Fibers and Related Procedures.* Tokyo: Academic Press, 1961.

Hughes, Sukey. *Washi: The World of Japanese Paper.* Tokyo: Kodansha International, Ltd., 1978.

Hunter, Dard. *Papermaking Pilgrimage to Japan, Korea and China.* New York: Pynson Printers, 1936. Edition of 370 copies.

———. *Papermaking: The History and Technique of an Ancient Craft.* 2d ed. New York: Alfred A. Knopf, 1947. Reprint. New York: Dover Publications, 1978.

Isenberg, I. H. *Pulp and Paper Microscopy.* Appleton, Wisconsin: The Institute of Pulp and Paper Chemistry, 1967.

Jugaku, Bunsho. *Papermaking by Hand in Japan.* Tokyo: Meiji Shobo, 1959.

Kaempfer, Engelbertus. *The History of Japan.* London, 1728. Later reprints exist.

Koretsky, Elaine. *Color for the Hand Papermaker.* Brookline, Massachusetts: Carriage House Press, forthcoming.

Kume, Yasuo. *Tesuki Washi Shuho.* Tokyo: Yushodo Booksellers, Ltd., 1980.

Kunisaki, Jihei. *Kamisuki Chohoki.* Translated by Charles E. Hamilton. Berkeley: The Book Arts Club, University of California, 1948.

LaBarre, E. J. *Dictionary and Encyclopedia of Paper and Papermaking.* Amsterdam: Swets and Zeitlinger, 1952.

Little, Elbert L. *The Audubon Society Field Guide to North American Trees: Eastern Region.* New York: Alfred A. Knopf, 1980.

Loeber, E. G. *Supplement to the Dictionary and Encyclopedia of Paper and Papermaking.* Amsterdam: Swets and Zeitlinger, 1967.

Machida, Seishi, and Mitsumasa Inano. "Chemical Studies on Polyuronides. VI. On the Mucilage of *Nori-utsugi* Plant, *Hydrangea Paniculata,* Sieb." *Bulletin of the Chemical Society of Japan* 28, no. 9 (1955): 629–32.

Machida, Seishi, and Sadanori Nichikori. "Chemical Studies on Wood Hemicelluloses. II. On the Hemicellulose of Gampi Bast Fibers. I." *Bulletin of the Chemical Society of Japan* 31, no. 9 (1958): 1021–23.

———. "Studies on the Dispersing Agents of Fibers. Part I. Part II." *Bulletin of The Faculty of Textile Fibers* (Kyoto University of Industrial Arts and Textile Fibers) 3, no. 2 (1961): 267–89.

———. "Studies on the Dispersing Agents of Fibers. Part V." *Bulletin of The Faculty of Textile Fibers* 4, no. 3 (1965): 436–42.

———. "Studies on the Mucilaginous Solution Concerning Japanese Hand-made Paper. Part IV. On the Dispersion of Bast Fiber of Gampi Plant" (in Japanese; one page in English). *Bulletin of the Paper Pulp Technical Society* 18, no. 3 (1964): 127–30.

Machida, Seishi, Sadanori Nichikori, and Tadashi Ueno. "Studies on the Mucilaginous Solution Concerning Japanese Hand-made Paper (Part III). On the Change of Papermaking Properties of Tororo-aoi Mucilage in Preservation" (in Japanese; one page in English). *Bulletin of the Paper Pulp Technical Society* 17, no. 149 (1963): 501–4.

Machida, Seishi, and Norito Uchino. "A Summary of Chemical Studies on Polyuronides. Part I. On the Mucilage of Tororo-aoi Plant, *Abelmoschus Manihot,* Medic." *Bulletin of The Faculty of Textile Fibers* (Kyoto University of Industrial Arts and Textile Fibers) 1, no. 1 (1954): 116–26.

Machida, Seishi, and Yasushi Yoshino. "Studies on the Dispersing Agents of Fibers. Part III." *Bulletin of The Faculty of Textile Fibers* (Kyoto University of Industrial Arts and Textile Fibers) 3, no. 3 (1961): 583–90.

———. "Studies on the Dispersing Agents of Fibers. Part IV." *Bulletin of The Faculty of Textile Fibers* 4, no. 2 (1964): 236–42.

Mainichi Newspapers. *Te-zuki Washi Taikan.* Tokyo: Mainichi Newspapers, 1974.

Metcalf, Harlan G. *Whittlin', Whistles, and Thingamajigs.* Harrisburg, Pennsylvania: Stackpole Books, 1974.

Mikesh, Robert. *Japan's World War II Balloon Bomb Attacks on North America.* Smithsonian Annals of Flight, no. 9. Washington, D.C.: Smithsonian Institution Press, 1973.

Narita, Kiyofusa. *A Life of Ts'ai Lung and Japanese Papermaking.* Tokyo: Dainihon Press, 1966.

Parkes, Harry S. "Reports on the Manufacture of Paper in Japan Presented to Both Houses of Parliament by Command of Her Majesty." London, 1871.

Petrides, George A. *A Field Guide to Trees and Shrubs.* 2d ed. Boston: Houghton Mifflin Company, 1972.

Poyser, J. Norman. *Experiments in Making Paper by Hand.* Pointe Claire, Quebec, 1975.

Rein, J. J. *The Industries of Japan: With an Account of its Agriculture, Forestry, Arts, and Commerce.* New York: 1889.

Shimura, Asao. *Early Chinese Papermaking.* Tokyo: Bunseido Press, 1980.

Swanson, John W. "The Science of Chemical Additives in Papermaking." *TAPPI* 44, no. 1 (January 1961): 151A.

Symonds, George W. D. *The Shrub Identification Book.* New York: William Morrow and Co., 1963.

Takeo Company, Ltd. *Handmade Papers of the World.* Tokyo: Takeo Company, Ltd., 1979.

Technical Association of the Pulp and Paper Industry. *Freeness of Pulp T277.* Atlanta, Georgia: Technical Association of the Pulp and Paper Industry, 1958.

Tindale, Thomas Keith and Harriet Ramsey. *The Handmade Papers of Japan.* Tokyo: Charles E. Tuttle and Company, 1952.

Trier, Jesper. *Ancient Paper of Nepal.* Jutland Archaeological Society Publication, vol. 10. Copenhagen: Copenhagen Royal Library, 1972.

Tsien, T. H. *Written on Bamboo and Silk.* Chicago: University of Chicago Press, 1962.

U. S. Department of Agriculture. Agricultural Research Service. *Common Weeds of the United States.* New York: Dover Publications, 1971.

W. J. Barrow Research Laboratory, Inc. "Permanence/Durability of the Book, VII." Richmond, Virginia: W. J. Barrow Research Laboratory, Inc., 1974.

Yanagi, Soetsu. *The Unknown Craftsman: A Japanese Insight into Beauty.* Tokyo: Kodansha International, Ltd., 1972.

For more information on handmade paper, consult the following bibliographies:

Bidwell, John. "Paper and Papermaking: 100 Sources." *AB Bookman's Weekly* (February 13, 1978): 1043–61.

Bird and Bull Press. *An Exhibition of Books on Papermaking.* A selection of books from the collection of Leonard B. Schlosser, The Free Library of Philadelphia. North Hills, Pennsylvania: Bird and Bull Press, 1968.

Hunter, Dard. *Papermaking: The History and Technique of an Ancient Craft.* New York: Alfred A. Knopf, 1947. (See pp. 585–602.)

Index

The "weathermark" identifies this book as a production of John Weatherhill, Inc., publishers of fine books on Asia and the Pacific.